the
Reluctant
Fathers'
Club

the Reluctant Fathers' Club

(or How I Learned to Stop Worrying and Cautiously Embrace Parenthood)

Nick Duerden

First published in 2009 by

Short Books
3A Exmouth House
Pine Street
EC1R 0JH

10 9 8 7 6 5 4 3 2 1

ISBN 978-1-906021-50-4

Every effort has been made to obtain permission
for copyright material in this book. If any errors have unwittingly occurred,
we will be happy to correct them in future editions.

Printed in Great Britain by Clays, Suffolk

Cover photograph © Getty Images
Cover design: Emily Fox

For Amaya and Evie,
who taught me everything I needed to know

Prologue

The mother of my child has her legs in stirrups, the hospital-issue gown cast carelessly about her thighs. It's not her best look. There is blood on the floor, and a masked doctor sits between her legs, halfway through another interminable shift, a needle and thread in hand, ready to stitch. From beneath her mask, I watch her yawn.

It is dark outside, the moon high over an almost-Christmas night, but neon-lit and unforgivingly bright inside. A midwife, another one, I've lost count how many by now, is leading me with encouraging words away from the hospital bed and towards the corner of the delivery room where a contraption comprising a small tray and some heat-giving light sits, humming with electricity. In her hands she holds a baby: mine. There is no sound coming from the baby, despite what I would have expected, if I'd had the presence of mind to expect anything. She places it on the warm tray and, her eyes drawing me in, begins to count the fingers of its hands. There are four fingers on its left hand, four fingers on its right, an opposable thumb on either. She counts them by placing each tiny digit between two of her own and registering them aloud, as if the exercise required considerable concentration, which perhaps it does. She then repeats the process further south. Its feet have five toes, also tiny, perfect and fully formed, complete with toenails that already need trimming with a pair of scissors we have yet to buy. From the baby comes a noise:

1

a sigh, a weary grunt. It is then placed into my hands and I'm told to take the six steps back towards my girlfriend, who lies dazed and expectant, but differently so now. She takes it from me and holds it against her breast. We look from one another to it, and back again.

"Happy?" says one of the midwives.

From outside comes another noise: the mother-in-law, Spanish, beseeching, her previously impressive patience now at a justifiable end. She has been waiting for this moment in the corridor, the hospital canteen and outside on a freezing Westminster Bridge, for almost ten hours now. She wants in, and is duly beckoned. Her joy is exultant, immediate and profound, and it colours the room just as vibrantly as if she'd had paintbrushes in each fist. Now there is celebration, and it comes exclusively from her. A couple of years shy of her 60th birthday, and she is a grandmother at last. It is infectious, her happiness. It infects the two doctors who, until moments before, had been in a squabble that I had worried would put my then undelivered baby's life in danger, and it puts a smile of complicity on the faces of the midwives, the nurses, the assorted hangers-on.

Suddenly, I am invisible, mercifully so, and perhaps now I can finally leave this claustrophobic room. I need air, the toilet, some respite, and a mobile phone. I stumble out into the corridor, which is pale and empty, its walls the colour of oatmeal, and I blink in the harsh overhead lighting. I burst briefy into tears, then walk past people who ignore me, who have no idea what I have just gone through, and into the garden area, seven floors up above London with its views of the big clock, the Houses of Parliament, a churning, licorice river, the moon and a few stars. There are plants here, and I sit amongst them. Underneath a sign that says No Mobile Phones, I turn on my mobile phone and call first my grandparents, ailing and aged in Milan, and eager for news. In broken Italian, I tell them what I have to tell them, and try to drink in their quiet satisfaction, which I hope sparks something in me. I'm exhausted and spent – and relieved, definitely that. My girlfriend, who I had thought was in serious trouble back there, moments away from the kind of tragedy that litters the newspapers day after day, is alright, likewise the baby that finally saw fit to come out, take its first lungful of air, and cry. *Mother and baby doing well*; the first of countless clichés sure to follow. But as I impart the news to my grandparents and then to a succession of friends late on Christmas Eve night, I realise that I am numb to it, entirely numb. At some point very soon I will have to begin my new life, my old one now consigned to history, a part of my past.

I make several more phone calls, five, maybe six, aware that I have big news to convey, a war story of sorts, and everybody likes a war story with a happy ending. I concentrate solely on this for the time being: the war story, the survival of. When I have made the calls I most wanted to make, I put the phone away and take my first step back towards the room, where there is Spanish sound and noise, a girlfriend who wants me back and a baby who will surely make demands on me that I cannot, at this point, even begin to anticipate.

I have no idea what will happen next.

One

I am woefully unprepared for this, I'll admit it, albeit secretly, to myself. And though I would like to search around for someone else to blame, the fault is ultimately mine alone. The guidebook did strongly advise an acclimatisation period of at least two days but, with a cavalier arrogance that has rarely served me well, I insisted we'd be fine regardless, my assumption based on the loose logic of us being young, fit and healthy. So we turn up with barely twenty-four hours to spare, and to hell with it. The guidebook also suggested to go easy on alcohol the night before, due to the effects of the altitude on our already diminished constitutions, but I order wine with my dinner regardless, then something shorter and stronger to follow. I go to bed dizzy.

The following morning, barely an hour into our first mountain trek, and the oxygen is thinning exponentially the higher we climb. I find it increasingly difficult to breathe. My legs tremble fiercely. By lunchtime I have the makings of a headache and, a couple of hours later, the sun already beginning its abrupt descent behind a mountain range I think are the Andes, and the cold setting in, the headache is clanging inside my skull like a hammer. Altitude sickness, says my guide. Strange you have not acclimatised, he continues. People normally do so after the allotted two days. I say nothing in response.

Night-time in my first tent for over a decade (and, I can confidently predict, my last) is close to freezing, the solid ground beneath me hardly a balm for my myriad aches and pains. By the middle of Day Two, the point at which we cross Warmiwañusca, or Dead Woman's Pass, we are a full 4215m above sea level. The air is anorexic up here, barely a rumour, and my headache is now a malleable, pulsing thing, pushing at the back of my eyeballs with all its heft. It is only the prospect of great embarrassment in requesting helicopter rescue that keeps me staggering forward, one uneven step at a time. The thought that we could instead be on a beach in Greece doesn't abate.

We are in Peru, en route to Machu Picchu, one of the wonders of the world, which is located just north of the beautiful terracotta-coloured city of Cuzco, high up in – and I'm sure of it now – the Andes. Like thousands of people each year, many of them older than me by several decades, we are doing the Inca Trail. Though it scales to peaks so high that, at certain points, we are looking *down* upon the clouds, this is actually a fairly tame adventure for the hiking enthusiast, but we are not hiking enthusiasts. There are twelve of us in our group, hailing from as far afield as Australia, Europe and America. Each of us, with the exception of me, is wearing the kind of rugged 4X4 walking boot that requires of its thick shoelaces a manly double knot. My Nike trainers are paltry in comparison, something our guide, a mocking smile on his face, points out several times over the next few days.

Though I don't know it yet, this is to be the most unhealthy and calamitous holiday I've ever had, a Norman Wisdom film made real, hardly what my girlfriend Elena and I would have chosen had we known, given its significance. Peru was to be something of a watershed for us, our last holiday as a couple. We'd been together for eleven years by this stage, and with Elena now into her early 30s, she had decided that she wanted a baby. After protracted discussions that had dragged on for almost two years, discussions often curtailed by me in a gulp of panic, I had eventually given in. We would, I agreed, at the very least *try* and see what happened. Several years previously, back in her native Spain, a doctor had told her that it was likely she would only ever be able to conceive with medical intervention, and even then it could prove difficult. I won't pretend here and now to know why exactly, except to relate that it had something to do with nodules and Fallopian tubes and irregular periods. But since arriving in London back in 1994, her periods had found a regular pattern and all seemed well. And so before she made an appointment with her GP, who would doubtless refer her to the local hospital and to countless invasive procedures that would turn our contented life into one of complication, she wanted us to try naturally. The novelty of Peru was largely for my own benefit, the prospect of sex in exotic climes a way to lessen the fear that we were no longer using protection. We would remain in the country for nineteen days and nights. All going to plan, we would return home having conceived.

It is only now, with the benefit of hindsight, that I begin to wonder whether the successive physical mishaps that took place within and upon my body during that time were designed, in some deeply subconscious way, as an attempt to thwart her hopes and dreams and keep me free of parental responsibility. I posit this only as theory because, really, who am I to say for sure?

Nevertheless, I have my suspicions.

● ● ●

The two years of discussions that led us to this point were entered into diplomatically, Elena employing some carefully honed feminine wiles with deadly precision. It was early one September when she first raised the subject, in a restaurant somewhere in the centre of London, a bottle of wine and a dripping candle between us. She looked healthy and tanned from a ten-day break back in the Basque country, her home a pinprick-sized town with easy access to nearby beaches. She had brought with her some photographs of friends that I was required to show a cursory interest in, but was sly enough to first steer the conversation towards other things, subjects that focused largely on me, and to which she was as attendant and responsive as ever. But also she was plotting. This is something that women the world over very necessarily do at certain stages in romantic life: they choose their moment with cunning before embarking upon the topic that will conspire to change things for ever.

She chose hers to coincide with the arrival of a second bottle of wine. The photographs came out, featuring friends she had known since childhood, many of whom had recently got married and were now either in the advanced stages of pregnancy or had recently given birth. Here was one now, of a lady named Ana, an IVF twin in the crook of either arm. And here was another, of lovely Susana, pregnant and beaming.

Pictures of pregnant women have never done much for me, likewise those of cradled infants. I am never sure how I am expected to respond to them, perhaps as I have no real frame of reference to even begin processing the information contained within. None of my friends were in similar states, none married, none with kids. I was uncle to no one. Consequently, a picture of a newborn elicits no greater sentimental reaction in me than one of a lollipop or a washing machine, a deckchair or a Little Chef. But I was aware that Elena was looking at me in a strangely provocative fashion, her chin tilted towards the table, eyes peeking out from beneath their lids, her irises an expansive chocolate brown in the flickering candlelight. There was nothing sexual about it, but rather manipulative in some more profound way, and that made me uncomfortable. I changed the subject.

I have nothing against children per se. I neither hate nor hold them in any kind of negative light. I liked them well enough back when I was one myself, but ever since adulthood I have had precisely nothing to do with them. I come from a tiny and now virtually non-existent family. I have no aunts or uncles and, consequently, no cousins, nieces or nephews. There is a half-sister somewhere, younger than me by a generation, but we've never met, and likely never will. I don't know any children personally, and those I pass on the street I do so blindly.

8

They don't permeate my universe in any way, nor I theirs. The only time I come into any kind of contact with them at all is on aeroplanes, where I find their incessant need for stimuli incredibly wearying. In such situations, I fold into myself, wanting nothing to do with them and hoping that, in time, they will retreat.

I was on a plane to America recently, an interminable eleven-hour flight from London. I had managed to nab a bulkhead seat, which meant no one reclining in front of me and welcome extra legroom. The seats beside me were triumphantly empty until, shortly before the doors closed, a mother and her young son hurried down the aisle and plopped themselves next to me, grinning in impish victory. The woman was attractive and blonde, vaguely hippyish, and spoke a combination of Dutch and English to her boy, whom I judged to be anywhere between the ages of three and seven. He too was blond, with his mother's good looks, and wearing a hand-knitted jumper of the kind one used to see on fishermen. We were delayed by an hour and a half on the runway, a torture in itself, but the boy contented himself with a colouring book and some crayons. I myself was deep into a novel and barely registered his existence. By the time the plane finally climbed heavily into the air and straightened itself, I was ready for food, wine and some other kind of distraction. As was the boy, who was becoming increasingly fidgety. His feet kicked my knee; his elbow wrestled mine for armrest space. He started singing a tuneless song, stood up on the chair, sat down again, slid sideways. Finally, the films started and I gratefully slipped the headphones up over my ears, but as the opening credits began to roll, I became increasingly aware that he was now very still and looking squarely at me from a distance of no more than six inches. A lifelong Londoner, I'm not particularly fond of my personal space being invaded and so, ignorant of what was required of me here, I simply continued to concentrate exclusively on the film, which opened as all aeroplane films do: with a car chase. A hand then reached over and draped itself on my arm, warm to the touch. It belonged to his mother. I pulled the headphones down and turned to face her.

"He just wants you to say hello to him," she said, her face alive with maternal love.

On my TV screen, Jason Bourne was running from an explosion. He exchanged oddly calm dialogue with somebody on a mobile phone the size of a credit card. I caught none of it, my headphones useless around my neck. The boy wanted me to greet him. Fazed and rather discomforted by the strength of his prolonged stare, I spoke. "Um, well," I began. "Hello."

Somehow, this upset him. He retreated instantly, spun around and threw himself into his mother's ready embrace, his head nestling under her armpit, struggling to wriggle as far from me as his seat would permit. I've no idea what I'd done, but she was looking at me now as if I'd struck him with the back of my gloved hand and challenged him to a duel.

"Don't worry," she said, speaking very slowly. "We won't be bothering you again."

I later thought of this incident as some kind of litmus test designed to appraise my suitability or otherwise with regard to children. Clearly, I had failed. But if I were to suggest that the results bothered me, I'd be lying. They couldn't have concerned me less.

In the days and weeks that followed the manipulative dinner with Elena, she continued to bring up the subject about her friends and their new babies and about how nice they were, how appealing and covetable, until one night, in bed, she turned to me. Instinctively, I knew what was coming, the same way they say animals know when a storm is imminent. And yet, when it did, it still took the wind out of me.

When we first met, more than a decade ago, she told me that she would never want to have children. It seemed a strange thing to say to a man she had only just met, but then in so many ways Elena was an enigma to me: pleasingly foreign, yes, but otherworldly with it, and bestowed not with a mania for neurosis, as several of my previous girlfriends had been, but rather an implacable calm, a woman entirely comfortable in her own skin and seemingly impervious to judgement. This quiet confidence of hers both aroused and unsettled me; she was like a puzzle I couldn't quite work out but very much wanted to. We'd met in a cafe in Soho where she had spent three weeks working unhappily, enduring punishingly long hours and the unwanted attentions of her Middle Eastern boss who clearly believed that all women should be immediately supplicant to his charms, especially those on his payroll. She had recently split with her long-term boyfriend back in Spain and was here in London to learn English for a period of not more than six months.

We started talking after I'd ordered coffee and cake. More specifically, I posed a series of questions to which she offered succinct, clipped answers with just a hint of an encouraging smile. But even a hint was more than I was used to, and so with the caution of a bomb disposal unit, I pursued the conversation. There was eye contact, and lots of it. She was interested. There was also, minutes later, an incident with a banana but, fourteen years on, she'd rather I didn't write about this, still convinced I'd got the wrong end of the stick, a lovesick Englishman adding two and two and coming up with *sex*. But there were less ambiguous signs, too. I ordered another coffee, and this time she initiated the conversation, asking my name, where I lived, smiling, showing teeth, a flash of tongue. Initially, I had hoped she was Italian, a language I was once sort of proficient in, but no. Undaunted, I ploughed on, and although men would hit on her all the time in the café, she seemed receptive enough, or at least sufficiently unappalled, to accept my phone number.

It took two weeks before she finally called. Our first date coincided with the suicide of Kurt Cobain. "Kurt Cobain?" Elena said when I told her gravely. "I've heard of him, I think." We met at a bar, then went for dinner and finally coffee, an evening in which I seemed to do all the talking in the face of an enigmatic silence. At one point, she did speak. She leaned in and asked with concern if I was nervous. "You seem nervous," she said a little too bluntly for my liking. I failed to take it as a compliment, and promptly resolved that our first date would also be our last. Much later, I tried to explain to her that if I did appear somewhat jumpy that night it was only because she seemed so aloof, so very detached. She countered that she had been neither, but rather was simply nervous herself, still unsure of her command of the English language and that, besides, I had been talking so much and for so long that she'd thought it rude to interrupt.

It was on our third date that she told me of her determination never to have children, referencing an already unhappy world and her reluctance to add to its woes by swelling its population however incrementally. We hadn't even slept together yet. Back then, I rarely looked past tomorrow in terms of my own future, and so this sounded just fine to me. Also, having helped my own mother bring up my younger brother after my father left (I was ten when they separated, and promptly promoted to co-parent of a sibling who needed two), I had reached my mid-twenties in the grip of a second childhood, and was perfectly content to see it prolonged indefinitely.

Initially, ours was a relationship never meant to last. We would have six months of fun and then she'd return to Spain and I to the lonely life of an anxiously single male. But within weeks, she was moving her fat suitcase across London and into my cramped bedsit. She quit the café and I started missing work in order to stay at home and explore her more, the electric sexual relationship I had for so long pined for finally a vivid reality. One lazy afternoon at the very height of summer, in one of the capital's prettier parks, we sat on the parched dry grass, legs entwined. Bees buzzed nearby, confident ducks approached in search of lunch. I held her hand in mine and told her that I thought I was perhaps falling in love with her. She smiled her unreadable smile, and I awaited a reciprocal gesture. "I know," she said.

Her six months elapsed, and though neither of us wanted to draw attention to the fact, it became clear that not only was she not making immediate plans to return to Spain, but also that it seemed unlikely she would. A job opportunity had become available in Holland, arranged through her Basque university, a position she had previously craved.

She turned it down without a second thought. My bedsit was becoming increasingly claustrophobic, meanwhile, and we began talking about renting somewhere bigger, together. The relationship that was never supposed to endure was now looking like it might in fact do just that.

And then, as is sometimes the curious way with these things, an entire decade went by. In that time, we'd gone on many holidays and had moved from bedsit to rented flat, then crisscrossed London from one mortgage to another. She'd been with me throughout the slow death of my mother, and I'd been with her at her father's. She'd come to accept the cat I had previously shared with an earlier girlfriend as her own, and we were not just content but proactively happy. She never asked for any more commitment, and I certainly never offered it, marriage an unnecessary state that only other people seemed to require. And as for children, well, we both knew where we stood on that subject.

And then, peer pressure prompting the body clock that we had considered forever faulty, everything changed.

"Look," she said to me that night in bed, "I don't want to have to convince you on this, I simply want you to come around to the idea yourself, and willingly. I want you to want children." The light was out and the room was dark. I could see nothing of her, but I could feel the heat of her breath on my face. "And don't worry, I can wait."

In the end, of course, she couldn't wait, and after a couple of years of belligerent resistance on my part, of being incapable even of giving the prospect any serious *private* thought, much less discussing it openly, I found myself relenting and saying yes, fine, whatever, my offhand manner suggestive that it was still too big a subject for me to fully grasp. And it was. All my agreement really entailed was the acceptance of unprotected sex. We'd see what would happen after that.

With typical understatement, she received this news more with relief than excitement, explaining that she hadn't suddenly gone soft and weak at the sight of every child she passed in the street, but was simply obeying a mounting biological need. Ostensibly, she still felt the same way about children as she always had, but that this new base requirement was one that wouldn't go ignored.

I'd had no change of heart myself, and wanted children now as little as I ever had before. I had said yes to please and appease, and because the alternative wasn't worth thinking about. I knew someone once who had split up from his girlfriend after she had made a similar request of him. They were apart for eight months, during which time he became increasingly unhappy, convinced he'd made a terrible mistake. He tried to move on with his life, but desperately wanted her back. Fortunately, she felt the same, though the condition remained unchanged. He weighed up his options, and realised he had none. They have two children now and, last I heard, he regretted nothing.

I didn't want to split up with Elena, didn't want to have to find myself another European waitress to inexpertly woo. I told her this. She wished I could be more positive about it, more optimistic that this could be a good thing for us, and I suppose I wished it too. We signed no contract to mark our pact, though we may as well have. This wasn't a game for her, but rather a businesslike resolution. No more hot baths, she told me. Testicles on ice.

A couple of months later, I read Rachel Cusk's disquieting *A Life's Work: On Becoming A Mother*, a remarkably candid memoir which documents the writer's own experiences of having a child, which were fraught with doubt, confusion and a mounting depression. Happiness became elusive, domesticity an anvil that weighed her down and moored her. Her long-term prognosis seemed bleak, and I read this book as if it were a foretelling of the very end of the world, all thunder, lightning, earthquakes and eventual apocalypse. It scared the life out of me. I passed it on to Elena in the hope that she would perhaps feel likewise and reconsider her position. I told her that if she did, I'd buy her a dog, a holiday on the Trans-Siberian Express, Moscow to Beijing like we'd always planned, anything she wanted. She read it, but it changed nothing.

Continually, and only slightly tongue-in-cheekly, I liked to claim myself still too young to settle down. But then who was I kidding? I was 36 years old, and old enough to know better.

What, then, did I have to lose, apart from everything?

● ● ●

Even before the Inca Trail could lay waste to me, I was already stressed and embattled by Peru. An hour after landing in the capital city's airport, we were involved in a road accident. Our taxi had run into the back of another on a busy ring road, and though no one was hurt, with only surface damage to a pair of already surface-damaged bumpers, both drivers decided to have it out with one another in the middle of rush hour. We didn't make it to our hotel until well past ten o'clock at night, and were so exhausted from the fourteen-hour flight that I didn't have the strength to complain about our room, cramped and grey, and with all the charm of a prison cell.

The following morning, I overruled Elena's suggestion that we head to Cuzco for the required acclimatisation period and insisted we stay to investigate Lima. This proved a bad idea because although Lima is big and busy in a manner not unlike Bangkok or Bombay, cities I love, it possesses neither the charm nor illicit musk of either. The following morning, we headed back to the airport where, over seven of the most frustrating hours we have ever spent in one another's company, we slowly learned that our flight to the gateway to Machu Picchu would not be leaving until the following morning due to poor visibility.

A sleepless night followed in a wretched hotel situated opposite a blaring nightclub, and I rose to my 5.15 wake-up call with a terrific crick in my neck, a slab of stress-induced muscular pain running down its entire left side and making left-turning mobility impossible. As Cuzco finally swam into vision through the passenger window of the aeroplane, which was delayed that morning by just a single further hour, I experienced hot fury that I could not turn to look at it without first standing up and rotating my body slowly through 90 degrees.

Cuzco was freezing but beautiful, its streets dotted with woolly alpacas and laced with the sharp scent of their urine. After checking in with the booking agent for the following day's trail, we breakfasted in a quaint café that looked out onto the main square and the hills beyond. It looked ravishing. We held hands over coffee and croissants, our first tangibly romantic act since arriving in the country. I would have leaned in for a kiss at this point were it not for my neck, which was still solid and intractable and wouldn't ease until halfway through the first day of our climb.

By the time I reach the 4000-feet mark above sea level two days later, my neck soft and loose again, I am by now breathing through the eye of the needle and experiencing proper, thigh-shredding exhaustion. Night draws in early this far up and brings with it a biting wind. We collapse into our (separate) sleeping bags in our two-man tent by nine o'clock at night, grateful for the opportunity to at last be horizontal.

"Sex?" Elena says into the darkness.

But I'm asleep already.

And when, 45 kilometres and four thoroughly chaste days later, we finally reach the mystical, 600-year-old forgotten city that has bewitched the visiting world since explorer Hiram Bingham brought it to international attention back in 1911, we find the entire site engulfed in fog, a thick pea-souper that refuses to lift.

"Is very common such things," says Adril, our indefatigable guide. "But do not worry. You can buy postcard from giftshop over here. Come we go."

We take the train back to Cuzco. The journey lasts no more than three mocking hours, each of them passing in comfort. For our first night back in civilisation, I have managed to secure us a room in the best hotel in town. Our room is a shagpile luxury replete with overstuffed sofas, satellite television and a bed so high you have to take a running jump at it. The bath is built for two. But we are sapped of all energy and in no fit state for any kind of further exertion. We fall quickly into a thirteen-hour sleep, waking late the following morning to the acute realisation that the only bus to Arequipa, our next destination, leaves within the hour, and that the bus station is way across town.

We pack up and check out, jump into a taxi, and arrive with minutes to spare, collapsing onto the ancient bus as it pulls out of the station amidst a stink of leaking petrol. Five hours of potholed roads stretches out before us, promising much discomfort. In the seat in front of us is a beautiful Peruvian child, moonfaced and sombre, his skin the colour of drinking chocolate. He regards us with a mixture of interest and confusion, his generous eyebrows quizzically arched. Under his nostrils run two tramlines of thick green snot. He sneezes, and I get all of it, in my eyes, my nose, the back of my throat.

By the time we shore up at our hotel in Arequipa, I am in the grip of what becomes a brutal 48-hour flu, and I'm consigned to bed. I have a fever and can barely raise my hot head from the damp pillow. By now this whole situation has become ridiculous, as if someone, somewhere, is having a huge cosmic joke at our expense. Our anticipated babymaking holiday has descended into laughable disaster. Peru itself may be a rich and varied land but our tour of it is not conducive to romance. Over the course of almost three weeks, we manage sex on probably no more than three occasions and, due to my successive fragile states, it is never particularly great. I've been better; we've had more forgiving mattresses. After bruising my shoulder in Huachachina, the astonishing desert oasis in the south of the country where the inexperienced can snowboard down endless rolling dunes at their own risk, my flu downgrades into nothing more sinister than a miserable cold, and by the time we check into our final hotel, just a day before returning home, I spend much of our last evening on the phone with an editor organising a forthcoming job that will require me to fly to New York within twelve hours of arriving back from

Peru. New York will then keep me away for four further days, after which there will be deadlines and jet-lag and all manner of other diversions.

You'd think consensual sex between a loving couple should be an easy enough thing to muster, not least a couple who live together and have unencumbered access to the bedroom whenever they want. And mostly it is. But occasionally, life gets in the way and more important things get put on hold, sometimes indefinitely.

TWO

We live in a heavily fortified flat in an area of south-east London where the indigenous population, Millwall supporters mostly, exist in an uneasy detente with the steady influx of monied city types who can't quite afford Shoreditch and so have decided to transform our neighbourhood into the Next Best Thing. The local vet makes for a fascinating sociological study. On one side of the waiting room sit the natives with their tattoos and their pitbulls, their shaved heads and their sneers; on the other are perched the fashion designers and media tarts in Diesel and DKNY, shampooed Airedales at their feet. The twain rarely meet. Eye contact is ill-advised. Up the road, the pie-and-mash shop has recently found itself with a new neighbour, a café-slash-art gallery selling Damien Hirst originals for inflated figures that could probably pay for the few remaining council flats around the corner.

Ours is a gated apartment complex, with CCTV and a 24-hour porter who deals with everything from plumbing concerns to the postman, and successfully keeps the Jehovah's Witnesses and ex-offenders selling sponges at bay. The four low-level apartment blocks are arranged around a landscaped garden that boasts its own palm tree, though quite how a palm tree survives and thrives thousands of miles from California remains a mystery. There is also a rippling pond that certain neighbours here refer to as a *Japanese water feature*.

It has its own jetty, which people sunbathe on in the summer. Our flat is in the cheap block, three floors of MDF and plywood, mostly, but it looks the part, and its warehouse-style windows give out onto the common area and allow views into the proper warehouse abodes across the way, with their high ceilings, exposed brickwork and circular staircases. Curtains are very rarely drawn here, with good reason. The underground car park is home to Audis and BMWs and pastel-coloured Vespas. At night you can hear the chopping sound of police helicopters circling above, their strobe lights picking out the burglars and the rapists on the lam.

The day we moved in, eighteen months previously, the large billboard outside the front gate was dominated by a poster alerting locals to a temporary gun and knife amnesty. Hand in your weapons with no questions asked, it encouraged. The message went largely unheeded: barely eight weeks later came news that the local bank had been held up at gunpoint. The bank robbers cleared the vaults and fled unchallenged.

There are no children within our complex because, frankly, it's not that kind of place. After we've been here a year, one woman in our block does give birth. She soon moves out. Instead, there are small, compact dogs, carefree young couples and handsome gay men. Pop bands come here for photo shoots and to film videos on the roof of the main building. In warmer months, people gather around the pond with wine glasses and corkscrews and picnic baskets and sections from the *Guardian*. Litter is frowned upon, dog shit an absolute no-no. We make friends with a couple across the way who rent out our car parking space for more money than seems good sense. They ski each winter, and it is from them that I first hear the phrase *Japanese water feature*.

We have a tiny kitchen in our flat in which sits a hip-high fridge that's mostly empty. We eat out a lot. Our bookshelves become cluttered with travel guides after holidays to India, Vietnam, Mexico and Zimbabwe. It's always nice to come home here, a ridiculously pretentious place, granted, but then we are going through a ridiculously

pretentious phase. We like it. Elena develops an interest in inte-
rior- design magazines and talks of things I have never previously
taken any notice of: minimalism, wooden floorboards, an armchair
designed by somebody called Charles Eames, which will become
the single most expensive item of furniture I hope I will ever feel
required to buy. But soon she craves a more fulfilling project.

Peru now a distant memory, we begin to try for a child in earnest.
It is not as easy as I had been led to believe. Despite a fairly decent
education, I come to find I am largely ignorant on the finer points of
making babies. Where I grew up, a stone's throw from our pseudo
penthouse flat, common consensus had it that teenage girls were
forever getting pregnant around the back of bike sheds, one quick
zipless fuck almost inevitably resulting in conception, which in turn
would secure them a council flat, housing benefit and a satellite dish. I
read recently that England has the highest rate of teenage pregnancy
in all of Europe, but for us, well past our teenage years, it proves a far
more convoluted business. Perhaps we should have been prepared for
this, because a decade's worth of the rhythm method has never once
resulted in the need of a morning-after pill. After several months of
not failure exactly, but rather *un*success, Elena buys something from
the chemist that tells her when she is at her most fertile, and she suggests that I, if you like, store myself up beforehand to help maximise
our chances of conception. It's a question of mathematics. The more
sperm I produce in one climax, the more theoretical likelihood of
launching at least one swift and determined swimmer. It's as close as
we come to tantric sex.

But as the months tick tauntingly by, nothing happens, and a dis-
appointing pall begins to infiltrate our collective mood. Tellingly for
a couple who previously seemed so happy to discuss almost anything,
this is something we choose not to dwell on. We hear that stress can
be a major factor during this process, and what a nasty Catch-22
situation that is. The more you obsess over becoming pregnant, the
less likely you are to do so, and so you invariably obsess all the more.
Throughout it all, Elena's yearning has not in any way diminished,

and I begin to fear what will have to come next, should the worst-case scenario be confirmed. The idea of cripplingly expensive IVF or the long bureaucratic road to adoption hardly seem like attractive alternatives to me.

In the meantime, she has become increasingly industrious in her efforts. She has cut down drastically on her drinking, while in the kitchen cabinet I find a dual pack of something called Pregnacare Plus, which, I read, contains 300mg of DHA, whatever that may be, which helps support the brain and eye development, the level recommended by international experts. It's the science of it, I think, that really grips me by the throat and reminds me I'm being led in a direction that will never make very much sense. The front of the box features a heavily pregnant woman, smiling with pride at her prominent bump. Will my girlfriend ever strike a similar pose? Do I even really want her to? I put the box back in the cupboard, then sit on the Eames chair and stare into space.

The seasons change, and each month brings with it a fresh need for more tampons. The ghost of an old conversation reminds us that she had once been warned of this fate, despite the fact that everything that wasn't once working as it should now clearly is. Ultimately, she remains pragmatic because pragmatic is her natural state, but we now both make appointments with the doctor. I am not necessarily a pessimistic person, but I feel increasingly that the fault could be mine. A good friend, Peter, has recently got his girlfriend pregnant within the first month of trying. So what, precisely, am I doing wrong here?

• • •

The morning I take my testicles to the doctor for examination is, of course, a wretched one, the experience painfully redolent of sitcom cliché. It has been almost a year now of unprotected sex, and while that in itself has had its benefits, our repeated inability to conceive has become difficult to bear. If it does prove to be my fault, then I won't at least be alone. Over the last decade, men's sperm counts have declined by a mighty 29 per cent due, as I understand it, to the multiple ills of modern life. It's all down to smoking and drinking, to obesity and anorexia, the excessive use of mobile phones. Even exercise can prove somehow harmful. I'm guilty of just two of these things: I drink, but not particularly to excess, and I use my mobile phone *a lot*. I don't smoke, I'm not not too fat or too thin, and while I swim for twenty minutes a day (because I haven't the strength for 30), that hardly counts as proper exercise. Apparently, a man should drink four pints of water daily to keep hydrated, because hydration is as good for the sperm count as it is the rest of well-being. I tried that for a while. I spent more time peeing than I did working, and it made visits to the cinema terribly awkward. But it's all too late now. My fate could already have been decided. All I want to be told today is that my sperm count is that most covetable of states: normal.

I am sitting in the surgery's waiting room alongside cancerous old folk and scabrous youth, in a symphony of lung-rattling coughs and the sound of mucus being sucked down from noses and noisily swallowed. My legs are drawn together at the knee. My right foot is bouncing up and down furiously. I'm wearing my anxiety like a coat. I know I'll be crushed if I'm told I shoot blanks, and though this doesn't exactly mean I'd rather it was Elena's womb at fault, I think secretly it probably does. There are masculinity issues at stake here, dumb, ignorant ones perhaps, but important ones nevertheless. Elena would cope much better with such news. I'd collapse into a self-obsessed depression. She would simply brush it off with a sad resignation but quick acceptance, and then steer me instead to consider our options. She'd insist on adoption; I'd refuse for reasons I've yet to analyse. We'd split up. I'd have to flatshare all over again.

The sound of my name, mispronounced as ever, through the tinny Tannoy sends a lead weight from my heart to my feet. I shake it off and rise. An old woman beside me shouts at the receptionist that she was here first.

The doctor's room is cold. I've never met him before, an Indian man younger than me and, though it surely can't be possible, more nervous. He nods his head hello without making eye contact, and asks me the reason for my visit. I explain, and he requests that I remove my trousers and boxer shorts. I have never shown my genitals to another man before, at least not willingly. I'm not quite sure of the etiquette. A sharp snap of rubber gloves onto elegant fingers that I like to imagine could play the piano rather well, and he sinks with ceremony to his knees before me. I look down on him, feeling briefly papal, and notice dandruff on his thinning crown. The room feels as if it's getting even colder, which concerns me for obvious reasons, but it's too late now, and what should I care anyway of any conclusion he may draw? (I care terribly.) I concentrate on his dandruff while he does what he does with a tenderness I am silently grateful for. He moves my penis to one side, then places ginger fingertips on each testicle, squeezing gently and tickling the hard spheres within the sacs. I do not get an erection, which I decide can only be a good thing. Five minutes later, I am discharged with a preliminary clean bill of health, and am given an appointment for a sperm test in four weeks' time. I view this as a stay of execution, and am grateful for it.

The following day, I fly to America for work, where a colleague tells me that excessive air travel can play havoc with one's sperm count, while another says that my jet-lag-banishing sleeping pills of choice will also greatly reduce my chances of natural conception. I wish I'd never spoken of this, a private matter, to them. Before I left, Elena told me that three more of her closest friends back in Spain have now had to undergo IVF treatment, a statistic that to me seems unbelievably high. When did it all get so very complicated?

In America, I endure three mostly sleepless nights thanks to my new avoidance of the sleeping pills, and I arrive back from my trip exhausted early on a Sunday morning. I fall into bed alongside a drowsy girlfriend, but on the bedside table I see a predictor kit, a familiar sight to me by now. It has been used, the results gauged, and I fully understand what is expected of me. Sex, of late, has become

24

strangely mechanical, which isn't necessarily unarousing in itself, but we do approach the task now much in the same way we would the washing-up, as something that has to be done. We are quick and quiet, necessarily so because a friend visiting from Spain is still fast asleep in the next room. As I withdraw and begin to slip towards slumber, I watch as Elena inverts herself into an almost yogic pose, her legs high up on the wall, abdomen arched, fingers crossed.

Rather perversely, I find I am looking forward to the sperm test. Not the results, of course, which I fear with the dread of one learning that he has cancer, but I imagine the process itself to be an interesting experience, something I can joke about with friends in a safely distant future. I expect a clinical cubicle within a hospital and a pile of well-thumbed pornographic magazines. But then I realise that there is something indubitably dated about this image. It speaks of Leslie Phillips and Hattie Jacques, of Robin Asquith, an unlocked door and a hilarious misunderstanding. I wonder, then, whether the process has updated itself for the 21st century. Perhaps in place of the magazines there is now a keyboard, a mouse, a flat screen monitor and a credit card reader. If that's the case, I could spend *hours* in there.

I confide in a friend about my impending appointment, and he tells me to anticipate something entirely different. He says that I will be expected to masturbate at home, and will then have no more than an hour to get my warm sample into a safe pair of hospital doctor's hands. My GP never told me this, did he? Thinking of it now, I'm not sure he said anything about it at all. I don't like the idea of phoning and asking the receptionist. So what do I do? And if my friend is right, what happens if I were late with my delivery? Do I live within an hour of the hospital? The bus outside my flat is notoriously unreliable, often stuck in traffic or else delayed because children from the local school have set fire to one of the seats on the upper deck again. And even if I did reach the hospital in time, how would I find the particular department? I never know quite how to follow all those coloured lines on the dull linoleum flooring. I tried it once for an ingrowing toenail appointment and ended up in oncology. And if I did miss the 60-minute deadline, what then? Another cup, and a suggestion to repair to the nearest public toilet? I'm not sure I could perform in a public toilet, not at my age.

Elena's own hospital appointment is still several weeks off. Apparently, they are terribly busy with a great many women in identical situations as hers. She is told, and presumably the pun wasn't intended, to be *patient*.

A job comes up, but it clashes with my sperm test and so I am forced to turn it down, unusual for me because work always takes priority. That's £600 down the drain, or rather spunked up the wall.

And then, three days before my appointment, Elena begins to exhibit the classic symptoms of PMT. By now, I know the signs.

But this time, I am wrong.

• • •

It is a clement Saturday afternoon in late April and we are in Covent Garden to see friends, to wander around the shops, have coffee and then make our ambling way back home. Nothing is pressing today, which is just how a Saturday afternoon should be. But Elena is acting strangely, and I don't know why. She has trouble paying attention to anything I say, her mind somewhere else. En route back to our bus stop, she spies a chemist and says she needs to pop in. She re-emerges a minute later with a flush to her cheeks and a smile I fail to recognise.

"I bought one," she says.

"One what?"

"A pregnancy testing kit."

My Adam's apple dips low as I swallow hard. I tell her she is foolish, building up hope unnecessarily when we both know precisely why she is experiencing these mood swings, but she just shrugs her shoulders and offers me another curious smile. We arrive home with a bottle of wine and a video, but dinner passes with an uneasy feeling of anticipation. She wants to do the test, but I keep stalling. My reasons, admittedly, are weak ones: I point out that we have a video to watch. If she takes the test now and it turns out to be positive, then that would make actually sitting down and paying attention to the film I just paid £3.50 for virtually impossible. Couldn't we do it first thing in the morning instead?

She strides purposefully to the toilet, pees, flushes and comes back into the living room with the radioactive stick held tightly in her hand. She sits next to me on the sofa, the cat purring quietly between us, and asks if I am ready. The honest answer is that I have never felt less ready for anything in my life. She turns the stick around, a thumb covering the circular display.

"Now?" she says.

I make her first explain to me how the thing works and what we are looking for, and she says that a + means pregnant, an unbroken | means that I will keep my sperm test appointment this coming Tuesday morning. I nod my head in a close approximation of the affirmative. My mouth is dry. The video, which I'd loaded into the machine while she was in the loo, is on pause, the picture holding fast. It will stay that way for a good while yet.

She slides her thumb away and we see a +. It says everything to me in one powerful, tumbling instant, an approaching tsunami of total comprehension. At the same time, it means absolutely nothing.

"And…?" I ask.

She is smiling a small, neat smile. She looks pretty and radiant.

"You're going to be a father," she says.

I am not proud of my reaction; it simply is what it is. If anything, I'm outside myself, merely a helpless bystander watching on. I place my head between my knees like in an aeroplane about to crash, and the room spins, not in a figurative sense but somehow literal, picking up speed and flinging me violently about, a wet rag in a gale. A strong wave of nausea reaches my throat and I open my mouth, tongue exposed, to vomit. An empty wretch. I look up into Elena's lovely face, which is bright and hopeful, and I burst into howling tears. They flow with a force that scares me. I don't usually cry. I bury myself in her embrace and hide.

"I was hoping for a better reaction," she says, her voice cracking. "I mean, this is good news, after all, right? What we've been trying for for over a year now?"

I laugh, and then I start crying again. I have no idea why. The cat senses something bad is happening and leaves us, her stomach pressed low to the floor. The video, still on pause, suddenly times itself out and the television bursts into life. Ant is chasing Dec up some stairs surrounded by an excitable studio audience waving banners. He is laughing loudly, practically hooting.

Three

So what, exactly, was my problem? Why such an exaggerated reaction to something we had, after all, been actively chasing for a dispiriting amount of time now? My reasoning, perhaps predictably, will err towards the simplistic here but will be, I hope, no less pertinent for that. In the past twelve months, I had been doing something that was, to all intents and purposes, for the benefit of my girlfriend, not me. I enjoyed all the sex, and I also liked the idea of striving towards a specific goal. He shoots, he scores. But once we'd actually done it, once we'd hit the back of the net and *conceived*, the full ramifications were beginning to dawn. It seems incredibly obvious to state it now, but *I was going to become a father*, a sentence so loaded with threat and suggestion that I didn't quite know what to do with it. It meant that everything I had come to appreciate in my life was about to end and be replaced with an unimaginable level of change. There were other concerns, too. My own family had hardly been an ideal model. Would I be condemned to repeat the pattern?

I remember several years ago now interviewing an up-and-coming band who would go on to become one of the most successful, and respected, of their generation. More intelligent than many of their peers, both then and certainly now, the singer told me that it was unlikely they would ever implode in the manner of their musical forefathers simply because they had spent their formative years devouring biographies of them and effectively taking notes from these bands of the 1960s, the 70s and 80s, for whom success came in a rush, went straight to their heads and ultimately proved their undoing. This will never happen to us, the singer insisted. We'll be able to recognise the warning signs, the point at which we need to step back, take stock and reappraise. It was a method that would serve them well. Fifteen years on, and his predictions have come true. They have yet to implode but rather have negotiated their career upon their own strict and idiosyncratic terms. In many ways, he said to me, this is a method we should all adapt to *all* areas of our lives.

By extension, then, if we can pinpoint where our own parents went wrong, we'll avoid their pitfalls and thrive, yes? It's a nice idea, all rosy and soundbitey and idealistic. If only life were quite so straightforwardly simple.

"The kind of man that is worried about becoming a father is actually your *average* man. And that's good, of course it is, because it's a sign of his deep sense of responsibility." So says Adrienne Burgess, Policy Director for Fathers Direct, the UK online information centre for fathers. Fathers Direct is where men can go for advice on every aspect of modern fatherhood, from the rigours of juggling the pressures of work and home to just how a new father can cope if he happens to be on drugs, drowning in alcohol or incarcerated at Her Majesty's pleasure. You can buy dad magazines from this service, starter help kits; you can also buy a book on how to get more connected to God, should a new father deem such a thing necessary.

I meet Burgess at her London home. She's small, Australian-born and middle-aged, a woman who seems to know not just plenty on this subject but precisely how to dispense it with vigour. She is feisty and declamatory, and very good company.

"To be honest," she continues, "I'd worry about the man who *doesn't* worry about becoming a father. It is, after all, a bloody big deal."

In her experience, she tells me, it is entirely normal for men to fret about every last detail of their partner's pregnancy, from the health of the foetus to the effect it will have on their lives. Most men cope; but many don't. On the day we meet, there is a report in the newspapers about a man who, having accompanied his wife to the three-month ultrasound of their first baby, then promptly committed suicide. Granted, this was something of an extreme reaction, but the point does echo Burgess's suggestion that it is a *very* big deal.

"Women, in the stereotype, tend not to think as far ahead as men during pregnancy," she says of the different reactions between the sexes. "They don't worry about putting roofs over their children's heads, but rather they concerntrate on things like nurture and love. I don't know, maybe there is a hormone that insulates women against that anxiety, but it certainly doesn't insulate their partners. If you talk to men about their feelings during pregnancy, they tend to tell you about all the worries they have, their concerns over the neighbourhood they currently live in and whether it's appropriate for raising a family. They worry about the future, about their children falling in with the wrong crowd, drinking, experimenting with drugs. Again speaking in stereotype, men are also often the main breadwinners. Unless you are in an extraordinary situation, your partner will likely be out of the workforce for a considerable amount of time and will never, on average, make up the loss of her earnings. So of course you will be the primary breadwinner. The trouble is, men often don't feel equipped to be, and so it is an unusual man indeed who *fails* to worry about how they are going to provide once the baby arrives."

I ask her if it's also expected for us to fret about our own upbringings, fearful of repeating the mistakes of our parents with our children.

"Absolutely. Of course," she says. "We all do. Look, no one sets out to damage their children, but what we all have to do is limit the damage as much as we possibly can by reflecting on our past experiences. That's the key."

One of the most damaging things that can happen to children during their upbringing, she continues, is role reversal, when the child suddenly finds himself taking on the mantle of co-parent. This usually occurs after divorce. I tell her that this was something that happened to me. She frowns, and so I ask her whether I'm irrevocably damaged goods.

"No, because you have a good relationship with your partner now and you are able to process your feelings. Also, just by being here and talking it over with me now suggests that you think about it a lot, which I'd say was pretty crucial. As the saying goes, 'Those that do not reflect on the past are condemned to re-enact it.' My advice to you?" Burgess says, hands bunched into fists. "Reflect. Always reflect."

And so I do.

Somehow, the combined strands of my upbringing, though mostly happy and positive, have conspired to mould me into the kind of adult male who bursts into tears when his partner gives him a piece of news that people the world over would pay good money to receive. In other words, it's my parents' fault.

In her lifetime, my mother rarely managed to sustain long-term happiness, not just because of an enduring clinical depression but also because of circumstance. She was born in Yugoslavia, the product of a reckless affair between her mother and an Italian soldier. My grandmother's pregnancy was not good news, given that, at the time, 1943, Italy was busy occupying the country. She was forced to flee across the border, ending up in a convent in Milan. Seven years later, she married an Italian (my grandfather), my mother now passed off to everyone as their daughter. But her presence was a daily reminder of a sin best kept secret, something she herself became increasingly sensitive to throughout adolescence and well into adulthood.

She arrived in London in her early twenties at the very height of Beatlemania, her intention to remain in the city long enough to become fluent in the language and to see a world wider than industrial Milan could ever offer. Fresh off the plane, she still pronounced Thames with a soft "th" and consequently had much to learn. She gravitated towards Hampstead, where for a while she worked as a live-in nanny, the separation from her parents, who had raised her with a sense of stricture more redolent of Victorian times, making her feel deliriously free. Soon, she met my father, a Yorkshireman by birth, and their whirlwind romance shortly afterwards began to develop an air of permanence about it. A year passed, then two, and she failed to return home. My grandparents were furious. In an attempt to assuage them, she took my father to meet them. They weren't impressed. He seemed remote, deliberately so. He didn't speak Italian, and showed few signs of ever wanting to learn. Shortly after returning home, they announced their engagement, my mother already pregnant with me. My grandmother was tearful. My grandfather, in his most stentorian voice, predicted an unhappy marriage that would surely end in divorce. He became even more certain of this a few years later when they paid us a visit. By now, my parents had two sons and were living in a brand-new estate in south-east London, nine floors up in a block of nineteen that would soon become a popular place for suicides. My grandparents quickly gleaned that my father wasn't about as much as he should have been, the euphemism most regularly employed that he was away on *business*. When my grandfather's sour forecast finally came good in 1978, my mother asking my father to pack his bags and my father doing just that, he couldn't help but crow. The daughter he'd raised as his own was now alone in a crime-infested estate in another country, with little money and desperately trying to provide for her children. He told her that she should give serious thought to returning to Italy at once, where at least she had friends, a support network, her parents. She refused.

To have separated parents was becoming increasingly commonplace at school, and though our teachers were mostly helpless in their ham-fisted attempts to placate the pain and confusion of these pupils, they did cut us considerable slack as a result. For reasons I wouldn't fully learn of for decades, my father never did become a weekend dad, but rather an entirely absent one. When he left, he effectively disappeared for good. We heard nothing from him after 1980: no visits, no phone calls, no letters. I took it all with a curious equanimity, perhaps desperate to hold it all together when my mother plainly wasn't, but my brother took it hard. He had always been prone to a quick and fierce temper, but this became more pronounced after my father left. The slightest thing would set him off and he'd rage magnificently, all eyes and hair and gnashing teeth. Someone at school would say something, he'd hit them, then bolt from wherever he was to somewhere else, sometimes missing for hours. He never went very far, most often to the nearest chip shop to play Pac Man, or else to my mother's office around the corner where he was immediately calmed and allowed to swivel on an executive chair. I, meanwhile, was invariably summoned to the headmaster's office for a quiet word, and here this otherwise terrifying man was unexpectedly sympathetic. We were from a *broken family*, he told me. What else was anyone to expect? Such conveniently mitigating circumstances would get my brother forgiven for plenty over the next few years.

My mother was forever melancholy and frequently angry, at herself and what she saw as wretched circumstances for a woman in her early thirties with still so much to offer, so much more to achieve. Outside of annual summer trips back to Milan, she routinely refused the offer of help from her parents, largely because it came with, for her, unfavourable conditions; but despite the perpetuity of her misery, she did manage to thrive. She got us out of the suicidal block of flats and into a council house on a better street. She bought on hire purchase a washing machine, meaning we'd never have to visit the squalid local launderette again. She bought a car, a Morris Minor, and we went places at the weekend. She had two jobs, one in an office during the day, the second doing accounts for a local chemist by night. Sometimes, she'd work as an interpreter for Italian companies at weekends. And she was there for us always, as strong for her sons as she was weak in herself. She confided everything in me, in matters I was far too young to fully comprehend, but I tried anyway, with a feigned sense of maturity that would come to define me. I was the serious and capable one, the good son, whether I wanted to be or not. I was my mother's confidant, her stabiliser, and increasingly my brother's arch enemy. Our father was lost to us. More often than not, I couldn't wait for childhood to be over.

Strange, then, to find myself now mimicking at least some of those patterns set down by my parents. The girl I had met and fallen for was also foreign and had also come to London, initially, for a limited time. And she, like my mother, had chosen to stay. Her own mother, far less Victorian in her attitudes, was mercifully more encouraging, happy in her daughter's happiness wherever it may lie, but was unavoidably disappointed in her choice of men. I wasn't Basque, wasn't even Spanish, but rather English, an *English* who didn't speak Spanish and, just like my father, showed little real intention of ever doing so.

But it was here, I very much hoped, that our similarities ended. Unlike my parents, we never felt any need to fast forward into marriage, much less an unplanned pregnancy, despite our often careless approach to safe sex. We took our time, we rushed nothing. More pertinently still, Elena and I, unlike both my parents and hers (who, though they remained married until her father's death in 2003, never seemed to like one another very much), were happy and content. Just like that band I'd interviewed all those years previously, we'd learned from the mistakes of others and had adjusted our own lives accordingly.

To then bring a baby into this equation was surely to throw everything off its axis. A baby would bring with it doubt and uncertainty, and it would also bring something I'd never very much wanted in the first place: a sense of responsibility. And tell me, what unreconstructed male in this day and age, an era in which arrested development is all but a global state of mind, would crave a thing such as that?

• • •

I decide to take things one step at a time. If I can simply focus on the business of today, then I'm hoping that that will help me muster the courage for tomorrow and the day after that. It is May, eight months until the birth, which comfortably feels like a lifetime away at the very least. We have committed to telling no one until the mandatory three months have passed. I'm not quite sure why they are mandatory, because even if the pregnancy were to end abruptly in miscarriage – and today's statistics suggest that one in five do – would we be expected to keep it secret from our closest friends? Despite all my reservations, our news is like a hot coal in the palm of my hand. I want to pass it around, and quickly. I'd like to know how friends' reactions will make me feel about it. But we've made a pact. Silence until summer.

A week later, I am speaking to my friend Peter on the phone, the same Peter who had managed to impregnate his partner on the first attempt. Like me, he was reluctant to start a family and did so largely at the wishes of his girlfriend. Though he doesn't know it yet, this gives us a new common bond. In fact, I very likely have a common bond with half the pregnant males in the world right now.

When I spoke to Adrienne Burgess about why the decision to try for a baby is almost invariably led by the woman, she explained to me that it wasn't that men didn't want children at all; they just wanted them *later*.

"Women tend to want to start a family much earlier, but by the time they have reached their mid-40s, many men we've questioned said they considered the importance of having them just as highly."

Which means that by the time men actively *crave* to start a family, they already have one. But, she continues, the age gap is narrowing.

"We are having children later in life these days, very often towards our mid to late 30s, by which time the majority of men have at least started to come around to the idea."

Burgess also suggests that in older age it is men who suffer more from childlessness than women. Men, more inclined to be loners than their partners, will experience a stronger sense of loss, perhaps because women are already more tied into family networks. We all have a desire to nurture the next generation. Women can spread this around their existing family, as teachers or nurses or carers, or else amongst the children of friends. But men would much rather nurture their own flesh and blood.

And so anyway, I'm on the phone to Peter. His girlfriend is six months pregnant now. He talks to me of his excitement, and then of his anxieties. He asks me how I am. I tell him our news. I can't help it; it just comes tumbling out. There is a moment's silence on the line, and then his voice, rising an octave, is joyful and congratulatory. He clearly means it, despite all his own reservations. This, I will come to find, is a typical reaction in all men, irrespective of our own personal feelings towards fatherhood. For whatever reason, we view it, in others, as fantastic news, worthy of a cigar, some champagne. I had been much the same with him. When he first told me of his girlfriend's pregnancy, I was full of good cheer in the face of his own bemusement. I later relayed the news to Elena as if I had impregnated his girlfriend myself. I have no idea why.

The following evening, I meet a friend for dinner. This is someone who has no interest in children himself and neither does his girlfriend (within the year, they will have an abortion, and it can't come quickly enough for both), and yet he too greets the news with happiness. There are tears in his eyes. A week later, I tell one more friend, then another. That's it: four. Now nobody else for the mandatory twelve weeks. I have no regrets in telling the people I've told. Their reactions have made me view my abilities in a new light. Me Tarzan. If it doesn't quite make me feel any better about the reality of impending fatherhood itself, then it nevertheless makes the here and now more manageable, and I couldn't ask for more.

I tell a fifth person, then one more for luck.

• • •

Suddenly, there are babies everywhere, as if transplanted into the neighbourhood specifically to taunt me. They do an efficient job. My local café, the one with the Damien Hirsts on the wall, has overnight become a magnet for upwardly mobile young mothers and their over-sized strollers, these bizarrely ergonomic prams and pushchairs that they wield the way a soldier does a machine gun, aware they could go off at any moment. And often they do, shredding the atmosphere of this small, cramped space with the sudden bleating sobs of a not-for-long unseen infant. It makes any reading I'd hoped to do impossible, and ratchets up my frustration until my temples throb. I become unavoidably judgemental, and hate them. They come in here, these beautiful young blondes and brunettes, many of them younger than me and all of them more financially secure, with an aggressive air of pride and self-confidence, as if the ability to procreate were worthy of a prize. Why else would they swan and strut about the place as if they owned it? And if I have to squeeze past them in order to fetch myself a muffin and a latte, then so be it. Will they inch their wheels forward to allow me better access? Of course not. They are far too wrapped up in themselves, discreetly breast-feeding while indiscreetly conducting their conversations at a pitch that suggests their hearing was destroyed during the hyena screams of childbirth. And so here I sit, day after day, with my book, unable to focus, and watching as one breast is unharnessed while another is hooked up again, each as heavy as meat. Gradually, I buckle, then break. I've had enough of pregnancy at home without being reminded of it here in my coffee break. I start going to Starbucks instead.

In the middle of July, we attend the three-month scan. It is a key moment, this, because it offers concrete proof of what has until now felt more theoretical than anything else. I haven't been to a hospital since my mother died in one, and the sense of déjà vu swamps me. We sit in the holding room, leafing through dog-eared magazines long past their sell-by date and wait until Elena's name is called. I experience flopsweat.

We arrange ourselves in a darkened room, Elena on her back, stomach bare, while a nurse puts a paper towel beneath the lip of her knickers, warning that the translucent gel she is about to spread over her belly will be cold. She places something plastic and medical on her by now definable bulge, which prompts a picture to burst into black-and-white life on the monitor screwed high up on the far wall. At first, it's snow, nothing more than television interference. It takes some time before an image settles, and when it does, it's of a body, skeletal, slightly curled and on its back, limbs floating weightlessly above, serene in peace. We see the umbilical cord trailing into murky darkness, and the outline of a face, a nose, a smudge of fingers and toes. The nurse flicks a switch at the monitor and suddenly we hear heavy sound: the rhythmic thud of a heartbeat, but quick and rapid, as if it were running a race rather than resting suspended in amniotic fluid. A limb jerks, and the baby moves, then moves back again and resettles, and yawns. It is alive. Measurements are taken, once, twice, seven times, and a conclusion is drawn: our foetus has a one in 1200 chance of being born with Down's Syndrome, which places us in a safety zone in which panic and further testing will not be required.

Elena is rapt and curious, unsmiling in studious concentration as if she were sitting an exam. We had been holding hands initially, but my palm has long since slid away from hers due to all the excessive sweat I'm producing. She turns to look at me now and finds me leaning forward, elbows on knees, and breathing fast through the open cave of my mouth. I am fighting an urge here to get up, kick back the chair and run.

"Oh dear," says the nurse.

Eventually, I regain some kind of composure and ask the nurse whether she can confirm something for us, that we are expecting *a* baby, as in just the one. She pays me little attention, wiping the smear of gel from Elena's stomach with a coarse paper towel in a distracted manner, and I am forced to repeat myself. I tell her that Elena's brothers are twins. Twins run in the family, right? *Right?* She turns to me. As deadpan as a stand-up comedian, she points at the now frozen image on the screen which will cost us two pounds to have turned into a photograph and asks how many I see. In response, talking quickly now, I tell her of a man I met recently who told me that at the three-month scan of his wife's first pregnancy, they were told she was expecting just the one child. But by the time of the five-month scan, it was revealed that she was in fact expecting two.

"Something to look forward to then," the nurse says, her pink tongue rudely exposed between pursed and poison lips.

• • •

I've said this already, but it bears repeating. None of my immediate friends are fathers yet, and none are married. Two have just ended long-term relationships and are wilfully single, one remains gay. I can't help but feel that if I had had greater peer pressure – *if he can do it, so can I* – then this process would be so much easier on me. Only Peter, whom until recently I had known solely in a professional capacity, is on hand to show me the ropes, as it were. He is six months ahead of me, and I follow his progress closely. He appears to be coping, and coping well.

I find I now crave advice, not the expert kind dispensed in the myriad How To guides, but rather from someone with whom I can more readily identify. I begin to seek out other fathers to talk to, to grill. Something strange happens in this regard: I am readily indulged, and often rather fulsomely, by both colleagues and strangers. It is, I come to learn, that kind of topic, with so much to impart and even more to share.

Men generally don't like to talk in the free and expressive manner of women. There are instead countless unspoken parameters to what we can and cannot discuss, and multiple no-go areas to which we are permitted access only when drunk and emotional. As a gender, we have difficulty opening up to one another, and deeper feelings remain tucked away in hiding, as if ashamed of themselves. Instead, we make do with the time-consuming business of discussing music and film, football and alcohol, and the women we would seduce were seduction something at which we excelled. But when I approach men for advice on fatherhood, it's as if the doors are suddenly thrown open to a secret club at which I have immediate membership. Within seconds, we are able to race towards an intimacy that would otherwise have remained out of bounds. During these conversations, I have had men admit things to me that they wouldn't ever to their partners. I have seen them well up and hold on to me for support. I have been given photographs of their children as keepsakes. It is as surprising as it is enlightening, and I'm grateful for it.

I speak to a tour manager who, though in his early forties, still acts and boasts the narcotic appetites of a 25-year-old. He becomes swiftly soft and gooey at the mention of his kids. He has two children, seven and three years old, "the best thing I've ever done in my sorry life", he says. He tells me their names, describes to me their characteristics, the difficulties but also the joys, and how much his heart aches every time he has to leave them. When I tell him I'm about to become a father myself, he places a meaty paw on my arm and suggests we get wasted in celebration. He gives me his phone number and says to call whenever. "I'm there for you, pal. Welcome to the club." Somebody else I speak to, a businessman in a bespoke suit who is more chatty on a long-haul flight than I would strictly like him to be, reveals to me that babies largely fail to engage men fully until they are at least a year old. If anyone tells me different, he insists, they are lying.

"Basically, until they are at least twelve months, it's all about the mother," he says. "And you can't help but feel shut out. But don't worry, because after the first year, they start to interact more and want to know who you are. That's when it becomes good and fun. They become lovable as well, which is just the most indescribable feeling. And it's a love completely different to how you feel about your partner. After that, more or less, it just keeps getting better. But do keep in mind that the early months, at first, are tough, very tough."

I am introduced to an acronym, OPK, uttered in a derisive manner: "Don't worry if you don't like other people's kids," I'm told.

"Nobody does. Generally speaking, other people's kids are horrible little bastards. That doesn't mean you won't like your own. Your own are something else entirely. Even when they have their moments of horrible little bastardry, and they will, believe me, you're somehow blind to it. And even if you're not, you'll forgive them in an instant, a click of the fingers. Eventually, they'll turn into the most wonderful people you will ever meet, and that is priceless. Every other relationship will pale by comparison."

I collect all these morsels and hold onto them, with hope and optimism. I'm particularly taken by the OPK disclaimer, and feel infinitely encouraged by it. I'll have reason to remind myself of it frequently.

We are invited to Sunday lunch at the house of a friend of a friend. It's a sort of dinner party thing, but in the afternoon, because evenings are dominated by their children's bath and bedtime. They live in east London, and we arrive to shrieking pandemonium, his children, three girls with pistons for limbs and a surfeit of energy, tearing around the front room and screaming at a level that could cause tinnitus. Because of the commotion, which is appalling in its constancy, ordinary conversation remains impossible. Elena looks at me long and hard, her gaze trying to transform my frown into an accepting smile. As we take our place at the dinner table, to be served a traditional Sunday lunch with all the trimmings (and Ribena), one of the girls sits on the floor at my feet, a notepad and green crayon in her hands. She looks up at me intently.

"Here," she tells me moments later, tearing the paper from its binding, which is now filled with green scribble. "I drawed you a picksher, see?"

At lunch, the children wolf down their small portions and then proceed to chase one another around the table, continually running into its corners and bursting into brief but apocalyptic tears, or else they clamber over my increasingly tense thighs and try to reach for knives and forks, the salt and the pepper. This makes them hot, and so they remove their dresses and continue with the running game. None of them having put on underwear this morning, they are now quite naked. Their parents don't bat an eyelid and neither does Elena. I become intensely uncomfortable. I don't know where to look, but I try not to look at them in case my gaze is misconstrued. At one point, one of the girls insists on sitting on my lap. Her mother whisks her away into the kitchen. I offer a silent prayer in thanks. She comes back in pants, and in tears.

As we leave, relieved at last by the comparative silence of the passing cars, buses and lorries, Elena reminds me of the last time we went to a house with children in it, at which I had a similar adverse reaction. It was several years ago, and my girlfriend was still ignorant of the unwritten laws of the British city dweller that decries we keep ourselves to ourselves and never mix with the locals unless strictly necessary. Rather Spanishly, she became insistent that we make friends with our next-door neighbours. She'd bumped into the woman at the shops recently, and they'd stared talking. Elena suggested we all meet for dinner, and we duly received a formal invitation.

Upon arrival, we learned that dinner had been downgraded at the last minute to tea and biscuits because the woman and her husband, a meek man whose eyes seemed to me full of unspoken pain, hadn't had any time to buy in food due to the demands of their newborn baby, tiny, wrapped up in wool, loud as war. I was starving. We sat perched on their stained white sofa while the woman breast-fed and the baby cried and coughed and vomited. She told us about the delivery and the epidural, words of which I had little understanding and no tangible interest. I quickly tuned out. In the kitchen, her partner made more tea. I went to help. He told me about his exhaustion, his son's incessant crying – he mentioned a word, *colic*, entirely unfamiliar to me – and that he was at his wits' end. He asked me if we were trying for children ourselves; many people in the street, by all accounts, were. He'd met them during coffee mornings, he said, and he'd never had a coffee morning before. "Overrated." Back in the living room, the woman asked if I'd like to cradle her infant. Elena encouraged me. It roared. I gave it back.

Tentative plans were made to later return their hospitality, but it soon became evident that this was never going to happen. We each had our reasons. For the next year, until we moved away into our fortified flat across town, I would occasionally see the mother and baby in the street. Our eyes purposefully never met. I would hear her child's colicky wails through the walls, and, once the colic had passed, I'd hear the reasonless crying in the dead of night, and the heavy footfalls of its parents pacing the corridor, desperate for sleep and respite.

I didn't envy these people and I didn't much like their children. But then, as I now knew, these were OPK and I was allowed to remain indifferent and uninterested.

"Be positive," Elena tells me regularly. "Ours will be different."

I try, I really do. I keep thinking of the man who told me that my child would turn into the nicest person I shall ever meet.

It's a nice thought. I sleep on it.

Ashley Walters, the young father

I go to meet Ashley Walters, the south London gangsta rapper turned actor, on a cold winter afternoon at the closet-sized office of his stepfather and manager, Richard Parkes. He is in the middle of another interview when I arrive, so Parkes takes me for a coffee in a nearby café, where he tells me that he has big plans for his stepson. He is keen to move him away from the invariably negative image that he had all but fostered for himself at the beginning of his career, an image that was bolstered inexorably by a spell behind bars, and into the mainstream, "sort of like a British Will Smith", he says

You can't fault the man's ambition, but Will Smith? Walters is nothing like Will Smith, the west Philadelphia dayglo rapper turned all-American family entertainer, thanks to an ability to be both goofy and endearing at the same time, an eternal child in a man's body. Walters is far too forcefully masculine for the comparison. He speaks in a voice that sounds like tar mixed with gravel, and lots of it. He isn't particularly tall, but there is plenty of stature to him. When he shakes your hand, it stays shaken. But, like his proposed American counterpart, he is given to easy smiles, is very friendly and is also gradually establishing himself as an actor of note, one desperate to break free from stereotype. Since the dissolution of his group, So Solid Crew, back in 2003, Walters has appeared in films that have required precious little stretch. He played young black men from the wrong side of the tracks in 2004's *Bullet Boy*, 2006's *Life and Lyrics* and 2007's *Sugarhouse*. He was impressive in all of them, often turning in performances that the films themselves didn't entirely warrant. Now he has set his sights, cautiously but firmly, on Hollywood.

"A British Will Smith," Parkes says again. "You'll see."

At just 26 years old, Ashley Walters is already a family man. He and his long-term girlfriend Natalie Williams have three children together: Shayon, China and Paniro (the latter's name a combination of his favourite actors, Al Pacino and Robert De Niro). In a community where, as recent statistics suggest, 49 per cent of black men grow up in single-parent families that are inevitably headed by the mother, Walters is one of the few positive male role models around. He takes it rather seriously, too, regularly giving speeches in inner London schools and youth centres about the importance of a paternal presence.

"I know this sounds weird but it's lucky my dad fucked off when I was a little kid," he says to me at one point, "because it made me want to be around my children so much more. Even though it was a shock when Natalie got pregnant the first time, I knew that I would never abandon this child, never."

In 2001, Walters was Asher D, one of more than 30 members of the UK garage act So Solid Crew. Taking their inspiration directly from American rap, they developed a bad-boy image with such clunking flamboyance that it resembled caricature. Songs were invariably about drugs, guns and bitches. One contained the line "Gonna put you in the morgue". Another, "21 Seconds", which was fast, feral and sinister, took them to number one in the charts. The *Daily Mail*, amongst others, was up in arms over the negative imagery they were feeding our young and impressionable. A typical *Daily Mail* response, you'd think, but one that the band did their very best to live up to. Seeing them in concert became an increasingly risky business: people got shot. Venues nationwide became too fearful to book them. Five of the collective, including Walters, would end up in prison for a variety of misdemeanours, one of them murder. They didn't so much split up as become irrevocably inoperable.

But before things went seriously awry, Walters was in his element, nineteen years old, financially flush for the first time in his life, the world at his feet. But then the girl he was sort of seeing and sort of not announced that she was pregnant.

"I was like, fuck off, that's not my baby, you must be mad, you're crazy," he says now. "Though to be honest, I only responded like that because I'd seen other men doing it all around me. I think basically I just didn't want to face up to it, to take that responsibility. It was just – just too big; I was too young. You know, one minute I didn't have a care in the world, I wanted loads of girls, I *had* loads of girls, and then the next thing I was buying Pampers and getting ready for a baby. My mum, let me tell you, my mum was very disappointed. After sitting me down and talking to me for, like, five hours and telling me how I'd ruined my life, she wouldn't talk to me. I hardly saw her again for something like a year. A *year*, man. But then, you know, she was 35, not ready to be a grandmother just yet."

Abortion, he says, was never an option.

"No, never. Subconsciously, I think, I wanted this baby. Why? Maybe to save me, but definitely for my own selfish reasons. I think maybe I needed something else to focus on, something positive that would make me feel like a man, something that needed me and would love me back. The love you get from a kid is something you can't get anywhere else, and a lot of people desire that, don't they? People who haven't had much love in their lives – well, having children is a surefire way of getting it. It's having another person rely on you, isn't it? When you see babies looking at their mums, it's like, *You are the shit, the Queen, the whole wide world to me*. I think I liked that idea."

His girlfriend, who had already been on the waiting list for council accommodation, suddenly found herself with a Guinness Trust flat in one of the roughest areas of Brixton, south London. Walters moved in with her, wanting the freedom a place of their own would offer, in the same week that So Solid Crew signed a recording contract worth half a million pounds. With a baby on the way and insurmountable responsibility looming, he did what any young man in his position would. He bought himself a car.

"An Audi TT, £35,000, brand new, no licence, no insurance, no tax," he says, laughing his wonderfully filthy laugh. "I got stopped by the police a *whole* lot. A young black man in a car like that? It was practically guaranteed that if I was going *this* way and a cop car was going *that* way, they'd do a U-turn and make chase."

At which point, Walters would put his foot to the floor and be gone: "Down a side street, park, jump out, disappear into a shop, up the nearest alley; whatever I had to do, basically, to avoid them." He shakes his head. "I hated living like that, I really did. I used to watch people with licences sitting next to police cars at traffic lights, music loud, not a care in the world. I'd seriously envy them, man, seriously."

And so why didn't he do something about it? Why didn't this father-to-be sort out his licence, his insurance and tax?

He smiles broadly, and in the smile is both pride and just a little shame. "No time, mate, never any time. Life was fast."

When he wasn't appearing on *Top of the Pops* with his band or touring the country, he was at home with Natalie in Brixton, getting to know the woman with whom he was now going to be forever connected.

"Pregnancy was basically our time to get to know each other," he says. "We weren't in love at the time, me and Natalie, and I hope she doesn't feel bad about me saying that, but it's true. We weren't. Instead, we grew to love each other, pretty much because we had to. We had a kid coming."

Though he would go on to miss the births of his second and third child, he was present for the first. The labour, he remembers, "was crazy, thirteen hours of pain and torture, and all of it just amazing and totally surreal. It feels like you've been waiting for it for ever by that stage, but when it finally starts happening, you can't quite believe it, like you were convinced she was going to be pregnant for the rest of her life. But her waters broke, we rushed her to hospital and then she started scratching up my arm and chatting loads of shit, evil stuff like you see in the movies. She was pushing and pushing, screaming and in pain, but nothing was happening – for hours."

Until suddenly, everything happened all at once.

"It was unbelievable, really. When he finally started to appear, the first thing I thought was that she was giving birth to a plastic bag. All I could see was black hair, lots of it, all shiny and slick where the blood had mixed in. I was terrified that my firstborn was a plastic bag! But it wasn't, it was a boy, my son, Shayon. He came out, and when he did, he didn't make a sound, never cried or nothing; he just looked around the room blinking slowly, taking it all in. And me? I was like, Oh, alright, so this is who you are, this is what you look like. Hello."

Returning home with a baby in tow, Walters had an abrupt realisation: he had no idea what to do next. His own father had been largely absent during his upbringing, and he still felt like a kid himself. But he wanted, swiftly, to assert himself in a manner he considered appropriate.

"My idea was that a man should be a powerful thing," he says, "something like The Terminator, Arnold Schwarzenegger, a body-builder; someone who could protect and provide. Because I saw little of my dad growing up, I had to look elsewhere for that kind of influence. My next-door neighbour was very successful, a drug dealer, loads of money. He carried himself well; people respected him, feared him. He was a man to me. And that's what I thought I had to become."

And so the nineteen-year-old emergent pop star became a drug dealer. He hardly needed the money – So Solid Crew, after all, were at the height of their success – but, he explains, being in that kind of band required an attendant reputation to match.

"Trouble is, I made for a crap drug dealer, one of the worst. It just wasn't for me. I didn't even really know how to do it, was just copying those around me, trying to live up to a certain image. So Solid were hard, were *street*; I had to be as well. In that situation, a lot of people, local people, wanted to test me. I'm talking about real gangstas, people who wanted to see if I measured up. I never did."

During his brief time as Britain's most hapless dealer, Walters was shot at, kidnapped and held hostage, and became increasingly convinced he was a marked man. Walking home one night with Natalie, his baby son in his arms, he was approached by another dealer who operated the same patch. He held a gun to his head. I ask why he simply didn't pack up and run like any sensibly terrified person would. Sighing, he endeavours to explain that such a thing for someone like him was never a viable option.

"Listen, mate, that's the last thing I could have done, trust me. If I'd done that, I would have alienated myself from everyone, my crowd, even the people I considered my friends. So I just tried to keep my head down. And it's not like I wasn't busy enough trying to cope with fatherhood, because I was."

At home, he says, Natalie didn't want to be a mum for at least the first six months.

"It was probably a post-natal depression kind of thing. She found it difficult to engage, basically. So I did everything; I was mummy: sterilising bottles, changing nappies, feeding him, putting him to bed – everything that she wouldn't do, in other words. It was really hard, but me and him bonded in those six months all by ourselves because of it. Natalie came round in the end and was then totally on it, but me and Shayon have a completely different kind of relationship to the one I have with my other kids today, and I think that's directly because of those first six months. We were everything to each other."

The climate of danger in his neighbourhood, meanwhile, showed no signs of abating. He was followed home on more than one occasion, and was regularly threatened to such an extent that, increasingly fearful for his life, he got himself a gun, "for protection. The people I had beef with, see, were right on my doorstep, my next-door neighbours. I needed to be prepared".

He fired the gun just once. It happened after a near confrontation on his estate. A group of men had been following him in his Audi, and so he parked up and got out to face them, gun poised. At the sight of it, the others fled. When he returned to his car, he found that he was shaking with nerves and slick with sweat. The gun went off, the bullet embedding itself in the gear stick.

Several months later, by now a father for the second time – China, a daughter, was also unplanned, he says, but proof that they were very fertile – he was involved in an altercation with a traffic warden. The police became involved, and his car was searched. In Natalie's handbag, stuffed deep inside a sock, was the gun. It was loaded and therefore deemed a deadly weapon. Walters was arrested, tried and sent to prison for nine months. He allowed his young family to visit him just once during that time.

"I couldn't cope with seeing them while I was inside," he says. "That one time they did visit, it shattered me. I went back to my cell and broke down. It was just too painful."

By the time he was released, China was coming up to two years old.

"I got home and she looked at me as if to say, *And who the hell are you?* And you know what? I wasn't in the mood for that. I'd just come out of jail, I'd missed so much, but I didn't need to be reminded of it like that. We have a very on-and-off relationship, me and my daughter, because of that, I think. That's what I put it down to, anyway; those missing months. No one else notices it, but for me, it's there. And I'm not surprised, because they were important months in her life, and I was absent. Don't get me wrong, I adore her, and I'm so glad I've had the chance to bond with her since. I'm with her, with all my kids, all the time now. I take them to school every day, I teach them to read, I cook their dinner, the whole lot, but you can never get back what you lost, can you?"

After Paniro was born in 2004, he and Natalie decided, somewhat belatedly, to take precautions. Three children were enough. Though he missed the birth of his second son because he was in Amsterdam with friends celebrating his birthday ("Natalie was *very* pissed off with me about that"), Paniro, he explains, is the one who seems to take after him the most. He is fascinated by his father's job, and loves to accompany him on set and in the studio, obsessed with both film and music, and wants to follow in his footsteps. I meet Paniro later that afternoon, when Walters picks him up from school. He is the spitting image of his father; they have the same panther-like eyes, the same easy swagger.

"Everyone says he's a mini-me," he says, "but I'll tell you something he has I never had at his age: balls. He has just the most incredible bravery to him. I'm telling you, if I'd had his courage when I was his age, I'd be much further along the line than I am now. He is one very smart boy and so, if anything, it's me that looks up to him. That's one of the greatest things about having children, isn't it? The fact that they can surprise you so much and in so many unexpected ways."

Walters never really got to know his father, a man who'd had five other children with five different women and was in and out of prison for much of his life. Whenever he did pay an unexpected, often unannounced visit to his teenage son, Walters considered him a stranger whom he had to get to know all over again. He felt a pronounced mistrust towards him, and a residual anger, too: why did he spend more time with his other children? Why were his visits so infrequent? And then, four years ago, Walters by now an adult, his father was diagnosed with lung cancer, his chance of recovery slim.

"He said he finally wanted to get to know me before the end of his life, but by now it was very much on my terms and so I said to him: okay. I had nothing to fear from him any more."

He invited his father to visit him in Canada where he was filming, and the young actor took the chance to make up for lost time by asking him all the questions he had stored up for so long.

"Basically, I knew this guy was going to go, and go soon, and I just wanted to get as much out into the open as possible, once and for all. I plied him with Crown Royal and he let his heart out. I'm so happy he did because I don't think I would have ever really respected him otherwise. But he explained himself to me, what he'd gone through in life, how tough things had been, the whole lot."

His father, Walters discovered, had been born into a comparatively wealthy family but had been overlooked in favour of his brothers and sisters. Feeling increasingly neglected, he fell in with a bad crowd and ended up first in borstal, then foster care and eventually prison. He would go on to be locked up on no fewer than seventeen occasions, prison clearly failing to rehabilitate him. Though he did learn how to cook, and would later prove this to his son while in Canada.

"That was something we had in common at least: we both learned to cook in jail."

His father died a few short months after their reconciliation.

"I didn't entirely forgive him, but I did come to respect him. And I'm glad about that; at least I have that."

Ashley Walters is in his mid-twenties now. He has a flourishing acting career, and is adamant about not failing his children as his father failed him. He's already had one hiccup, the nine-month stretch behind bars, but it's clear he takes the business of fatherhood very seriously indeed.

"We're not perfect but we get by," is how he puts it. "Natalie and I fall out all the time and she throws me out of the house a lot, practically every day sometimes, but if I didn't love her when we first got together, then I really can't get enough of her now. We've grown to love each other and we've bonded over our children. And that's the strongest bond of all."

He admits he would never have chosen to have had a family as young as he did, and that the pressures of having three now are daily and endless and fraught with anxiety and exhaustion, but his children also bring him a depth of pride the like of which he could never experience elsewhere.

"When it comes down to it, becoming a dad gets you more in touch with your feminine side, I reckon," he says. "You become more sensitive. I do, at any rate. I sit down with my kids every night and I write out stories with them and do comprehension with them. I'm certainly not going to rely on the national curriculum to push them as far as they could go, and by doing this, I realise that it's true what people say: what you put into your kids is precisely what you get out of them.

"It can be scary, sometimes, the power you hold over them. I mean, you could make them a murderer or a Nobel prizewinner, anything and everything in between. I just hope I'm doing an okay job. I like to think I am, mostly."

He regretfully admits, however, that Paniro, his youngest, has a pronounced terror of the police and Walters is convinced that this is a complex he himself has somehow passed down.

"Every time he sees them he gets scared and wants to make sure they are not coming for me. That's sad, but then it also has its uses." He is smiling now. "Whenever he is playing up and I need to get him back under control, I tell him I'll call the police on him. Works every time."

Meantime, he sits with his children every night watching them grow and watching them learn.

"My daughter is seven years old now and she is already reading books that I couldn't get my head around until I was at least eleven. I hear how fluent she is and it just makes me cry, tears rolling down my cheeks. It makes me feel — you know, flipping hell, this is amazing, really amazing. Know what I mean?"

Four

It is late summer now, the weather autumnal, and we are back in hospital for the five-month scan. Today is going to be an auspicious day, historical even, at least for the two of us, because today is the day I am going to propose to my girlfriend of eleven years. This does not mean I have succumbed to a freshly developed notion of romance – I have not purchased an engagement ring, for example – but simply that I have looked deep into myself and decided that I need to make some kind of gesture here, a public act of love and solidarity. This far into the pregnancy, I have been far from a model father-to-be, if such a thing exists, instead selfishly wrapped up in myself. Elena, in comparison, has been her customary tower of strength, but unerringly so, her capacity for coping in any given situation now almost SAS-like in its efficiency. Expecting a baby has not laid her low; the mood swings, mercifully, minimal. Morning sickness has been nothing more than a slight sensation of nausea around, contradictorily, dinnertime, while cravings – and I had been secretly looking forward to the cravings – have not centred around snails and coal and emery boards, but simply around fresh fruit, and lots of it. In films, men often have to make midnight mercy dashes to the all-night supermarket for ice cream and asparagus in an attempt to placate their craving wives; I had no such requests made of me, though I have cut up a lot of pineapple and mango, and presented it on a plate with a fork and a Kleenex.

Friends, meanwhile, say that she is glowing, largely, I'm guessing, because this is what one is meant to say in such situations. But is she really *glowing*? I looked the word up in the dictionary and found it means "to emit a soft and steady light, a rich, strong or bright colour, especially reddish or brown". She is neither reddish nor brown, and I haven't been aware of any radiating light. That's not to say I don't find her lovely to look at, because I do, and the levelheadedness she is displaying makes me increasingly happy that I ever managed to find myself such a woman, and wonder whether I fully deserve her.

I'm hoping she will say yes to my proposal, though I can't be entirely sure she will. We have never had any interest in getting married, not even in the wake of the many weddings we have attended back in Spain over the years, a country where marriage appears to be an unavoidable matter of course, Spaniards – or at least those I met – so much happier to follow tradition than trend-bucking Londoners. We seem not to be fully convinced by it, the reasons offered for getting hitched rather nebulous and vague. Can it ever, in the 21st century, still suggest real commitment, when as many as one in three marriages end in divorce? And haven't we already displayed all the commitment we'll ever need to? We share a mortgage together, the bills, a cat, the washing-up and our day-to-day lives. I actively *like* not being married, just as I like having a girlfriend rather than a *wife*, the word itself, rather like *pregnant*, loaded with a weight I'm not sure I could bear.

But then things are changing now, fast, and I am scrambling to keep up with them all. I can offer examples. We have reluctantly put our flat up for sale, having agreed that we now need more space as well as a neighbourhood with better parks, better schools, fewer knife crimes and less murder. We have booked a holiday that bears little relation to the kind we normally go on, and will soon head to an Italian beach where we will lie down all day and watch our alcohol intake closely at night. Amongst all this, then, marriage feels at the very least warranted, the sensible thing to do, grown-up. A friend of Elena's recently told us that enrolling your child into a school may prove harder were it to be born out of wedlock, bastards as socially malignant – in certain circles, at any rate – as they ever were.

I have rehearsed what I am to say over and over. I know my lines. I think I shall resist the temptation to go down on one knee, if only because I'm sure Elena will laugh if I do, but I decide to do it unconventionally, not in a restaurant or with low lighting and flowers, but rather within the hospital or at least nearby. It will take her by surprise, and hopefully in a good way. She will smile and melt, embrace me and say yes. Peter, someone who won't manage to propose to his own girlfriend for another two years (by which time they will have had a second child), thinks it's a fantastic idea.

I find I am less nervous at the five-month scan than I was at the previous one, and I mellow considerably more when it is conclusively established that the baby on the screen is indeed alone, no twin lurking in its shadow. It is bigger now, the foetus, but otherwise fairly unchanged. The screen is still dominated by snow and still looks more like a diagram than anything real or human or, for that matter, partly mine, but I'm beginning to feel almost good about it, as if the secret knowledge of my intended imminent proposal is engendering within me a sense of acceptance and perhaps even a certain buoyancy. The nurse asks if we want to know the baby's sex, and we both say no. I make a point not to look anywhere near its legs, and certainly not between them. Elena does, however, telling me afterwards that she couldn't help herself, and wonders aloud whether the fact that she didn't spot anything means it's a girl.

Afterwards, we are waiting by the lift, alone, just the two of us. I clear my throat. My stomach then plummets as we are joined on either side by several other people, one of whom is a patient in pyjamas with a tube snaking out of his left nostril and a drip attached to his right arm. In one hand he pulls the trolley upon which the drip's sac is suspended. I cannot possibly propose now, within his earshot. I tell Elena we'll take the stairs instead.

"But it's seven floors," she grumbles, "and I'm pregnant."

I had anticipated that the stairwell would be empty and therefore perfect for our intimate moment, but no. It's full of people running up and down in either direction, many of them medical staff with unlit cigarettes clamped between their fingers and a determined look on their faces. For four floors, we never have a moment's privacy. Perhaps I should just let it out, get it over with? Perhaps an audience, even one as unlikely as this, would make it more memorable somehow? I'd ask, and people would stop, stare and applaud. They'd tell their friends and partners later that evening; we'd be news. The four words are in my throat now, as fat as cancer, and I want to spit them out, but they won't budge.

Outside, we walk onto Westminster Bridge, the Thames flowing thick and brown beneath us. I think about suggesting a quick coffee, but I have an interview I'm already late for and simply don't have the time. Elena, also, has to return to the office. Her bus pulls up and so this is it, my last opportunity.

I turn to face her, holding both hands tightly, and lean in for a kiss. This seems to take her by surprise, partly because I don't do it as often as she'd like these days. By this stage in our relationship, I normally expect a kiss to lead straight to sex, because otherwise what's the point? Anyway, she beams at me beautifully, and right now I feel absolutely full of love for her. There surely cannot be a better moment than this. I open my mouth.

"Elena?"

She turns to look at the bus driver and holds up a finger in an attempt to stall him. He throws back an impatient look.

I falter. "Have a nice day. See you tonight."

She kisses me back, then turns, boards the bus and is gone.

Half an hour later, I find myself telling the actress I'm interviewing all about the scan and how I almost proposed, then botched it. This is highly irregular behaviour. A journalist should never tell the talent he is interviewing *anything* about himself whatsoever. Mostly, the talent is a person so self-enamoured that they can't see beyond their own noses anyway and, besides, they've only just met you, you are a stranger, and so what do they care whether you are in the middle of a crucial point in your life? They've a product to plug – the reason they agreed to do the interview in the first place – and would really rather get it over and done with so they can go and speak to the next journalist, and then the one after that. But all good sense goes out of the window today. I'm in emotional freefall, and vulnerable with it.

The actress, bless her, contravenes all expectations and proves a wonderful listener, her eyes bottomless wells of empathy, her words full of encouragement. After she has plugged her television programme and we have said our goodbyes, she reminds me to go through with it tonight, and to buy some flowers first. But by the time Elena gets home, late due to pressures at work and in the middle of a bout of nausea that will last all of a quarter of an hour, the moment has somehow passed. We have a quick dinner, I drink wine, we watch *ER*, then go to bed, have gentle sex and fall asleep. The morning after, I decide that the proposal can wait.

Two weeks later, I read in the newspaper that the actress has just announced her engagement to the actor boyfriend she has been dating for eight months now. They are actively trying for a baby.

"Seems everybody's doing it," she is quoted as saying.

● ● ●

Late September, and we attend something called The Baby Show in the kind of aircraft hangar space normally given over to cars and yachts and Miss World competitions. The place is vast. From ground level, it stretches out on pastel-coloured, static-inducing carpet for as far as the eye can see in every direction, apparently endless. From above, it looks like a beehive bisected, full of separate, tiny cubicles, each selling its own individual wares. The noise is tremendous, rising like heat. Our day here is a long one and completely knocks it out of me, of us both, like last-minute Christmas shopping but with added pressure.

Elena is six months now, and big with it. Across a crowded room, I can still have a moment's trouble picking her out, her new bulk a continually surprising thing to me and making her resemble someone else entirely, a stranger. She wears it well, though, and moves with the slow elegance of a hovercraft at low speed. Seemingly like all pregnant women, she has developed the habit of standing with both hands on the area of skin between hip and rump, palms flat, elbows akimbo, in an attempt to placate her new weight. She has also developed an air of quiet determination and unshakeable resolve. She decides upon something; we do it.

She saw an advert for this baby expo on the tube the other day and flatly decided we'd go, whatever my protestations. And there were protestations. My argument, grounded in a male logic that carried little truck with her, was that the baby was still months away. Why buy stuff now when, surely, we could simply visit a local department store a couple of weeks before the birth and get everything then? We don't buy a rack of lamb from the supermarket 90 days before we intend to eat it, do we? Also, we were still living in our small flat. Where on earth would we store all the clutter, the unfamiliar paraphernalia? Her response was silent tears of fury. I relented.

In one of the pregnancy books she now has littered about our home, I read about something called the *nesting instinct*, an entirely natural occurrence by all accounts in which the mother-to-be experiences an overwhelming need to get things ready for the baby's arrival way upfront of its due date. The book actively encourages this state, claiming it pays to be ready for a variety of reasons that I fail to fully ingest. It says that this normally happens around the fifth month, which is why Elena's desire to attend the show is so pronounced. In the days preceding it, she tells me that she was already growing anxious over our lack of preparation. We hadn't yet done anything for the baby, and we needed to remedy this immediately, today, *now*. We needed a cot, a cradle, a pushchair, nappies, clothes, toys, books, monitors, a changing mat, a changing table, mobiles, batteries, spare batteries. This all made little sense to me. Why would a baby three months shy of worldly existence require *books*, for Christ's sake, much less nappies and toys?

"Don't do this," she says, not so much a plea as a directive, an order. "Just agree with me for once in your life. It won't kill you."

My first thought at the baby show is of IKEA on a bank holiday weekend. There are too many lights and too many people, hundreds certainly, possibly thousands, the vast majority female and enormously pregnant, tight cotton tops stretched over arching domes, belly buttons straining indecently at the fabric. I feel as alien here as would a vegan in an abattoir. Gradually, through the melee of swimming hormones, I begin to spot men, too, fewer in number, perhaps, but present nevertheless, trailing their women the way we once did our mothers. Here, we can all be easily two-dimensionalised, each of us the same bulk of shuffling, sulky confusion following several footsteps behind our partners as they glide from outlet to outlet with clear-sighted cunning and skill, credit cards poised.

There is an abundance of product here, all of it pint-sized, microscopic. Elena holds up a babygro and asks what I think. She picks up muslin squares and asks whether I prefer them in magenta or cream. And what about a towel, a towel with a hood and ears, big fat cartoon eyes and a drooping nose with stitched-on whiskers?

At one of the pushchair stands there is the kind of scrum you see in town centres around tracksuited men selling fake perfume. We push forward. On a small podium is a man, large and bearded and wearing the kind of headset Madonna wears on stage. In one hand he holds a pram. The fact that he is holding it in just the one hand, he explains through a microphone that renders his voice robotic, is pertinent, because it means it is lightweight, which is good, a distinct bonus, you want lightweight in a pushchair, it's paramount, not least with a screaming load and a bag of shopping and you are tired and just want to get home, ha ha, isn't that right, ladies? He talks about the colours it comes in, all of which warrant the description *stunning* (the blue is stunning, the green is stunning; and the black? The black is stunning), its ability on a succession of terrains and just how comfortable baby — and he talks about them the way doctors and nurses do: just *baby*, minus the definite article, which unaccountably makes me take against him — how comfortable baby will be sitting in it, lying in it, sleeping in it, gurgling in it. I recall that the other day Peter mentioned an actual brand of pushchair to me. It was over the phone, and at first I thought he'd mumbled the word. But now I realise he wasn't mumbling at all. It's called a Bugaboo, and at the time of writing this particular pushchair is the equivalent of an Audi, a BMW, chic and stylish and popular in Chelsea. The one being demonstrated to us now looks sleek and sexy with its big fat tyres, reversible whatsits and all manner of smart addendums. A woman in front of us, whom I vaguely recognise from television, lunges forward now, her stomach guiding her and opening up the path ahead. She is brandishing her chequebook and requesting the use of a pen.

After an hour, I feel as if I've run a marathon. I'm tired, exhausted, embattled, bad-tempered and have an acute pain at the base of my spine. We have stopped for a coffee on my request (with hands pressed together as if in prayer) and Elena takes the opportunity to point out that we have yet to buy anything. I reiterate again that we can wait several more months yet, that we can buy whatever we need from somewhere local when, and only when, the time becomes necessary. She argues that by that time she will be in hospital in the *process of giving birth*, and I respond, with good reason, that *I* can go and buy them alone. All I will need is a list, and it's as good as done. I also point out that the towels, to me, seem superfluous. We have towels at home. Do we really need muslin squares? And what use, really, is a changing bag for the pushchair we have yet to purchase when everything the baby needs can quite easily be put into my shoulder bag, which I never leave home without?

Sipping at my coffee, I look around me, grateful to be temporarily out of the push and shove, and watch with empathy the face of the menfolk, each contorted into variations of Munch's *The Scream*. When I look back to Elena, I see that she is crying quietly but steadily, and appraising me in a cold, hard manner. I suddenly panic that she is about to cause a scene, another one. In my Damien Hirst café the other Saturday, she became dramatically tearful for no good reason, and these were not quiet tears. She complained that I wasn't being supportive enough, that perhaps she should return to Spain, where a ready support network was waiting for her. The next time I visited the café, alone, the staff looked at me with new scorn. Now she gets up slowly, heavily, and begins deliberately to walk away. Sighing, I get to my feet, about to follow, but she turns around.

"Don't," she says, and leaves.

Surrounded by hundreds, possibly thousands, I am all alone. I watch my girlfriend's back drift into the crowd, and soon I can no longer pick her out amongst all the other oversized women, unknowable to me now, the kind of person who somehow feels instinctively in place here despite the fact that, just a few short years ago, the idea of babies to her was anathema. Once again, I wonder what changed in her that still hasn't in me. At the next table, I see another man, also alone, methodically pouring sugar into his coffee and staring into the vague middle distance. We make the very briefest of eye contact, but in that fleeting moment, he is my closest friend in the world.

I find her eventually, and without words we make our way back to the stalls she has already, in her mind, picked out. There are many; it takes hours. We buy half a dozen babygros (in blue and white and yellow, but not pink; I refuse pink), we buy pyjamas and T-shirts and nappies and nappy bags and various creams and unguents and balms. We buy muslin squares, though I have no clear idea yet what function they will fulfil, and the funny towel with the hood, the ears, the eyes and the nose. We buy a changing bag, which has more compartments than any bag I have ever seen, and we go back to see the man with the headset and the overeager disposition. The Bugaboo really is the superstar pushchair here. Sales have been brisk. Only a few are left. We want one. But then I learn its ridiculously inflated price tag, and we end up buying something that looks not quite as good but for a fraction of the cost, a nifty little runaround equivalent, possessed of an unshowy and understated efficiency. It can also be picked up with just one hand.

We go home with arms full, bank balance crippled, Elena temporarily happy. Crucially for me, all is forgiven, for now. In the living room, we pull the sofa a foot away from the wall, and pile the baby stuff behind it. This is a good idea for many reasons, not least of which is that I don't have to see it staring back at me on a daily basis. For days at a time, I even forget it's there.

Two weeks later, the pushchair is delivered. It is black and trim and nippy, and we are happy with it, really we are. After Elena has shown me how it works, I play with it, sitting the cat on the seat and pushing it up and down the corridor, taking the corners at a clip. Under considerable instruction, I learn to fold it down within a couple of seconds, which is crucial, I'm told, for when you need to get it on a bus and the bus is full. It is a perfectly adequate pushchair, and so what if it has more substance than it does style? It's fully functional, perfectly fine for a newborn, and that, ultimately, is what counts.

But for the next two years, we will never pass a Bugaboo on the street without experiencing a keening envy and contempt for the smug bastard that pushes it.

●●●

I go to see a sex therapist, ostensibly for work, a woman who likes to promise that she can improve anyone's sex life with her open and tactile approach. She suggests we meet in an upmarket sex shop in the heart of London's West End. As an Englishman for whom a certain level of denial is practically mandatory, I feel compelled to tell her that there is, in fact, nothing wrong with my sex life. In fact, I have no complaints whatsoever. The sex therapist is standing so close to me while I tell her this that I can smell both her perfume and her breath, and she then asks me a series of bedroom-related questions, all of which I manage to answer with an affirmative yes.

"So tell me what you *would* like, then," she says. "Something new, something different, perhaps? We could all do with a little spicing up in the boudoir. Do you like whips, or perhaps being submissive?" She is standing too close now. I can see the tiny lines that reach from her puckered mouth to her nostrils. "Ever taken it up the arse? Many men haven't, but then rather like it. Try it." She shows me a glass butt plug, small but with ample girth. I swallow.

We take a walk around the sex shop, and she shows me things with feathers on them, peekaboo leather underwear with zips and flaps, no end of sex manuals and flavoured sex toys and, more ambiguously, an old-fashioned rocking horse. While I'm here, Elena, who is also taking part in the story with me, is across town, sitting on a cushion in a private members club, legs apart, at a sex seminar alongside twelve other women, each knickerless. An instructor is demonstrating how to insert a jade egg and to hold it there with a series of flexes. Such flexes, she is told, will help strengthen her vaginal muscles which she can then exercise upon me in a fashion not unlike a firm handshake. After the lesson, the instructor takes Elena to one side and tells her that this would have been much easier for her had she not been so pregnant. The fact that she is, however, is no bad thing, for she will need to exercise these particular muscles like she never has before if she wants them to work properly after the birth. It is a sobering, unpleasant forecast.

My therapist tells me much the same thing back in the sex shop after I reveal Elena's condition. If she had shown me a rather strict, almost dominatrix attitude before, she becomes quite mocking now. She laughs, and shakes her head with what I take to be equal parts pity and ridicule.

"Everything changes after childbirth," she tells me. "You should have mentioned that at the beginning, because we could have talked about that instead. If sex wasn't a problem before, it will be afterwards. You will never get a blow job again. You know that, don't you? She'll be too tired, for one thing, and anyway, what's the point? Also, after the birth, her vagina will go slack, loose. She'll get piles. And whatever you do, don't make her laugh, because she'll wet herself. She will. She'll have no control over that any more. Trust me, I know what I'm talking about. I speak," she concludes, and by now I can't wait to get away, "from experience."

She nods her head firmly and looks up as if I am supposed to respond to all this in some or other meaningful way.

Awful, awful woman.

Five

December arrives, a most fateful month for so many reasons this year, and everything happens at once, a fast-forward blur of activity only partly of our own making.

They say there is little in life as stressful as moving house. That's true, of course, though it is nothing compared to moving house *and* having a baby at the same time, and after the kind of experiences that seem to happen so frequently during these transactions – a desire to physically harm the people you are buying from, the estate agent too – we arrive at completion. Our fortified flat sold, we have had our offer accepted on a three-bedroom semi in an uninspiring but conveniently located (for Elena, for work) suburban town that clings onto London for dear life. The tube doesn't quite stretch this far out, but there is a train offering quick access to the centre of town, and though our new postcode doesn't have the usual SE, SW, NW prefix I'm used to, it does remain a Royal Borough Of and the telephone number still begins with 0208, which makes the transition slightly more bearable. I've lived in London my entire life, and to be leaving its heart now brings with it a wrenching that feels a little like death. Turning 30 was less painful than this. The family we are buying from, a husband, wife and two children ("You'll be just like us in a few years' time," the wife beamed at me, Stepford-like, when I first wandered in to appraise her kitchen), have required that we move in the week before Christmas, irrespective of whether Elena is due to give birth then. Should we even attempt to delay this, we are warned, the sale could fall through.

Three days before the move, we attend an antenatal class. Sometimes, these classes can be spread over the course of several weeks or even months in bite-sized portions of an hour each, but the NHS also offers a full day's course that usually occurs just a month before the birth. It's a little like cramming in as much revision as you can before a looming exam, or simply throwing all the relevant information at you before it's too late and seeing what sticks.

We arrive shortly before nine o'clock in the morning. The room is already filled with advanced-stage pregnant women and timid, gaunt men, and resembles a classroom to the point that it has a blackboard at one end, along which runs a line of chalk. The temperature inside continually fluctuates between either too cold or too hot, though in truth this may not be due to a faulty heating system so much as to the roller coaster of nerves the long, drawn-out dissemination of information produces. I gaze around the room and see several people who also look as if they don't fully know what they are doing here, or quite how they found themselves in this position. They are my kind of people: the bewildered.

Our tutor for the day is a middle-aged woman with a smiling mouth and a penchant for unbroken eye contact. She is a midwife of many years' experience and the encouraging manner of an art teacher. She greets all eleven of us, the uneven number a tell-tale sign that one woman's partner hasn't turned up (and won't), and she gathers us together on plastic orange chairs arranged in a circle so that we are forced to face one another in a display of like-minded community.

"One by one I want us to introduce ourselves to the group and also to say a little about ourselves, our partners and our feelings about our impending births, yes?" she says, stringing the words together as if they were a melody. Some of the men gathered exchange loaded looks. Others stare at the floor.

I've not yet needed to attend an AA meeting, but I imagine it feels pretty similar to this. Each of the women is confident and full-voiced when it comes to her turn, and they announce their pregnancy in weeks rather than months. The men appear able to speak only while repeatedly clearing their throats, and many of us resort to humour, man's ever-ready coat of armour when we don't know what else to say, which is often. Cheeks flushing, I explain to the group that I've never been very good at calculating my girlfriend's pregnancy in weeks, but I do know that she is due in under a month, and that the prospect terrifies me. This is greeted with gentle laughter and a general murmured agreement. Some gathered here elect not to talk at all, largely, it seems, because English is not their first language (we are a multicultural bunch: African, South American, Middle Eastern), but the power-dressing late 30-something Irish-woman whose husband will leave before the day is up addresses the room with such forceful confidence that I conclude she must be a prosecuting lawyer. She will prove the thorn in our tutor's side today, someone who has done her homework on childbirth, much of it online, and appears intent on challenging every one of the NHS's seemingly outdated methods. The rest of us sit in silence and wait patiently while she mounts her successive cases.

"There are always different dynamics in any given group," Julie Brown, a midwife at London's St Thomas's Hospital later tells me, "people who have researched things on the internet or watched all the wrong TV shows, Discovery Channel documentaries or simply heard old wives' tales, and it is our job to correct any misinformation they may have come across."

For the first half-hour, the tutor gives a general talk on what we can expect in our last month of pregnancy, about pelvic floor massages, optimum foetal positioning and something called perineal massage.

One of the women, who has otherwise remained silent, raises a cautious hand, her face set small within a large headscarf.

"A *what?*"

"Perineal, the area of skin between your vagina and rectum. Massaging it stimulates the blood supply and can help speed up the healing process after birth. It can also help to familiarise you with some of the sensations of childbirth, so you are less likely to tense up during delivery." She turns to look at some of the men. "Fathers, you can do this for your partners as well. It's a terrific way to get more involved."

For the next few moments, you can hear a pin drop.

She then moves on to the labour: signs of, the changes to the cervix, the difference between the latent and active phases; pieces of information that, for me at least, go in one ear and out the other. She mentions the phrase *coping strategies* and at least several men meet one another's eyes as anticipatory nerves mount. *Pain relief* is another morsel of terror she tosses out, and she demonstrates the mechanism of birth by using a toy doll and a plastic pelvis. The head is bigger than the opening through which it must pass by a great many inches.

"Muscles," our tutor explains. "Those, and the miracle of nature."

The mid-morning tea break proves awkward. Though many of us attempt to strike up conversations, they mostly fail to take hold. It's difficult to know where to go after *hi, how are you?*, and none of us is yet fully conversant in this subject to really go anywhere at all.

"Alright, mate?" one man, a publican, says to me, leaning forward as if about to whisper something conspiratorial. "Pass the milk, yeah?"

When we reconvene a quarter of an hour later, we are separated into groups delineated by sex. Momentary alarm spreads like wildfire throughout the room. Without our partners, the sole reason we are here today, we feel helpless and adrift. What will become of us without them?

"An activity," says the tutor, clapping eager hands together.

The women are told to write down things they would like their partners to provide during the delivery, the men likewise, and we then recongregate to discuss the results. The men have written down things like *helping with breathing* and *support* and *bringing tea*. The women have suggested *lower back massages, understanding* and *love*. For the first time today, we all seem properly engaged.

Midwife Julie Brown tells me that the practical side of the day is the part men like most.

"They are all curious, inquisitive and scared, but when we get to the more practical side of things, they come to life, realising they are not going to just be left sitting in a corner but that there is, in fact, a lot for them to do, to be a part of if they want to," she says. "And of course we encourage them in this regard as much as we can. The practical activities also help men open up a little bit more. Generally, men don't articulate their concerns within this kind of environment as easily as women do, but we have found that they don't actually mind talking about their vulnerabilities, especially when one starts the ball rolling."

Traditionally, she continues, men keep their feelings bottled up, "and it's only recently that they have been encouraged to fully express how they feel. But they are doing this now. What we hope to impart in these classes is that men should feel comfortable about being in the delivery room with their partners, and that's why it's so important that they attend things like this. The more we can encourage them to talk freely about their fears and concerns, the more likely they are to overcome them."

By the time of the mid-afternoon coffee break, the day looks like it's going to stretch on until Christmas at least. Everyone is beginning to itch for freedom. The power-dressing Irishwoman wants to have an argument about something called Vitamin K, but elsewhere a certain cameraderie has by now broken through, sparked largely by male-generated jokes, a necessary leveller after a succession of lectures on the topics of pre-eclampsia (hypertension in pregnancy that can, in some cases, be fatal) and the various ways to endure labour manually, the apparatus for which could spawn an entire sub-genre of the modern-day horror film. We are told that if the baby is refusing to come out or, worse, gets stuck en route (and this could happen for a variety of reasons, none of them good), then the doctors could use a vacuum (effectively a toilet plunger which sucks hard on the baby's soft, malleable skull with what looks like an ability to extend its forehead to comical proportions) or forceps, a pair of which she holds up for appraisal now, cold and clinical and sinister enough to prompt shivers. She discusses Caesarean sections, a six-inch incision into the lower abdomen by steady scalpel, and while one doctor pulls the heavy flesh up and open, another attempts to pull the baby free without bringing with it any of the mother's vital organs. The room, now, is sweltering. One father-to-be gets up to open a window. Another excuses himself to visit the toilet, and takes for ever to return.

"I saw this terrible thing on TV recently," one woman begins, and our tutor listens patiently, nodding her head and sighing.

"TV dramas really don't do us very many favours here," she says. "They obviously need excitement to get the viewers in and so they add a lot of drama, but what I want you all to remember is that the majority of women go through childbirth without any problems whatsoever and have perfectly healthy babies. It's important not to forget that, and to focus on it."

Finally, we are given a tour of the birth centre, the beds and rooms and, in one case, the small swimming pool we can, may or will give birth in when the time comes. The hospital's maternity ward is brand new. It still shines and sparkles and looks much more inviting than the often dilapidated NHS hospitals we remember from our youth. From this we all draw a certain reassurance.

Out in the foyer as we wait for the lift, we each raise eyebrows at one another and chuckle, strangers with a now tangible bond and a collective level of anticipation far higher than those ordinary, non-expectant people back out on London's streets. We wish each other well and say that we might well meet again a few weeks hence once waters have broken and the process has begun. One of the women wonders who will be the first amongst us to deliver. The publican says he will invite us all to his pub to wet our respective babies' heads and we all respond affirmatively, yes, definitely, we must, most of us knowing, of course, that none of us actually ever will.

It is raining as we leave, and dark. Our bus arrives. We run for it.

● ● ●

It is a dilemma that brings me more sympathy from men than it does from women. Elena has been given a due date of December 20th but we read somewhere that the majority of first pregnancies are far more likely to conclude in overdue births than they are premature ones. And so when a job offer comes in that requires me to leave the country for seven full days, not returning until the seventeenth, I am sorely tempted. Not just because it is work, and I do not get paid if I do not work, but because, with the very cruellest of ironies, it is perhaps the most exciting job I have ever been offered. I've been asked to go to Colombia with a British charity to gauge the damage the ongoing drug wars have had on local communities, particularly its child casualties. We will fly to Bogota, then travel upriver by canoe to small villages to see how lives have been affected by the cocaine trade, and examine ways in which their futures can be improved, or at the very least how the risk to their day-to-day lives can be lessened.

Much of my job over the past ten years has involved travel, visiting bands and actors on tour and on location wherever they happen to be in the world. This is, of course, considerable fun, an absolute privilege in most cases and an opportunity that grants you temporary licence to suspend real life in favour of living in a bubble of contrived self-importance, where food and drink and partying is free and roundly encouraged. But while it's an invitation that never fully loses its allure, it is also true that after a while one chic New York hotel looks much like its West Coast counterpart, and one doom-laden indie band begins to resemble another. Colombia, however, is something else entirely. I want desperately to go.

I do hesitate, though. My girlfriend is close to full term, and we are moving house in just ten days' time. If I board that plane, I won't be here to help. But then, I wonder, is my presence really needed? We have hired a removal firm, after all, and Gil, my friend, has already offered his assistance, a much stronger and more capable man than I. Last time we moved house, I was relegated to making tea in the kitchen and feeling like an increasingly spare part while sweating men around me got on with the masculine job at hand.

In Colombia, I'd at least have something active to do and, crucially, I'd be getting paid. But still I prevaricate. I ask my editor whether I can get back to him within 24 hours. Kindly, he agrees. I pick up the phone to call Elena but cut the connection before it rings, and call instead the doctor, desperate for some kind of prediction, a likely forecast and, with it, a guarantee.

I explain my situation to him, and the statistic about first pregnancies resulting in overdue delivery. "I mean," I say, "she could still feasibly be pregnant well into next year, couldn't she?"

His response is clipped and curt.

"Firstly, she could not be pregnant, as you put it, *well into next year*. It's true that she could still be pregnant in early January, maybe, but at that point we would induce the birth anyway. Secondly, as it stands today, your wife is already full term. If she gives birth right now, this evening, tomorrow morning, it will not be deemed premature. So while, statistically, first-time pregnancies *can* be late, it is by no means a given. Only yesterday one of my patients gave birth six full weeks earlier, without any prior indication or tangible reason."

"And it was her first?"

"It was. Listen, I understand your predicament, and I'm sure it would be just *wonderful* to visit Brazil —"

"Colombia."

"— Colombia, and how very lovely for you, et cetera, but I can in no way give you your guarantee that you won't come back to find your wife having already given birth. Think about it carefully, young man. Do you want to miss that? Does your wife?"

I phone Elena next, hoping for a more understanding ear. I tell her about the job offer, and this kind and gracious woman who continues to amaze me daily tells me that if I really want to go, then go: I have her full blessing. She sounds entirely genuine. I finish my call with her committed to doing just that. House, birth, travel; bring it all on in one multitasking avalanche, I can take it all, will juggle it all perfectly. I can address the topic of settling my life down *after* the baby arrives. But now, it's business as usual.

I Google Colombia, and it sounds fantastic: vibrant and exotic, with high levels of violent crime, kidnapping and homicide. Stick to the main tourist areas, I read, and avoid any off-the-beaten-track areas, which I can only presume includes paddling up river in a canoe. I tell myself that I'll be reachable by mobile phone at all times, and should anything occur while I'm away, I can be home within two days, three days, *five* at the outside, and that everything will be alright.

I call my editor, and he says hello. The *yes* is sat there plump on my tongue, just waiting to be spat out and to hell with the consequences, but it won't budge. Instinctively, I know this is the wrong response. I've known it all along; I've just ignored it. Even someone with my blinkered vision knows that this is a key moment in my life, an axis on which so much else might rest. My actions today could resonate for ever, and so perhaps it is time to put something else before my own concerns. I am terrified about the birth of my child, it's true, but at the same time I wouldn't miss it for the world. I'm even prepared to be here for the house move, to feel unnecessary and emasculated, and to pay for the takeaway pizzas in the evening which we will eat in an unfamiliar kitchen that hasn't had its cutlery drawer arranged yet.

And so I say to my editor what I have almost never said to him before: "No."

It feels oddly liberating.

• • •

December 20th arrives, bringing with it no baby and the now hollow realisation that I could have gone to Colombia after all, without incident or the need for redress. There is another arrival to contend with in the meantime, however, and that is the mother-in-law from Spain, here to dispense help and wisdom at our time of need for a full 30 days and 30 nights. This had not been in response to an invitation, but rather a decree of her own making, her daughter not wishing to cause offence by suggesting that, actually, two weeks would be ample. When I told friends of the length of her proposed stay, they all responded similarly: with raised eyebrows, a sharp intake of breath and a whispered *"How long?"*. I take comfort from this, as it convinces me that my reaction to her presence, which will grow and swell like a pustule that wants bursting with something hot and sharp, isn't exaggerated.

I feel it expedient to make clear here that I have nothing against the mother-in-law, that I believe her ultimately to be a kind and decent woman with her heart in the right place. She is not a nightmare, not a monster, and not as overbearing as she so easily could be were we not separated by all of France and a good thousand miles. Nevertheless, her plus points become pronouncedly less easy to appreciate when she moves into our still unfamiliar house and begins promptly to rearrange our lives within it. The kitchen swiftly becomes her domain alone, and she presides over it in a lordly fashion, forever frying things in pools of olive oil, diced onion and fiery peppers. She cleans everything everywhere all the time, and washes clothes constantly, both hers and ours. In the bathroom, she likes to dry her smalls, a word that, in this instance, is a touch misleading. One enormous pair boasts a leopard print.

The awkwardness that exists between us is due largely to the fact that we have never been able to communicate freely with one another, given the absence of a common tongue. The English and the Spanish are much the same in this respect: we expect the rest of the world to be conversant with our own language if only because so much of the world already is. But we aren't, and it has proved harmful. We had our one and only faltering conversation years ago, a complicated exchange that basically boiled down to *hola* and *no hablo español*. Now we fail, by and large, to even make eye contact, passing the salt when it needs to be passed and wishing each other good morning, but little else, separate entities existing for now in too-close quarters.

We first met twelve years previously at the wedding of a Spanish cousin during a baking Madrid summer. I was an evident oddity in a borrowed suit, the only foreigner at a traditional ceremony that had drawn over one hundred people. Being the sole reason her daughter had failed to return home as promised after those initial six months, she was curious about me at first, keen to get to know me better if only to understand why Elena had chosen to stay. We smiled, kissed each other's cheeks and attempted to meet somewhere in the middle, my passable knowledge of Italian, similar in so many ways to Spanish, allowing me to understand at least some of what she was saying, if not quite providing me with the tools to say anything comprehensible back. The recurring theme of that day was that when we were next to meet, at Christmas time, I would have played my *Teach Yourself Spanish* CD endlessly and memorised the accompanying book. Only when I became more fluent could she hope to understand me better, thereby drawing a more comprehensive conclusion of me.

Christmas came, but I had somehow failed to get past chapter one of *Teach Yourself Spanish*. Over the longest festive meal I had ever encountered (prawns and paella and chicken and potatoes and cheese, and then grapes, a great many grapes), I was able to tell my future mother-in-law what I'd learned, namely that I was a nurse (*soy enfermera*) and that I wanted to book a hotel room in Buenos Aires. This amused her but only fleetingly, and she took my inability to learn her language as a personal affront. We had reached an impasse which, although we didn't know it then, we would never quite breach. Unexpectedly, I began to imagine how my father must have felt with his Italian in-laws when my parents were still together.

For me, it brought waves of self-loathing and a sense of failure, emotional states that I soon began to identify irrevocably with Spain. And so I did whatever I could to avoid feeling them again. I rarely went back.

As far as I was concerned, this was the best thing under the circumstances, and certainly the most practical. True, it would mean that Elena would have to live a separate life, of sorts, because at big family gatherings in her Basque village, she was the only member not to be accompanied by her partner. But in this way I avoided feeling like a sore thumb, ignored after the initial introductory smiles, then left to wallow in an incomprehension of my own making. Why provoke such protracted awkwardness further when it could, in fact, be neatly sidestepped by simply staying away? This was my argument, hardly the best of scenarios, admittedly, but to me at least a reasonable and manageable one. Every two years, I give in and go back for a weekend, smile my way through every situation and am so keen to make a good impression that I eat whatever is put in front of me, then sit quietly at the table while the noise and activity grows around me and I become increasingly invisible.

But now she was here on my turf, streamlined with purpose and energy and bullishness, anxious to help feather the nest her daughter was already busy laying herself. After two days, she paid an emergency visit to the local household store and came back with a toilet brush, which she was at pains to point out to me. Later, I asked Elena why she'd bought it, and winced as she told me her mother thought I had a habit of leaving the toilet in a state she didn't find acceptable.

On the wall behind my side of the bed, I start marking the days of her tenure, like a prisoner counting down his time until release.

• • •

Moving into an unfamiliar house in an unfamiliar neighbourhood, where all the connotations of *home* are conspicuous by their absence, brings with it a heady sense of dislocation. I hate it. As we wait for the big event with a combination of trepidation and boredom, boredom because the nine months by now feel like nine years, I busy myself by running errands to the shops while Elena and her mother primp the house in attempt to make it ours. We have replaced our former neighbourhood of vigorous urbanity in favour of soulless shopping centres, department stores and 24-hour supermarkets, with ample parking attached. Street buskers stand outside The Gap with a guitar, a violin and, in one case, a xylophone, where they reinterpret Christmas carols with a nod, a wink and a Santa's hat cocked at an angle on their heads. Chuggers prowl the pavements, craving credit card details in exchange for leaflets on UNICEF, the World Wild-life Fund and Barnardos. I come across something called Eden Café, which is so erroneously titled that someone somewhere must be having a joke. It's a hollowed-out cave down one of the quieter side streets where microwaved *baked* potatoes come served with baked beans that spill all over the side of the plate and coagulate thickly on cigarette burn-pitted Formica tables. It seems to attract only old men and the occasional single mother. On the streets, there are families everywhere, the parents wrapped up in parkas and weighed down by heavy shopping, each pushing brand-new children who cry and scream and sleep and snooze, noses streaming. Walking between them is like negotiating an obstacle course, like a salmon swimming upstream against the current to its inevitable demise. I am struck by the sheer volume of them, and become quickly convinced that what people do more of here than they do anywhere else is have lots and lots of unprotected sex. If the birth rate in the UK is falling, then I appear to have settled in the one neighbourhood where we, because it is *we* these days, are proudly bucking that trend by conceiving with flamboyant ease.

I feel just as disorientated at home as I do out there, and not just because of the mother-in-law's presence. Our new house is a modest semi-detached affair, spread out over three floors, the upper a converted loft space that soon becomes my office. We have stairs, a novelty in itself as I have not lived anywhere with stairs since leaving home eighteen years previously. It feels sensible and adult, befitting of a 37-year-old. The aging cat doesn't quite know what to do with all this sudden space, having had to accustom herself to the cramped confines of a succession of bedsits throughout her poor life. She sits huddled in a corner in the kitchen so meekly that I cannot look at her without experiencing a piercing guilt at having not been able to provide all this for her sooner. Though I don't know it yet, she is already growing apart from me, becoming distant and alone and increasingly ill. She'll be dead within a year.

We have no fridge yet, and because of the pre-Christmas rush and the imminent post-Christmas sales frenzy, it appears likely we won't be getting one until well into the new year. The window ledge, consequently, is crowded with pints of milk, margarine and cheese that the day's bright sunshine duly curdles, later prompting in me much diarrhoea.

Elsewhere, we can't quite get the heating to work properly, and it's a raw December, the wind whipping itself up through the gappy floorboards, the ancient window frames and down the chimney stack. Elena sits in the kitchen warmed by the oven while her mother talks and gesticulates with Almodovarian fervour, and I retreat to the freezing living room, its walls painted bright green by the idiot previous owners, clicking aimlessly through the TV channels, the picture unsteady and flickery no matter how much I tweak the aerial. I switch it off and read instead, fearful that a mocking friend's pre-diction – that I will never have time for books again once the baby is born – will come all too horribly true.

December 20th gives way to the 21st, which in turn creeps inexo-rably towards the 22nd. Nothing, quite pointedly, is happening, nor does it seem likely to, Elena doomed to remain pregnant for ever and hailed a freak on daytime television. At night, she asks repeatedly if I'm okay, says that I'm unusually quiet, and I tell her yes because that is what I think she needs to hear right now. She is lying on her back beside me, her stomach a cathedral dome that creates a tent out of the duvet and encourages yet more draught in this already draughty house. She is exhausted all the time, heavy and sick of it, desperate for it all to be over.

The imminence of Christmas seems doubtful somehow, a fact for other people to get excited over (or dread), but not us, not this year. Everything is different now, real life remote, a memory, and we are here together, quietly, the two of us suspended in a kind of limbo, unable to fully appreciate or entirely prepare for the mystery that is inevitably to come, and come soon, hopefully soon. We join hands, holding tight.

From the darkened room down the hall that will one day belong to the baby, Elena's mother lies, dead to the world, and snoring with the might of an angered Pamplona bull.

Alex James, the contented father

In his 2007 autobiography, *Bit of a Blur*, Alex James writes: "No one can be wise until they have been properly foolish, or feel well at home until they've spent time wandering in the wilderness."

For almost fifteen years before he wrote these words, James was proactively foolish, his career an excuse for grand and gleeful folly. He was the bassist in Blur, one of the UK's best-loved and, for a while, biggest acts, the architects of Britpop and the band whose chart battle with Oasis for the number one position back in 1994 will live on in the memory long after that decade has faded into the realms of murky nostalgia. Blur won that battle, but it ultimately proved their slow undoing. Singer Damon Albarn had been a difficult, diffident character long before "Country House" had placed them squarely on the cultural map; he became increasingly more so after it, the glare of fame bewildering him to such an extent that he began to remove himself from it, ending up first in Reykjavik, then Mali and, more recently, as a two-dimensional cartoon rendered lovingly by his friend and Gorillaz collaborator Jamie Hewlett. The band's inspirational guitarist, Graham Coxon, was even more undone by their moment in the spotlight. In James's summation: "Graham felt he'd gained the world and lost his soul, that the juggernaut of attainment had compromised his principles." In 2002, Coxon quit the band. Drummer Dave Rowntree began spending more time indulging his passion for flying aeroplanes and nurturing an interest in politics (he would later join the Labour Party). And Alex James? Alex James, long the world's most carefree bassist, was having fun, pure and simple, on champagne and cocaine, and sleeping with as many girls as took his fancy. A great many did.

"I was the bass player," he shrugs in mitigation. "There were already very intense characters in our band as it was; they didn't need another one. My role was simply to join in occasionally, and occasionally I did. But mostly I didn't have any responsibilities or angst about whether we were doing the right thing or not. That was covered by the other two. As far as I was concerned, being in a band was just about the best thing in the world. You jump on a tour bus, you travel constantly, you play your guitar loudly and you shag and booze your way around the world. What, frankly, is not to like?"

He laughs as he says this to me, a great, filthy, Sid James type of laugh, with a throatful of nicotine. His mad, lank hair falls over one eye as his shoulders shake. He rearranges it with an impatient hand so that it falls over the other eye instead.

"I had a blast, the time of my life."

James is 39 years old now, to all intents and purposes a former member of Blur (though the band has never officially split up), and is today the self-proclaimed lord of his own manor, a working farm, alongside his wife of four years, Claire. They have 400 sheep, some pigs and chickens. He has a growing cheese empire, and is a ubiquitous presence in the media. He is also the proud father of three children, and it is this role he has, perhaps surprisingly, taken to most of all: fatherhood.

"I love it, it's just the best thing. We want more kids. At least one more, maybe two. We've set down our roots now; we're here to stay. May as well fill the place."

He bought the farm in 2004 just as he and Claire were getting married. No mere show home for the rich and famous, this is still very much a work in progress, but then farms invariably are. He takes me into his den, a large, self-contained room which he uses to write from and also, whenever the mood takes him, to record music. There are banks of computers here, and a row of bass guitars. The ashtray on the low coffee table is overflowing, and as we chat, he rolls himself another cigarette on brought-together knees, smoking his only vice these days.

"At first I thought I was being quite wild and reckless by leaving London and my friends for a farm in the country and a woman who, for all I knew, could turn out to be Heather Mills, but then I realised that I was in fact simply conforming to type. It's what aging rock gentlemen do, isn't it? They buy farms."

He has fulfilled another aging rockstar stereotype, too. With what one can only presume was his wife's full backing, he has given his children names only the most outlandish rocker would applaud. Their oldest boy is called Geronimo, the twins Artemis and Galileo; Momo, Arty and Gali for short.

"Well, we wanted them to have memorable names," he grins. "Job done."

In many ways, Alex James makes for an unlikely contented father. At the height of Blur's success, he was vigorously burning his candle at both ends. It had quite a wick. He was young and pretty, with a fringe he was justifiably proud of and a libido he could do little to stem. He attended parties he was invited to, and many others to which he wasn't. He got a pilot's licence and flew aeroplanes to France, for lunch. All of London's glitterati knew him, or else coveted his acquaintance. They bought him drinks, drugs, and he invariably returned the favour, the boy born in the seaside retirement town of Bournemouth now making Soho his new home. He hardly slept, had great reserves of youthful energy. Much of every night was spent at the Groucho Club with the likes of artist Damien Hirst and actor Keith Allen.

"In London, the Groucho was *the* place, the place where anybody at all might walk through the door," he writes in his book. "In fact, everybody always looked up when the door opened, to see who it was. Everyone was friendly. They are when you're number five [in the charts]."

When the Groucho either eventually closed its doors for the night or else ejected the trio for bad behaviour, the party simply continued at James's nearby flat, often picking up enthusiastic new stragglers en route. He likes to claim now that he spent over a million pounds on drink and drugs during this time, and he dealt with each new crushing morning after not increasingly convinced that he had a problem but rather in the way he does everything in life: with a crumpled, self-satisfied smile and a shrug of the shoulders.

"Was I an alcoholic? Truthfully, I really don't know," he says now. "Signing a record deal is rather like getting on a transatlantic flight. There is a drinks trolley the whole time wherever you go, and you never have to pay for any of it. Alcohol is such a good drug for travelling; it makes everything interesting and it gives you confidence. So much of the music industry has its business conducted in and around pubs and clubs, and so music and booze are virtually inseparable. If your use of alcohol is, as the World Health Organisation suggests, merely continued use of a substance despite its negative impact on your body, then that probably means everyone is, to some degree. All I know is that once you have drunk like that, in extremis, you have to be categorical when you choose to give up. And I did."

So what, precisely, happened to turn his life around? Many things, it transpires. Blur were falling apart, and James had fallen headlong in love.

"I stopped drinking properly around the time I met Claire," he says. "And everything changed in my life after that. When you are a heavy drinker and you suddenly stop, then very quickly you lose all your boozy acquaintances. That's fine; I could handle that. And anyway, your more intimate relationships can stand up to something like that. But then, my more intimate relationships were the ones that suffered when I fell in love. It rattles your closest friends when someone else comes into the picture, doesn't it? It's hard for them to cope, I guess, because it means they are going to lose you a little bit. But then I really did swoon for Claire. Claire was all I wanted, and once I got the girl, I was happy to go anywhere, as long as anywhere was with her."

They soon married, and marriage, he suggests, is a leap of faith, "and once you've done it, you rather go along with everything that follows, don't you?"

He certainly did that. It was on their honeymoon that Claire fell pregnant.

"I was over the moon, but was I ready for children? I don't think anyone is ever properly ready," he suggests. "Have you come across a woman called Susan Greenfield? She's a brain specialist, and she said that falling in love is basically a mechanism for the bringing about of madness. And you need that madness if you are to have children because if you didn't, you'd never agree to have them in the first place. Having kids just doesn't add up unless you're in love, and that, effectively, according to Greenfield at any rate, is what the function of love is: to make you mad enough to want kids."

Duly maddened, the man who had never previously thought of himself as father material now needed to shape up fast. Until recently, he had lived a life in which everything was done for him: "My management company even looked after *my laundry* until I was 30, for Christ sake. I was clueless, in so many ways."

But the new desire to become a dad was powerful and, he felt, entirely instinctive.

"I realised this one night while we were having sex," he says. "The condom split. Normally when that happens, your reaction is one of absolute horror, but I found myself thinking that, hang on a moment, if she were to get pregnant, then that would actually be brilliant. It was like an epiphany, like: Fuck! I want to have your babies!"

But then came the complications. When she was still just a toddler,

Claire's older brother Robert died of a genetic condition. Doctors informed her mother that had she had more boys, then they too would very likely have had it. When Claire herself fell pregnant, she was automatically high risk, and had to undergo a succession of tests. If the foetus she was carrying was male, there could be problems. They soon learned their fate.

"It was a boy," James says. "Of course it was."

They were told that she had a 50–50 chance of passing the condition on to their son: not great odds. The prospective father, however, was determined to remain philosophical about it, to not panic, to wait and see. There was so much else, after all, to be overjoyed at.

"I surprised myself just how quickly I came around to the idea of being a dad, how much I loved the anticipation," he says. "Everything about it was wonderful, really, even those uncertain times, because they are just a part of it all. I adored seeing the woman I loved becoming increasingly pregnant – she was just so cuddly – and I felt that the whole notion was just so incredibly romantic. I don't think I was prepared for how much you can love something straight away. But even before he was born, Geronimo felt like a member of the family; we had all these hopes and dreams for him. I guess if you've never really wanted kids, it's hard to appreciate just how much you can love a baby before it's born, but I did, I really did. And when he arrived – healthy, thank God – well, the love was instantly overwhelming and all-encompassing. I got all the totally corny dad moments, and it was all just lovely. I was suddenly in this whole new world: not in London any more, not in a band any more; everything different. And it was then that I started to realise what had actually happened here, that having a son had probably been a lifesaver for me. Yes," he says, nodding quietly, as if to himself, "Geronimo was a lifesaver."

He soon wanted to go through the whole process again, quicker even than his wife did. He proved persuasive. Within two years, she was pregnant again, this time with twins, and this time with even more complications, and not simply because they were also boys.

They were born twelve weeks prematurely. When he first held his new sons, in the hospital ward where they would spend the next three months successfully fighting for their lives, each tiny body fit into the palm of either hand.

"They were tiny, so very fragile. I was halfway through writing my autobiography at the time, but real life just promptly disappeared," he says. "We visited the hospital twice a day at least, for hours at a time, and it was hard, really hard. We were surrounded by all these other parents, some of them really very young, and many of them being told that their children weren't going to get better. A horrible situation, and the kind of thing you can never quite prepare yourself for. But then when it does happen to you, you cope because you have to. It's fight or flight, and that's no choice at all."

It was only when they were permitted to take their sons home at last that their doctor informed them that twenty years previously, had they been born in similar circumstances, they almost certainly wouldn't have made it. Twenty-first century technology had saved them.

"I'll be forever thankful to the NHS," he says. "They were amazing."

Life would never regain its previous course for Alex James, but then he no longer wanted it to. Briefly, he and Claire considered giving up their jobs in favour of full-time childcare, but because both of their careers are vocational, they instead went, in his words, "the nanny and au pair route, which I know a lot of people will criticise, but hey". Meantime, fatherhood was teaching him more about life than he'd ever learned before.

"I guess that's what fatherhood does at its very essence, doesn't it? It makes you a more rounded person, it gives you a big jolt into the real world. And let's face it, I needed it. Being in a band is all about self-gratification, thrill-seeking and avoiding responsibility. And when you are a *bass player* in a band, well, that occupies an even more lowly position of responsibility. I never made any decisions before my kids came along. Now, I'm making them all the time. It's a little like driving a car: there are always decisions to be made, and always so many arguments to have over each one of them. But they are necessary arguments, I suppose, because everything is just so very important."

W.H. Auden, he says, once suggested that there were four basic human needs: the need to love, to be loved, to be a teacher, and to be a pupil.

"And that's why kids are so brilliant, because all four are fulfilled right there, in one convenient package. If I hadn't had kids, I'd still be trying to be one, I think, still trying to pretend to like the new Arctic Monkeys album. But now, I'm perfectly comfortable to admit I'd rather be listening to Boney M, simply because the kids love Boney M. They love music in general, and through them, I'm rediscovering all my old favourites. Geronimo's favourite song right now is "I Fought The Law", not the Clash version, but the Bobby Fuller Four one. It's brilliant.

"Want a tip?" he says. "Try your daughter out on The Ramones, The Stranglers. Kids love a good beat…"

We leave the den and walk to the kitchen. The scene here is familial and domestic. Claire is answering some questions posed to her by a man in overalls who is hunched underneath the Aga, and the nanny is dishing up lunch for their three sons. James makes me a coffee, and we wander into the living room. Sitting in their highchairs with plastic forks in their chubby fists, the unidentical Artemis and Galileo appraise their father under curling blond locks and offer quizzical half-smiles. He reaches for a nearby ukulele and starts up an impromptu version of "Bob The Builder", while Geronimo insists on drowning out the racket by informing everyone that he wants to watch *Transformers* on the television.

Later, James tells me that Blur were recently offered the Saturday night headlining slot at Glastonbury 2008. It was an irresistible offer, and the band members, even Graham Coxon, were all immediately willing, with one exception: their lead singer.

"Damon ummed and ahhed for a while and then decided he was busy," he says, his shoulders shrugging in a helpless approximation of defeat, Albarn having stumped band progress once again (though in 2009, he would finally come round and Blur would temporarily reform). "Yes, I was disappointed, but then Geronimo asked me to come and play a show at his local playgroup with some of the other parents. I have to admit, it was a terrifying prospect and I was incredibly nervous, but you know what? It ended up being the best band I've ever played with – and, on reflection, much better than Glastonbury could ever have been."

As he so often does, Alex James grins expansively, employing every last tooth in his head. It's as if he is trying to convey the sense that life for him is nothing but a breeze, an existence unencumbered by stress or strain, anxiety or even the mildest apprehension, and that he is simply thrilled by each new successive challenge that comes his way. He stands, hands on hips, in his living room under a winter sun in a pair of farm-muddied boots and a creased, button-down shirt, half tucked in in the manner of an overgrown schoolboy. The hair of which he is so proud ("a rock star, even a former one, should always have good hair") is all over the place, and he needs a shave. Two of his sons smile at him, the older one hangs onto his leg. Their father barks with laughter. He looks very much at home.

Alex James will be 40 soon. He will reach this milestone having achieved everything he ever set out to and more, and so no wonder this current contentment suits him. But, I ask, surely he misses some of his old existence? Is it possible that anyone who led a life of such heady excess could so easily leave it all behind? His smile comes back at me now, with added force.

"I'm not sure I miss anything, really. I just see this as the next stage in things. I mean, of course, I miss plenty, but then we all do. I miss Father Christmas, I miss being ten years old, I miss having a go-cart and being in a band and having no responsibilities. You know, for a while, I thought that being in a band was the hardest thing to let go of, but the more I think about it, the hardest thing to let go of is actually being young. But then that would be much harder if I didn't have my kids. They make you happy to grow up. Adults make babies but babies make adults. That's true, isn't it?"

A carrot drops from Galileo's fork. The Aga man gets up, dusts down and leaves. Through the window in a distant field, a sheep, one of his, baas.

"This is exactly where I want to be," he says.

Six

Experience has taught me that I rarely feel much in the way of anticipatory nerves or excitement for almost anything that comes my way in life. Instead, I tend only to fully react to something when it is already on top of me and demanding a response. Perhaps inevitably, I am then rather prone to *over*reaction. During my footballing career, for example, truncated at the age of fourteen due not to a crippling injury but a general lack of talent and stamina, I would feel nothing of the encroaching anxieties enjoyed by my team mates for a forthcoming match until I was standing on the pitch itself and watching the referee place the whistle in his mouth, poised to blow. Only then would I feel an urgent need to pee, a factor that subsequently hampered my ability to play with anything approaching full mobility. Similarly, while I look forward to going on holiday in a manner comparable with everyone else, I don't develop the mandatory butterflies until bags are packed and we are hurtling in a train towards the airport, at which point it comes in a drunken, lightheaded rush.

And so being nine full months into Elena's pregnancy has still not prompted in me any of the white fear I thought I would by now be drenched in. Because if any event were ever to bring about such fevered anticipation within me, I figured, it would be this. Instead, I feel a stillness that has nothing to do with calm. It's a denial of sorts,

I realise this, but I'm trying to convince myself that I am, in fact, squaring up to the inevitability with admirable pluck and fortitude. The plain truth, though, is that even at this late stage, I cannot quite make the mental leap that, in a matter of days, possibly hours, I am to become a parent.

• • •

Richard has come to see me, a surprise enough in itself as Richard normally avoids public transport if the ticket will cost him more than two pounds. Relieved to have an excuse to get out of the house, I meet him at the station and we walk together through my new neighbourhood, past an endless stream of underdressed young women on their way to a Christmas drinks party. We end up down by the river, which I presume looks more appealing in the summertime than it does now, the ducks and swans grey and wan and gripped by the cold, and find ourselves in an uninspiring chain restaurant whose chips come fat and fluffy and whose disproportionately cheery waiting staff sit you in booths rather than at tables. The menu comes laminated. I go for chicken and chips, Richard a burger and potato wedges. We order wine.

At the next booth, six women are loudly consuming cocktails with umbrellas in them. They are young, their flesh spilling over tight fabric. Two of them have Rudolph antlers on their heads, one of them a Christmas cracker crown, each carefree in a manner I can no longer be. Watching them, I feel the sad lust and envy of a country and western song. The wine comes and my phone rings. It's Elena, which is unusual, as she normally wouldn't bother me on a night out. In an instant, the penny drops.

Now, out of nowhere, my mind finally chooses to make that unbridgeable mental leap, not in words but sensation. I visibly deflate, growing soft and weak, my bones putty. And I haven't even answered the call yet. Richard looks at me in mounting alarm. I bring the phone to my ear.

"I don't want to startle you," she begins, speaking quietly, "but something has happened."

She goes on to say that ten minutes previously, she became aware of a small discharge in her knickers. Vaguely, from our one antenatal class, I remember the term *plug*. At least I think it was *plug*. It's all hazy now. Elena tells me that she hasn't told her mother because she doesn't want her to worry, but that she thought I should know. I ask if it was her waters breaking, but we both know that this cannot be the case. We've seen such events on TV before, and it always seems to be a major, and quite unambiguous, event, comparable to an upended full bottle of Evian. I suggest she phones the hospital just in case, but Elena, perhaps in a kind of denial herself, insists it's nothing and says she'll wait and see what, if anything, happens next. If I'm not mistaken, I detect an underlying panic in her voice. I have never heard panic in her voice before. It unsettles me. I slump forward in my bench seat.

The food has arrived, but I've lost all appetite. Richard, who is normally averse to public displays of emotion and intimacy, is suddenly a tower of strength, taking me by the arm and talking lucid good sense. It's ridiculous, but I am shaking, and feel quite faint. His words are strong and defiant, oddly brave, and I'm aware of an overwhelming sense of gratitude towards him. In the months to come, our friendship will re-establish its usual pattern of good-natured bickering that regularly loses all trace of good nature, but right now I am glad to have him. I get a lump in my throat over the realisation. What on earth is happening to me?

"Eat," he instructs.

The chips are fat and fluffy, the waiting staff irrepressibly cheery. I'll never come back here again.

A full day later, the minicab pulls away from our front door, at which the mother-in-law stands anxiously, in her heavy blue housecoat, waving. She won't be coming to the hospital with us until we know something more conclusive. There is also the unspoken fact that I don't want to share her daughter on an occasion like this. As we pull out into the empty, darkened streets, Elena slips her hand into mine almost surreptitiously. If we are going to do any panicking here, she seems to be suggesting, then we are going to do it with understatement. I lean towards the driver and say the name of the hospital, then tell him its location, all the way across London and opposite one of the city's most famous landmarks.

"Big Ben?" he responds in broken English, clearly confused. "What is this?"

The journey will take us almost an hour, and relieve me of £50. Because we ended up moving house just one week before the birth of our child, we never had time to register with our local hospital, and so this mercy dash takes us through five travel zones and a distance of almost twenty miles. It is eight o'clock at night, the roads mercifully deserted. Unrecognisable parts of unknown suburbia race past the window, and for at least 40 minutes I have no idea where we are. The driver hasn't put the radio on. The silence is deafening.

Elena eventually conceded to my wishes and phoned the hospital earlier this evening. She was put through to a midwife, whose voice was clearly not predisposed to empathy.

"You're telling me that your waters broke?" she asked.

Elena tried to explain exactly what had happened, and her lack of certainty.

"You're telling me that your waters broke," the midwife said again, this time without the question mark. "Come in, *now*. Your foetus could be in danger, and potentially has been for the past 24 hours. I suggest you hurry."

Between palms, still pressed tightly together, our sweat commingles. Right now, it's our sole form of communication. The only time I speak out loud is to direct the driver. To assist him, I mention that Big Ben sits alongside the Houses of Parliament.

"Tony Blair!" he cries.

Shortly before nine o'clock, he attempts to drop us off outside

Downing Street until I gently suggest he carries along Whitehall, then left onto the bridge and over it. If at any time during our journey he has discerned that one of his passengers is heavily pregnant, he shows no outward sign of it. He parks up, and I collect Elena's overnight bag, the new unfamiliar bag with the new and unfamiliar clothes for the soon-to-come new arrival, and then I lead her by the elbow through the automatic doors and into blinding white light.

The lift to the seventh floor rattles loudly and smells strongly of disinfectant. Two nurses stand alongside us, laughing nicotine-laced laughs. The lift arrives, but my stomach is still on the ground floor, my wits scattered all around me.

Arriving at the maternity ward, we sign in, wash our hands and follow the yellow painted signs on the linoleum floor beneath our feet to a reception desk where, after several minutes, a nurse looks up and checks us in. We are placed in what looks like a private room – there is just one bed and, in the corner, an unfolded sofa bed – whose windows give generous views over the Thames. Elena gets changed into a hospital-issue gown, blue and frayed and gappy at the back, and sits on the rubber mattress. We are told that because her waters have indeed broken, waters that were protecting our unborn baby, the foetus could now be exposed to all kinds of infection.

"We'll need to do a couple of tests," the midwife says. "Then you'll probably be sent home, and you'll come back tomorrow when your contractions have started. No point staying the whole night if you don't have to, eh?" She offers a smile of reassurance, then leaves.

I look out of the window, at the famous clock and the river, then sit down, crossing one leg over the other, trying to will myself into a relaxed state. Elena lies back on the bed, staring at the ceiling. The seventh floor remains almost spookily quiet, seemingly bereft of all human life. Time passes, an hour, two, then three. It is now midnight, and while I'm not looking forward to trying to convince a cab to drive us all the way back across town, I am looking forward to being home. Friends are due to arrive tomorrow, Christmas Eve, and will be staying with us until Boxing Day. We've food to prepare, bottles to uncork.

At half past twelve, I venture out into the corridor again, unaccountably nervous, to look for our midwife. I see no one. The reception desk is now unmanned and ghostly quiet. I walk up and down, around corners and into another reception area. Nothing, no one. CCTV watches me impassively.

From behind a closed door, I suddenly hear a strange noise, more animal than human. It uneases me. I hurry back to our room, just in case, and sit alongside Elena for comfort. Together we hear the sound grow louder. It is reminiscent almost of a dog, possibly a wolf, a yeti even, in what appears to be its final death throes. It starts deep and low, then gradually climbs the scales until it has transformed into a helium, bleating shriek, no consonants, just unending vowels that stretch out like elastic and finally snap. It sounds like all the pain in the world and beyond, and then abruptly stops. Then it starts again. It is the necessary noise, we come to realise, of a baby being born.

"That won't be me, will it?" Elena whispers, her voice querulous.

I have no idea.

"Of course not," I say.

At two o'clock in the morning, I make another tentative search of the ward, and actually find someone. A nurse. I explain our situation. She nods. She tells me to wait, to be patient, and that she will come and see us shortly. Like a fool, I take her at her word.

The sun rises early, full of sparkle and glitter over a cold, cloudless Christmas Eve morning. We try to doze a while longer, Elena on the rubber mattress, me on the unfolded sofa bed, but the truth is that neither of us have slept more than half an hour uninterrupted, either by worry or disorientation. I venture out to Starbucks for coffee and a croissant, and a Saturday newspaper whose magazine has an article of mine on the cover. I want nothing more than to sit down with my breakfast and read it, but when I return to the ward, the improbable has happened. A nurse has finally visited Elena, and I find her now being hooked up to a drip which, shortly, will bring about the contractions that don't appear to be happening of their own accord. This, I am told, will speed up the delivery, which means that we are going nowhere now until the baby is born.

A midwife enters the room and starts to make conversation. I tell her that we have friends coming over and that we haven't much time.

"They'll have to wait," she says, a hand on Elena's stomach, "because baby won't."

Defeated, I sit down on the sofa and open the paper.

"Close that," the midwife snaps, "and come here. Your wife needs your support."

"We're not married," I tell her. Her eyes glower.

I get up to stand beside Elena, apologising meekly, and hold her hand. The coffee grows cold, the croissant stale. I won't be sitting down again for another thirteen hours.

● ● ●

Once the contractions start causing a level of pain gas and air do little to counteract, Elena doesn't swear and scream at me as films would have us expect, but is rather entirely focused on the task at hand with a determination that floors me. She is absolutely and utterly focused. Her eyes stare ahead at nothing, the vein that runs down her forehead pulsing steadily. It's like I am here but also not, meekly whispering encouragements that I am convinced she neither needs nor hears. After a while, she turns to me, suddenly fearful that she is squeezing my hand too tightly.

"That's a first," the midwife deadpans. I don't like our latest midwife. Derision oozes from her like garlic fumes. She clearly considers me an idiot. Earlier, she told me that she goes off duty in a couple of hours. I can't wait.

It is to become the slowest day of our lives. I want this all over quickly; it feels imperative to get out of here as soon as possible. I am reminded of the story a friend told me when his girlfriend was in hospital waiting to give birth. A haughty, and very pregnant, woman in the next bed was loudly impatient with her doctors, issuing instructions in a honking voice.

"Can we if at all possible get a move on?" she complained. "I've a ski catalogue to write."

The drip has been feeding Elena for six hours now, and though the contractions have gone from seven minutes apart to five, to three and now to once every 90 seconds, she is far from ten centimetres dilated and so a good way off from delivery just yet. This explains the offhanded disdain the succession of midwives has shown us. They are, clearly, bored and impatient. Each time another contraction occurs, prompting more ravaged howls of pain, they offer vague words of encouragement but their hearts aren't in it. One of them spends 30 minutes in our room, not at the bedside but rather in a corner on her laptop, filling out hospital forms. At one point, she even disappears for a full quarter-hour, during which time she misses several further contractions, each one of which I'm convinced will result in abrupt, slippery birth, leaving me holding the baby and utterly ignorant of what to do next.

Initially, Elena had wanted as natural a birth as possible – most women do – but then, as the hours progress, the pain worsens, and no discernible end swims readily into sight. Finally, she has decided that the agony is too great and that the sensation of ripping vaginal fire has to stop. She wants an epidural. The moment we inform our current midwife of this, we lose all her respect completely. Beforehand, she had been fairly friendly, a squat Scottish woman with broad shoulders, thick arms and a bluntly amusing manner. But now she is scowling, looking at me with something like contempt. She shakes her head and transfers her gaze to Elena.

"It's only pain, Helen," she says. "Women go through this every day; it's no big deal, trust me. You'll be fine. An epidural will only delay the birth even more, and anyway, I've a feeling baby'll be born inside of ten minutes."

An hour later, the head is still refusing to crown, and repeated pleadings – merciful from Elena, but whispered from me for I am scared of the woman – prompt her to go and fetch the anaesthetist. She is back inside of a minute.

"Doctor's busy; she'll be here soon."

No more words pass between us.

When the anaesthetist eventually arrives, she is all kindness and light. I like her immediately. She makes what sound like genuine apologies and says that she understands we want pain relief. But before Elena can answer, the midwife interjects, talking not to us but directly to her colleague. There appears to be tension between the two, and neither attempts to conceal it from us. The midwife argues that the epidural really isn't necessary, that the baby will be born much quicker without it, and that if Elena has suffered so admirably these last many hours, what's another 30 minutes? Elena, tired, emotional and weak with exhaustion, so much so that she falls into seconds-long sleep in between each new contraction, gives in.

"You're sure?" the anaesthetist says. "Because I'll happily do it right now. The pain will be history. Just say the word."

"She's sure," the midwife says.

The anaesthetist leaves. The midwife smiles.

"Do you know what time Tesco's closes today?" she asks.

It is shortly after seven o'clock in the evening. Our room is suddenly full: a couple of doctors, two midwives, several nurses. They have been summoned because there are – and it's a word I've heard many times before on many medical TV dramas, and it terrifies me now to my marrow – *complications*. Eight hours into the drip feed, and the baby still hasn't arrived. Crowning appears to be under way at last, though I can't see anything for myself due to the number of bodies crushing in for a view of their own. Somebody mentions forceps, someone else a Caesarean. One doctor wonders why, despite the patient's evident discomfort, an epidural wasn't administered. Our midwife, about to finish her shift, says nothing. I hear the word *tearing*, and the likely requirement of scissors. Bickering breaks out between them over which method to go for, and how soon. I've seen this episode on *ER*, and I know just how it will pan out. It won't be good.

"*Quick!*" somebody says sharply, pointing at me. "Get him a chair. He's going to faint."

From somewhere a chair is thrust into the back of my knees. My legs give way and I fall heavily onto my behind. But I don't want this; I want to be beside my girlfriend. And so I get up again, reach over to her, hold her hand and squeeze it for want of anything more proactive to do. I am feverish with panic, while Elena herself seems unreachable: in a tunnel of pain and pushing, still intensely focused and so very desperate for a conclusion.

Now, abruptly, a rush of activity. Medical implements are picked up and cast aside. I cannot be clear who is doing what, or why, and I have lost my voice, incapable of asking. Every 60 seconds, Elena lets out another depth charge, sodden hair stuck to her forehead. *We're going to have to cut her.* I hear it without realising I've heard it, and then immediately I play it back to myself: *We're going to have to cut her.* And right now, amidst the noise and the tumult, the fear and the hope, a terribly selfish realisation dawns. I become vividly aware that if they are going to cut her, then our sex life will suffer later down the line. I'd read this once in a book, a magazine, and it stayed with me more than anything else I've read on the subject of childbirth. The vagina, when cut, can remain slack afterwards, failing to regain its elasticity and consequently not quite as snug as it previously was. There was a statistic quoted, I can't remember the figure, confirming that anal sex becomes much more common in couples after childbirth than it ever was before, and for this very reason – the arse now considerably tighter than the fanny. I've tried anal sex; it didn't do much for me. But now a doctor, scissors in hand, is going to condemn me to a lifetime of back-passage entry, or else propel me into the arms of another woman yet to endure the butchery of childbirth.

I switch back to the present and realise there has been a development. The scissors have been cast aside, unused I think – oh sweet mercy! – and a doctor is saying, "One more, one more push – *push!*" Elena screams louder than ever, a mighty prolonged roar, and in a liquid flash, no slow crowning now, just a *whoosh*, there comes a flash of movement, of life, slick limbs, a single cry, and I am shocked to see a baby being placed on Elena's stomach and one of the nurses or midwives holding the umbilical cord taut while another nurse or midwife reaches for the scissors, then cuts. Shouldn't I have done that? On television, it's the father that does that. I've been robbed. The doctor is talking now, saying words – to me.

"Tell her, tell her the sex."

Elena looks at me eagerly, her position low enough and the baby far away enough for her not to see the detail I can. So I look, briefly, registering the shortened umbilical cord dangling, confusing it, and I tell her, I say to her: "A boy."

The doctor laughs. "Look again," she says, moving the cord to one side, and I see now an absence where previously I thought I'd seen something else entirely.

"A girl," I say.

A girl.

Somebody places scissors in my hand, and I'm encouraged to make a sort of ceremonial cut of the truncated umbilical cord. I do so. Elena is spent, smiling but relieved. Here we are, then, finally, at ten to eight on a moonlit Christmas Eve night in 2005, with a baby.

We are three.

• • •

I'm on the phone. Gil is talking.

"So what time will you be back? Dinner'll be ready by five, so we'll pick you up at – what? – three, three-thirty?"

"Sounds good. I'll call you later."

It's Christmas Day, noon. I've been home for the night, slept surprisingly soundly and come back to collect my girlfriend and my daughter. It has been a strange night in my new, and currently very full, house. The mother-in-law was overjoyed but disappointed that her visit last night had been so short, just an hour with her new granddaughter for whom she felt nothing in the way of ambiguity: hers was an instant and overwhelming love, an emotion she felt able to lavish with a loud and public extravagance. My own feelings remain somewhat confused, but then I expected the confusion and I'm fine with it, for now. We left the hospital, the mother-in-law, Gil and myself, and shortly after eleven, came home and opened a bottle of champagne while I recounted my evening's bloody war story.

"So, wow, you're a father now," Gil said. "How do you feel?"

Avoiding the question, I requested another glass.

In the morning, our final guest for Christmas lunch (by now already postponed to Christmas dinner) arrived. Motorbike helmet in one hand, a bottle of champagne poking from his backpack, Stuart offered congratulations while I told my story again over a breakfast that ran leisurely into brunch. The phone rang. It was Elena, unhappy that I wasn't already at her bedside. The truth is that by perpetuating the male ritual of celebrating childbirth with alcohol, I had completely forgotten her. I apologised profusely and told her I was leaving immediately.

The plan was this: to get to the hospital, help pack, dress the baby, come home, do Christmas. But as I arrive at the ward, there are more complications, almost certain delays and further inevitable changes of plan. Gil returns home to await instruction and to deal with the mother-in-law on my behalf.

Time grinds to an eventual standstill.

• • •

Christmas Day unfolds tentatively, minutes stretching into hours into what feels like days and months. We are ready to go, but we need to be appraised and signed off by a nurse before being permitted to do so. There is a depleted staff today, for obvious reasons, and the boisterous West Indian women on duty appear both busy and leisurely at once. Someone will be with us soon, I am repeatedly told. Every hour, Gil phones for an update, and tells me that while Paul, a former chef, is cooking up a storm, the mother-in-law, for whom the kitchen is usually her exclusive domain, is watching him from a distance of just two feet, continually asking questions in Spanish, to which Paul can only smile, shrug and blush.

"She doesn't look best pleased," he tells me. "She's cleaned the Venetian blinds, the skirting boards, the windows; she won't stop. When the hell are you coming home?"

It's a good question. Elena hardly slept last night, and is happy now to doze. Meanwhile, our new daughter Amaya is sound asleep in her transparent plastic cot, a tiny thing in a tiny babygro. Hard to believe she was the cause of all that agony yesterday. I peer into the cot, waiting to feel the same rush of emotion that clearly assailed her grandmother the previous evening. Nothing comes.

Elena had to give up the private room after I left last night, and is now in a ward of four people. One of them is a silent 30-something woman with her silent infant. Neither have visitors. In another is a Muslim woman surrounded by an extensive family, all of whom covet privacy, and so conduct their whispered business behind permanently drawn curtains. In the remaining bed is a light-skinned young black girl, pendulous breasts unconstrained by the hospital gown she doesn't bother to do up whether breast-feeding her newborn or not. Her nipples are huge, the colour of dark chocolate, and with the constituency of rubber. On average, she spends 50 minutes of every hour on the phone to friends and family, and she says the same thing over and over again to each person she calls, a Groundhog Day of endless repetition.

"Eight pounds four ounces, he's doing really well, and already has a great big willy, so he's clearly his father's son…"

There is a stench in the ward of body odour and sour breastmilk, a combination the air conditioning doesn't quite know what to do with. I breathe through my mouth. Gil phones. I palm him off, then rip some skin from one of my cuticles with my teeth, watching as the blood bubbles up.

"Helen, right?"

A loud, booming voice, sticky as rum, promptly wakes up mother and daughter. Finally, someone has been sent to sign us off. The latest midwife is in late middle age, reading glasses clamped across her eyes and a clipboard in her hand from which she misreads Elena's name. She peers down at the baby and seems joyful and unfussy. I have a good feeling about her. She'll have us out of here in no time, I'm convinced. But then Elena spoils it all by telling her she is having trouble breast-feeding. The admission brings with it tired tears.

"Now now, dear, don't fret, let's see what we can do about it."

She gives me the clipboard, then picks up Amaya and holds her aloft, clamping the baby's spongy skull in each of her five fingers. With her left hand, she frees Elena's breast from the gown and all but smacks the baby onto it with a practised skill that almost prompts within me a round of applause. The baby suckles.

"Easy, see?" she says.

Elena tries and fails, repeatedly. There are more tears. I check my watch.

"Okay, girl, don't worry, we can try again later. What you need now is sleep. You look terrible tired, terrible. Here, father," she says, turning to me and depositing the swaddled bundle into my suddenly out-thrust arms, "go bond with your daughter in the corridor while your wife she get some rest."

I wander into the family room which, to my relief, is empty, no one there to watch and appraise me. My daughter lies compactly in my arms, eyes open but unseeing. I walk around the room's perimeter in a generous circle, and gradually her eyelids begin to lower. I decide to sing to her, but quietly so that nobody can hear, a song called "Beautiful Friend" by Sebadoh's Lou Barlow that I rediscovered on my iPod recently. It's about a man who wants to rekindle his relationship with an old girlfriend, and though hardly suitable material for a father to sing to his daughter, it is beautiful, with a lullaby quality to it. And, besides, the lyrics are fresh in my mind at a time when nothing else is. "I'm still in love with you," Barlow sings, in a pleading voice. "And I only want to be with you/I only want to be with... *you*."

I grow self-conscious, feeling increasingly like a man auditioning for a part in a romantic comedy, a new father doting over his new daughter in a New Man kind of way. It's hollow and fraudulent. But then right now, *everything* is hollow. Nothing feels natural; I've no idea what I'm doing. I never got around to reading the pregnancy books for one reason or another, and now that I need their knowledge, I'm wallowing in a self-imposed ignorance. She sleeps and I fall silent, standing by the window watching trains arrive and depart at Waterloo Station, some of which will take their passengers on to Paris and beyond, a world of untethered possibility.

Boxing Day follows a similar pattern to Christmas Day, but unfolds even more gradually. It becomes increasingly clear that we aren't going anywhere in a hurry. Though this is monumentally frustrating in itself, it is also rather encouraging. I'd grown up being led to believe that the NHS was always keen to get rid of new mothers as quickly as possible. But here they are actively requesting this one to stay.

By the day's eventual close, at the stroke of midnight, I am on Westminster Bridge waiting for Gil to pick me up and drive me to his place in the Barbican, rather than back home to the anxious but sympathetically patient mother-in-law. I am so very tired, and fall asleep on the living-room sofa bed in an instant.

Early the next morning, I leave a note of thanks and close the door behind me quietly, then walk the 40 minutes across town to the hospital for what I very much hope is the final time.

The new day brings with it a light falling of snow. The streets are entirely empty, as if in my distraction there has been a mass evacuation of the city's inhabitants, serving only to further my general sense of dislocation. At Moorgate, I unexpectedly find a branch of M&S open. I go in to buy, as instructed by text message, two pairs of knickers and a packet of extra-thick panty liners (for what, precisely, I'd rather not know). The girl at the till, bored until I arrived, gives me a wry look.

The hospital lift's rattle is, by now, uncomfortably familiar. On the seventh floor, I go through the usual rigmarole of signing in and washing my hands, then walk down the corridor and into the ward. The beds have different women in them now, mothers having achieved what we haven't. But Elena is looking better.

"Amaya's feeding," she says with a smile. "We can go home."

My heart leaps. "Now?"

"As soon as the midwife comes to see us, yes."

Four hours later, we leave the hospital. Ria, a close friend, is waiting for us with her car and, from somewhere, a baby seat, which is more complicated a contraption than it looks. The drive home takes another hour through largely deserted streets, and we arrive to a scrubbed and spotlessly clean house. The mother-in-law has bought flowers for the kitchen. The windows are clean, the blinds thoroughly dusted. The television screen shines. The window ledge boasts fresh milk, new margarine. She is beyond content that her granddaughter is at last home, and starts to make the noises women of a certain age cannot help but make in the face of a bemused infant. I make coffee, we talk, Ria leaves, a new kind of life begins.

• • •

The following morning, Elena and I are gathered around a Moses basket in which our daughter, finally, sleeps. We've had a long night of it, Amaya stirring throughout and making sticky, mucus-y noises like soft leather in wet mud, noises that Elena tells me the handbooks say is quite normal. The baby looks at peace, completely still.

"Is she breathing?" Elena says, growing concerned.

I bend down to place a finger under her nostrils, but do so clumsily, and manage to hit her in the mouth. Her eyes pop open, filled with instant alarm. Her face crumples. Now she is screaming, the racket completely disproportionate to the tiny vessel that generates it. I apologise profusely as Elena, a gentle hand on my back, encourages me to pick her up, hold her and rock her back to sleep. "You can do it," she says. "Go on." But the mother-in-law has swooped suddenly into the room, without invitation, and has pounced. Amaya is now in her arms, still screaming.

"Ja ja, alla, alla," she says in metronomic repetition, a form of nonsensical Spanish babble designed to calm, rather than a vocal celebration of the Muslim God. I am thunderstruck with pique – Amaya is *my* baby, not hers. Elena gives me a sympathetic look of apology, but it's too late. I'm sulking now. I pick up all 900 pages of Gregory David Roberts' *Shantaram* from the bedside table, stalk upstairs into my room and close the door.

Of course, all along I had had no firm idea of how I would react to parenthood, or quite what it would bring out in me.

But I hadn't expected this.

Seven

I'm not sure if it's morning or night, the middle of the day or approaching dusk. It could be Thursday, Monday, or we may already be into the weekend. Christmas is over and New Year looming, that's all I know for sure, but then in many ways it doesn't matter, all sense of time having temporarily lost its significance. In the kitchen, Christmas crackers are unpulled and presents unopened, while next to the draining board and under clingfilm sits remnants of the three-course meal Paul and Gil slaved so hard over days previously.

We are in the bedroom, the four of us, the blinds down, curtains drawn. Amaya is wailing in her cot, Asiatic eyes closed, chubby red cheeks stretched, mouth a perfect O. Elena is alongside her, dressed in the same nightgown she had on in the hospital and which she seems to wear all the time now. There are dried breastmilk stains on its front, alongside other stains too: snot, saliva, upchuck. She stands with her hands at the base of her back, the top of her bum, much like she did when pregnant, her habitual pose now and the only one that keeps her upright. Her stomach has deflated but not yet by much; in a week's time, when the washing machine is delivered, one of the delivery men will look at her swell and ask when the baby is due. Her hair is unwashed, her skin a deathly pallor. She hasn't slept for more than an unbroken couple of hours now for at least a week, and looks drained and helpless. Beside her is her mother, issuing advice and instruction, the only one of us in any way capable or knowledgeable, or not in some way overawed. I'm on the edge of the bed, peering into the cot from a safe distance. The baby has been crying intermittently for hours; in fact, she has done just that for much of her life so far, milk and rocking and mollycoddling bringing only an all-too-brief respite. The mother-in-law is the first to take action, picking her up and onto her shoulder where she gagas her to fleeting slumber, marching up and down the hall and babbling incessantly. A small miracle: the crying stops, at which point Elena immediately climbs back into bed and into instant sleep, leaving me alone.

They say that in the weeks immediately after the birth of a child, levels of testosterone in fathers drop by more than 30 per cent. The reasons are strictly evolutionary: once deprived of testosterone, men are less likely to search for new mates to inseminate. They are also less aggressive. Perhaps this is why I feel so depleted, so aimless. I'm half the man I used to be.

Upstairs in my room, I find my watch and learn that it is Thursday, December 29th, shortly after eleven in the morning. I have nothing to do, no work to occupy me and certainly no immediate paternal requirements to fulfil. I get dressed and go out into the cold streets, walking with my head down, hands in pockets. My daughter has been home from hospital for two days now, days that have brought with them an exhaustion and confusion I have never previously known. I remember reading somewhere that the first few weeks of your baby's life are crucial to the bonding process, to the extent that it could determine your future relationship, perhaps, some argue, irrevocably. There has been no bonding between us yet, nothing even close. I am still too bewildered by her, and far too infuriatingly timid to assert myself in the face of her dominant grandmother. If this failure of mine does bring with it repercussions, will I ever be able to forgive myself? Moreover, will I look for someone else to blame, Elena perhaps, for not ensuring that this defining period in our lives should have been fully and exclusively our own?

•••

Avoiding the multitude of coffee shops and restaurants that my new neighbourhood offers, I seek out instead the gloomy interior of the Eden Café. Its continued existence this far into the 21st century is a triumph of sorts, a belligerently anachronistic greasy spoon that has stubbornly refused to update itself, despite all the shiny modernisation springing up around it. Step inside the Eden Café and you can convince yourself that Starbucks and its ilk exists in another universe altogether, a soft-sofa'd fantasy for fops and wimps and women laden with shopping and children. Eden is for men, workmen, and the place *is* predominantly filled with just that, many of a certain age, with donkey jackets thrown over chairs and inch-long roll ups smouldering from between fingertips, creased tabloids spread out before them. There are just eight tables here, seven of which hug the far wall under framed photographs and paintings of, amongst other things, a china doll with a poignant tear in its eye, and an image of Eden itself, in delicate pastel, Adam and Eve appraising the fateful apple. The remaining table sits squarely in the middle and appears to be for the exclusive use of the hirsute waiters, who congregate here between orders, reading tabloids of their own and lighting one dog-end from the dying embers of its predecessor. (When the smoking ban comes in several months later, it will hit Eden hard.) Today, Christmas carols are being piped through a speaker system riven by tuberculosis, and so "The Frog Chorus" comes with great spluttering coughs and a sucking, wheezing death rattle.

I plump for Eden's signature dish, baked potato *with*. The *with* can be anything from chilli con carne to cottage cheese, sausage and beans, coleslaw or corn, or even chips. I opt for the sausage and beans, a heavy dish that will sit with me for hours, and I take the window seat, the permanent smear on the pane of glass conspiring to soft-focus the world outside.

I have a book with me, something Peter had recommended that he thought I'd find useful. I need to read something useful, having failed with the various hectoring parenting guides during Elena's pregnancy. During those nine months, the only books I read were the ones I wanted to: novels mostly, memoirs, travelogues. From time to time, I did pick titles that at least had parenthood as their subject. The aforementioned Rachel Cusk's *A Life's Work* filled me with terrible foreboding. Lionel Shriver's *We Need To Talk About Kevin*, which takes the form of a succession of letters a mother writes to her incarcerated teenage son who has just committed a Columbine-style massacre, was a queasy, if brilliant, treatise on just what utter sick, sadistic bastards your children can grow into, despite your very best efforts. Peter Carey's *Wrong About Japan* did convey some lovely, tender things about being the father of a teenage boy, but this was hardly much help to me. It did make me want to revisit Tokyo, though.

Peter's recommended read, Oliver James's *They F*** You Up*, is hardly the balm I was looking for under my present circumstances. As far as I can surmise, it suggests that irrespective of our very best intentions in bringing up our children, we will still afford them a lifetime's worth of insecurities for which they will never fully forgive us. Making deliberately slow progress with my baked potato, I go through 100 pages in slack-jawed unease.

When I return home several hours later, my mobile phone having not been troubled once (my extended absence clearly not a cause for concern), I find the mother-in-law cooking in the kitchen, Elena dozing upstairs in bed, Amaya at her breast. I try to engage her in conversation, but she is not quite with it. The baby is refusing to suckle properly, requiring all of her focus.

Upstairs, now deep into Oliver James, I read about personality disorder, about the people he defines as either Avoidants or Clingers, and how parents can project onto family members an unhealthy level of aggression and depression. I have never been remotely aggressive but now, quite suddenly, I'm aware of a rising – not *depression*, exactly, but certainly a kind of creeping melancholy, a sense of distress that sits low inside me and rumbles upwards. I close the book and reach for my iPod, music the only thing to keep this rising sensation at bay.

It's another restless night, the baby tossing and turning and making those strange noises of hers, Elena feeding at regular intervals, meditatively shushing her cries, the mother-in-law coming in to see if she can be of assistance, lights going on and off, lots of pacing and the continuing grumbles of an infant whose needs are consistently not being met. But I hear none of this, not consciously at least, and become aware only when Elena tells me about it the following morning. These past few days, and in fact, for the next few weeks to come, I sleep deeper and more profoundly than I ever have before, an utterly dreamless unconsciousness impervious to interruption, a merciful escape. And yet despite this, I awake each new morning brutally exhausted, and have to drag myself from bed as I would from the bottom of a well, had someone thrown down a rope in the hope of rescuing me.

• • •

Tempting as it is, I can't quite face another lengthy incarceration within Eden today, and so I head into the centre of town instead, to London's Oxford Street, ostensibly to look for bargains in the sales. But mostly this is just an excuse for me to get out of the house and to create a tangible distance from its clawing claustrophobia. Home has become rather suffocating of late.

Last night, I had asked Elena if she could perhaps politely suggest to her mother that she didn't continually interrupt us whenever we were speaking but rather waited until we had finished. She means no harm, of course, but whenever her mother wants to talk, and she is voluminous in almost eternal chatter, she does so whether those around her are already engaged in conversation or not. It makes communication between us impossible. And so Elena asked. It didn't go down well. She burst into tears and then mounted a counter-attack.

Didn't we realise that this whole situation — a foreign country, a foreign language and, though it went unspoken, *me* — was so difficult for her too? All she wanted to do was help, but that if help resulted in all *this*, then she wanted to leave, to go back to Spain, immediately. She would do as well, were it not for her granddaughter. I removed myself from the kitchen, wretchedly, on tiptoes, while Elena did her diplomatic best to backtrack. Later that night, she and I were talking in the living room, the TV murmuring quietly in the background, Amaya asleep upstairs. Her mother strode in to ask a question before catching herself, realising her error, turning on her heel and running into the kitchen. We could hear more tears.

This morning, over an awkward breakfast, Elena and I finally exchanged Christmas presents. I had bought her a cashmere jumper, a baby manual she had wanted and an Ayurvedic massage coupon she could cash in at will. She, in turn, gave me a pair of socks, specifically ankle socks, to be worn in the summer with shorts, six months and a whole lifetime away. Socks. I hadn't realised our relationship had descended to this. As she watched my face collapse into what very nearly became a torrent of childlike tears, she quickly explained that this was just a gentle joke. Holding one of my hands in both of hers, she told me that she would have got me something else but that she simply didn't have the time, what with the baby and everything.

The baby and everything.

And right there, in that instant, I felt it for the first time: resentment.

Oxford Street is the perfect place to lose yourself in a crowd, and I'm always happiest in the percolating chaos of a busy city street. But today I feel detached from it all. I have no interest in clashing elbows in overcrowded department stores simply for the sake of a pair of jeans, and even my usual bookshops fail to detain me for long. I wander aimlessly amongst the frenzy, my footsteps far slower than usual, far more hesitant.

It is a cold, bright day, cloudless and blazing blue, a new year imminent, a buzzing optimism in the air. The surface noise is huge: engines, horns, belching exhaust pipes and the merging voices of a hundred thousand conversations. I reach Oxford Circus, where a human traffic jam has developed at the lights, while heavily uniformed police officers try to direct the flow of bodies against the flow of bumper-to-bumper buses. And that's when it happens.

From my stomach comes a wave of pressure that travels up my oesophagus and gets tightly lodged in my throat. My face grows prickly hot, pins and needles and splashy raindrops combined. I feel as if I am about to cry, and I want to cry, to open my mouth and roar. I'm uncomfortable in my skin and my clothes, and I need to flee, no, to run – run away. I make my way across the road and leave the crowds behind. I find myself in the comparative tranquillity of Grosvenor Square, where the gates to the little park are open and I sit on a bench and stare into the vague middle distance. Pigeons peck around me, a tramp sits alongside and asks if I have a light. I breathe in through my nose and out through my mouth, and I am numb, empty and numb. I think about Elena and Amaya. Nothing comes, and then abruptly it does: a definable sadness and a growing conviction that I cannot, and will not, cope, that I have made the single biggest mistake of my life. I am not going to be able to do this, somewhere it is written, maybe deep within my DNA, and so it is not my fault and yet all my fault entirely. Perhaps I should clear out, for everyone's sake, a clean break?

For the next three hours, I walk through the back streets of the West End visiting no shops and not stopping for lunch or coffee or pause. Life streams past me, all of it a blur, people actively going somewhere with someone, business as usual, same old same old, gales of laughter, another pint, cheer-up, mate, it might never happen. Already has. The lump in my throat never fades. My phone goes – Elena – and I ignore it. I don't respond to her later texts. I find myself at the train station, and I weigh up my options, more for the sake of fantasy than anything else. Ultimately, I have always been painstaking and responsible, a characteristic bred into me from a young age.

I am defined today, to myself at least, by my responsibility, and so it is not about to desert me, not even at a time like this.

None of the destinations flagged up on the departures board sound particularly alluring anyway, an enticing horizon for me to escape to. Certainly not Maidenhead or Feltham, not even Strawberry Hill.

I look at the board for ten, maybe fifteen minutes. There is nowhere for me to go, and so I buy my ticket and head home. It takes just 28 minutes, a detail I used to focus on as confirmation of its merciful proximity to the centre of town. Now I wish it were further, that I could sit on this train indefinitely. There are no delays tonight, and the journey flies by. I get out at my station and I walk home, I go into the hot bright kitchen and nod hello and then I take my coat off and climb upstairs to my room and, without turning on the light, I sit on the floor.

And five minutes later, still in darkness, this is where Elena finds me and where, too, she begins the process of rescuing me.

I have said nothing to no one for many hours now, and at first, when I open my mouth, no voice comes out. I try again. She asks where I was and I tell her. She looks worried now, her face drawn, and a powerful love races out of me towards her, unseen. I want to tell her how sorry I am, but also to tell her the truth: how miserable I feel, how shocked and stunned I am by it all. It's too much, I want to say. I'm not equal to the task, and I won't be able to do it: this now an absolute conviction, I've never been quite so sure of anything. Before, everything had seemed so uncomplicated, linear and predictable, easy. We had fun and we had arguments and we had everything in between, but we knew how to do it. This, however, is a learning curve too sharp and steep. What I wanted in Oxford Street reaches me with a force now and, for possibly the third or fourth time in my adult life (but, worryingly, twice in a week), I cry helplessly, the shock of my tears prompting even more tears, which soak through onto Elena's shoulder as she gathers me up and allows herself to cry too.

If I have had a hard time these past few days, then I can only imagine what she has gone through herself: the trauma of childbirth, and juggling the needs and wheedling complaints of a baby, a boy-friend and a mother, all in the unfamiliar surroundings of a poorly decorated house that still sorely lacks a fridge. We hug each other so very tightly, and say all the things we have to say in the hope that we will get through all of this, and do so together. Somehow, at least for the time being, it seems to work. I feel marginally better. As we prepare to go downstairs to the kitchen and put on a public face for the Spanish houseguest, she pleads patience and understanding. I promise to try, the very least I can do.

The markings on the wall behind my side of the bed tell me that the mother-in-law will be gone in 22 days. We travelled the length of Vietnam once in less time, and so this feels like a gloating eternity, but thereafter comes freedom. I know that she is hardly the real problem here, but she is nevertheless a convenient one for me right now. The moment she leaves, I convince myself, will be the moment I can try to become a proper father to my daughter, with full, unimpeded access as and when I desire it, and also the moment I can begin to make up for lost time, and to perhaps finally find a sort of footing in all this.

• • •

It is, I am quick to learn, a long-held tradition that when someone has a baby, particularly for the first time, friends from far and wide pay a visit, a variation of the three wise men story but in a kind of excitable conga line, and each bearing updated equivalents of gold, frankincense and myrrh. Elena reminds me that we have done it ourselves with friends of hers, and so now we are to be on the receiving end. For almost three weeks, we have a steady succession of visitors every evening, making us feel much more popular than we really are. All of them bring presents: none, sadly, for me. They come with their cuddly toys and colour-coordinated baby clothes and they congregate around the new arrival who looks uncomprehendingly up at them, the women keen to hold her, the men reluctantly accepting when she is suddenly thrust forward, though they keep her at arm's length as if she were a bomb that needed to be thrown through the nearest window at a moment's notice. Elena is operating solely for the baby now, and so when the baby needs feeding, she feeds her, whether we are in company or not. This causes some alarm amongst my male friends, suddenly seeing Elena's breast bared for the first time. It is a DD at the moment, and so is the other one, so there is a lot of breast to appraise. Most are thoroughly British about it, suddenly finding an interest in the far wall, the switched-off television set in the corner of the room, the hair on the backs of their hands. One friend, however, seems unduly fascinated, so much so that he gets his camera out and takes a picture of it.

One night, Julie and Mark come to visit, and Julie, one of my oldest friends, holds Amaya while we talk in the living room. But after fifteen minutes or so, the mother-in-law comes in, does her by now customary swoop and leaves. Suddenly, Julie's cradled arms are cradling nothing but air, so decisive is the mother-in-law's impatience to be returned to her own flesh and blood. I later castigate Elena, as if she were somehow responsible, but any residual anger soon peters out into laughter, a laughter of the increasingly maddened kind.

A certain routine begins to assert itself, though one that still has little obvious need for my presence. Gradually, the baby is beginning to settle more at night-time, she is less crotchety and makes fewer midnight farmyard noises in her slow transition from sticky foetus to nearly discernible human being. She is still overwhelmingly delicate, and whenever I do hold her, I am repeatedly reminded to protect her head, which is soft and squelchy, its weight too much for her neck – virtually elastic for the first few weeks – to keep upright. A succession of health visitors come to our door, three in as many weeks, each of whom contradicts the advice given by her immediate predecessor, one cold and critical, the next sympathetic and understanding, the last a confusing combination of the two. All accept the offer of coffee and spend much of their time ticking boxes on pieces of paper attached to a clipboard, a frown across their foreheads, something like suspicion in their eyes. But we appear to answer their questions correctly and competently, because we are allowed to keep Amaya. Even I recognise this to be a good thing.

After a long and drawn-out week indoors, Elena has decreed that it is safe enough to take our daughter for a walk in the outside world for the very first time. It is early January now. Amaya is nine days old.

It is a cold day, but dry and bright, and I'm immediately taken by the novelty of a family expedition, our very first. I slip on my coat and my trainers and hold the door open, ready to leave. Twenty minutes later, now impatient, I am still stood in the same position. Elena, increasingly impatient herself, instructs me to close the bloody door and come upstairs where I might be of some discernible help. When I get there, I witness more activity than I had anticipated. In order to get a nine-day-old baby ready to brave temperatures of five degrees centigrade, it seems that she first has to be wrapped in a succession of layers one would more expect of Inuits. By the time she is ready to be transferred downstairs, where another rigmarole awaits her, she resembles a pass-the-parcel package, a heavily bundled thing rendered twice her usual size and width. Only her pinched pink nose is visible beneath all the wool, cotton and polyester that bind her tight. Her hands are lost inside the sleeves of her too-long coat, her feet snug inside two pairs of socks. The coat itself is a series of Michelin tyres stitched together in bright red fabric, and it is zipped up to and beyond her chin. By the time she is brought into the kitchen to be attached, clipped and bolted into the pushchair, she is fast asleep.

"Ready?" I ask wearily.

A stupid question, for now the pushchair has to be prepared, a methodical business in itself. Into the changing bag that will attach to the buggy's frame, Elena inserts some muslin squares, three nappies, a pack of nappy sacks, baby wipes, anti-rash cream, a bottle of milk previously expressed from her breast with a contraption that I had thought would make the act rather alluring, albeit in a David

Cronenberg kind of way, but I was wrong, very wrong, and a full change of clothes should she implode in a shower of shit or sick en route to wherever it is we happen to be heading. I'd thought we were simply going for a gentle stroll, but all this preparation suggests we could be away till March. The mother-in-law, meanwhile, is assiduously folding the pushchair's waterproof cover in half and half again, then placing it in the underneath tray, where it sits ready for action.

"But there isn't a cloud in the sky," I tell Elena.

"Better to be safe," she says, suddenly transformed into the kind of woman with a maternal homily for every occasion.

Now, and only now, it is her mother's turn to get ready, which takes another age. I could have gone to the cinema and back by now. I could have enjoyed lunch in Paris.

When the pushchair finally touches down on to fresh pavement for the very first time, I feel heady with relief. Because she knows I want to, and because it is man's inalienable right to always control a machine no matter how basic, Elena says that I should push it. I'm excited at the prospect, and immediately experience a flashback to the aisles of Safeway through which I negotiated a trolley, aged twelve, with all the expertise of a Formula One driver.

But then a curious thing begins to happen in the battle of unspoken wills between the mother-in-law and me. It appears she wants to push it, too. We have all but stopped attempting any communication by this stage in her month's stay. Eye contact occurs only by accident. If I enter a room she is already in, she quickly departs. We address each other only in the third person, Elena a Kofi Annan working to build diplomatic bridges. Right now, we are walking three abreast on a narrow patch of pavement up towards the traffic lights. The sun, as it falls on our faces, is pleasantly warm, and I feel a quiet contentment as we make our deliberately slow process. At the lights, the mother-in-law begins surreptitiously to reposition herself, no longer on the outside of things but now in the middle. She continues to appear lost in conversation with her daughter, but her left hand strays with tacit determination towards the pushchair's handle, ignoring the fact that *my* hand is already there. The moment she makes contact, our hips clash, the bump forcing me to relinquish my grasp. She then uses an encroaching dustbin to her full advantage by effectively steering me into it with the heft of her, and I am forced to let go altogether – her clear aim all along – so that it is now under her sole control. At first, I want to laugh because this is funny, it's fucking hysterical, but I'm also furious, and vow instantly to wreak my revenge.

A week later, we take the baby on her first trip by train on a habit-ually dispiriting visit to IKEA, and the mother-in-law soon employs the same tactics with the pushchair. It happens when I am bringing it out of the train station lift. Our hips clash once again and her hand reaches out, but this time I stand firm, so firm that she bounces back off me and trips over the wheel, stumbling before managing to regain her posture, if not quite her composure. She quickly relents, strides ahead and links arms with her daughter as if nothing had happened. I too pretend not to notice, but inside I am screaming with the pure adrenalin surge of ecstatic victory.

●●●

Eventually, the long month duly passes, and the day for the woman to return home finally arrives like a benevolent gift from above. It is the morning of our final day together and I sit bolt up in bed, as instantly aware of the auspicious nature of the occasion as if it were a new smell in the room. Today will bring with it change. I am excited. I sing in the shower. I pick up the cat, hold her aloft and kiss her purring head. Downstairs, breakfast is business as usual. It would be rude to gloat, and so I don't. I keep my head down, heat the milk and spoon in my coffee, keeping my distance and allowing her full access to her granddaughter for the few precious hours that remain. For the rest of the morning, I hide upstairs with the Sunday papers, and when I come down again for lunch, I am polite and courteous. Elena looks at me with suspicion, her eyes narrowed into slits.

And now, the meal over, come preparations for her departure. Amaya has been readied and wrapped and harnessed; Elena dons her coat, her mother likewise. I see them to the door. I won't be accompanying them to the airport for my own selfish reasons, but then no one asked me to. We lightly kiss one another's cheeks in the European manner and I thank her for everything in Spanish, Elena having rehearsed the words with me previously. Suddenly, she looks me squarely in the eye, her light brown irises huge behind near-sighted lenses. At first, I think she is about to hit me, but instead there are tears there and she says to me (Elena translating) that she will be on hand to help us any time we need her and for as long as we need, that my daughter is wonderful, a delight, perfection, and that she will see us again soon, very soon. I didn't expect this, this sudden poignancy, this level of naked emotion. It makes me embarrassed and cowed, and slightly ashamed. As they walk up the garden path and disappear around the corner, I am filled with fleeting regret for my attitude towards this ultimately good and kindly woman, and I resolve here and now if not quite to fully embrace her future visits, then certainly never to pour scorn on them, to make more of an effort, and not just for Elena's sake. I realise that she will be a wonderful grandmother to my daughter, and I am grateful for that, I really am. In the visits that follow, she will prove this time and again, and though we will never come to be friends, never even manage a conversation that doesn't rely upon an interpreter, we will respect one another's roles in our awkward, stilted fashion. It could be worse, I say to myself repeatedly, it could be so much worse. I should count my blessings.

But right now, as I close the door to an empty and silent house, I feel only an onslaught of relief. I've cleared the finishing line; I've won. I can now collapse, relax, unwind, be me. I bunch my fingers up into fists, jump three feet into the air and cheer.

Time passes. In the kitchen I sit, and I wait. Soon I grow impatient. I want my girlfriend and my daughter to return home. I want things at last to *begin*.

Matt O'Connor, the weekend father

In 2003, Matt O'Connor, a creative design consultant from Kent, founded an organisation called Fathers 4 Justice to help gain greater contact rights for fathers separated from their children. He had recently gone through a messy divorce himself, his newly ex-wife suggesting, at one point, he be allowed no more than four hours' access to his two young sons every month. He wanted more, and so, first through the family law courts, but increasingly through the media, he fought for more, highlighting his case and those of other, in his words, "wronged" fathers, his voice so loud and so hectoring that he was soon difficult to ignore.

F4J became a ubiquitous presence nationwide, its increasingly outlandish antics splashed in bold print across newspaper front pages as they pulled off a succession of highly public, and highly disruptive stunts. Each featured a father dressed up as a modern day superhero, the reasoning being, O'Connor explained, "all fathers are superheroes to their children" (a suggestion that later prompted in many the pantomime retort of "Oh no they're not".)

Batman scaled the balcony at Buckingham Palace and set off a national security alert. Spiderman brought traffic to a standstill high above Tower Bridge. They powder-bombed the Prime Minister in the House of Commons, invaded the pulpit at York Minster and gatecrashed BBC1's National Lottery Draw live on air in front of ten million viewers.

"We became very good," he deadpans, "at grabbing the nation by the scruff of its neck and demanding attention. And guess what?" He puffs his chest out, bristling with pride. "We got it."

There are, and long have been, various pressure groups working for the rights of divorced fathers and pressing for a change in family law that many feel is unfairly biased towards the mother, but it was O'Connor's outfit that brought their plight suddenly and forcefully into the headlines. While he has yet to effect any change in the law that, in his eyes, denies fathers their fundamental rights when a marriage goes sour, he has nevertheless succeeded in creating serious debate on the subject, MPs even going on record to say they approve of the man's message, if not quite the manner in which he delivers it. In 2005, *GQ* magazine named him the seventh Top Communicator in the UK, and the 92nd Most Powerful Man in Britain.

"The Labour government," he says, "has done more in the past decade to remove the need for fathers in the modern family than any other government in history. We are viewed as little more than cash machines. You can, for example, walk out on your family tomorrow morning and nobody would give a damn so long as you continue to provide financial support for your children. No one seems to care whether you continue to provide emotional support; as long as you keep up your payments, that's all that matters. And if you want to continue seeing your children after the separation? That's where the fun begins."

Much of his campaigning attempted to challenge the view that fathers today are too easily demonised by the law, the media and, he insists, by mothers themselves. Upon the breakdown of a marriage, even if fairly amicable, the father is promptly cast out by the family law courts, now forever frowned upon and judged with suspicion, whether suspicion is warranted or not.

"There seems to be this idea in society that if you are a father and you stand up for fathers' rights, then you have to be whiter than white before you are even given a chance of a fair hearing," he says. "But if you happen to come with normal baggage in life [and O'Connor did], then you are in for some serious trouble. Fathers are being systematically undermined here. It's nothing less than gender apartheid."

As the F4J brand grew, so O'Connor's private life fell increasingly under the media spotlight. Revelations emerged, amongst them the suggestion that while married, he was anything *but* a model husband. He drank, he womanised, he was rarely home. Ironic, then, that he was now so desperate to see the very children he had had such little time for before.

In many ways, O'Connor got off comparatively lightly. A little character assassination, he says grinning cheekily, "never hurt anyone". Meanwhile, it came to light that several other key F4J members had even more to hide. Some had restraining orders issued against them, others convictions for domestic violence – factors that did much to remove any sympathy the cause might have otherwise engendered. Next came dissension within the ranks, some members convinced that O'Connor wasn't going far enough in the pursuit of justice. Splinter groups began to spring up. And then, in 2006, the entire organisation imploded when a story was leaked to the media that F4J's latest plan was to kidnap Leo Blair, the five-year-old son of the then Prime Minister.

O'Connor denied all knowledge of this at the time, and claims now that it was "all bullshit cooked up by the Labour Party". Whatever the truth, it proved the death knell (albeit temporarily) of F4J, which promptly ceased its public operations.

But by now O'Connor was already moving forward. In 2007, his autobiography was published, and the film rights quickly snapped up. F4J had given him a platform from which he could now operate in other, perhaps more effective ways, his confidence undiminished, his ambition undimmed.

"But while I still have a breath left in my body, Fathers 4 Justice will continue to carry the torch for fathers. I will never, *never*, let the matter lie," he says, bringing a Churchillian fist down on the table between us, making his coffee cup rattle in its saucer.

If many men can be described as reluctant, perhaps even fearful, at the idea of giving up their previous life in favour of fatherhood, then Matt O'Connor represents another extreme altogether. He was the kind of alpha male who barely gave it a moment's hesitation, the reality of his wife's pregnancy merely a blip in an already heady existence, and one to sidestep with a cavalier shrug of the shoulders. The arrival of his first son into his life gave him little pause for thought: "I'm not the most self-analytical person," he admits. "I'm always looking forward. Can't help it; I'm cut from a certain cloth; I'm a force of nature."

And so he simply carried on much as before, under the illusion that his wife would prove an uncomplaining homemaker while he remained the traditional breadwinner, with unimpeded access to a very full social life. His story may not be a particularly pretty one, much less, at times, a sympathetic one, but he is nevertheless representative of a great many men.

I meet him on a cold February morning in a library café in Winchester, near the house he shares with his new partner Nadine. He is a big, voluminous man with an expensive hairstyle, heavily framed designer glasses and a watch the size of a dessert plate. Like certain rock stars, he somehow manages to be almost winningly obnoxious, a proudly unreconstructed bloke who thrills in delivering sexist asides that leave you wondering whether he is being ironic or simply a fan of 1970s comedy. He has a supernatural confidence, and much like the man he befriended during his early campaigning days, Bob Geldof (another divorced father who took on the family law courts and won), he seems preternaturally disposed to starting an argument with anyone, with *everyone*, as if conflict were his default setting.

But behind the over-the-top gregariousness and the evident pride at having become so infamous, O'Connor is in fact just another divorced dad desperate to do right by his kids.

"If I'd met and married Sophie now, in my early forties rather than back in my twenties," he says, "I think we'd have stood a much better chance of lasting. But you live and learn, don't you?"

Fourteen years ago, he was a high-flying creative consultant over-seeing bar and restaurant designs, putting in long hours at the office, then entertaining clients long into every night. He had a string of girlfriends, all of them casual and from whom he craved nothing permanent. But then he met a Spanish woman called Sophie, the same woman he would one day refer to as "Franco in a skirt; a one-woman Spanish Inquisition". A whirlwind romance ensued, O'Connor wooing her with his customary garish flamboyance. It worked. They were quickly married, and she fell pregnant shortly after.

"My reaction?" he says now. "Delighted, completely delighted. Did it change my lifestyle? No, I have to say that it did not. My job came with certain demands that I wasn't about to walk away from. I lived a hedonistic lifestyle: birds, booze, hotel rooms..."

Even during his wife's pregnancy?

"Absolutely. Funnily enough, many of my friends from that time are still at it today, a full decade later. Well, actually, not all of them. My former business partner is dead. That tells you all you need to know, I suppose."

Inevitably, his marriage began to show signs of strain, Sophie pleading for him to be home more, his invariably flippant responses prompting even more conflict. Despite the growing animosity, they attempted to brave it out. A year after their son Daniel was born, Sophie then gave birth to another, Alex.

"I've worked out only recently the exact mechanics of where our relationship went wrong," he says, and I suggest that a fool could work *that* one out. But O'Connor, a touch defensively, is quick to claim that he wasn't always quite as self-obsessed as he sometimes appears, and that perhaps there were other factors at work too, one of which might just have been Sophie's post-natal depression.

"At the end of the day, it boiled down to this: we had a great relationship before the kids came along, but having two in quick succession put a big strain on the whole thing. Too big."

She asked for a divorce. He refused, asking for one more chance. But then he systematically failed to mend his ways, and so when she now demanded they separate, he decided, he says now, "to go out and embrace the female of the species with open arms. I had a harem going at one point, and that's when things began to get ugly, and I started to worry about just how damaging this could be to the boys. I didn't want that. I really didn't".

The day he left, he says, was the worst of his life. The divorce proceedings would soon become pronouncedly bitter, his ex-wife refusing him access to his sons, now furiously – and quite under-standably – angry at him, his conduct, his failings. His business partner died in mysterious circumstances; his company went bust, his savings all spent on legal fees. He was angry much of the time. One night, he ended up on Waterloo Bridge, drunkenly staring into the murky abyss below. But that nearly suicidal night was the moment he decided to stand up and fight back, in the most public manner pos-sible. Suddenly, he was re-energised.

But behind F4J, the necessary scaffolding that was essentially keeping him up, a more personal realisation was beginning to dawn. He was about to become a weekend dad.

The weekend dad is not a rare species. He is there on every high street in every neighbourhood, the forlorn figure in McDonald's hoping that a Happy Meal lives up to its billing, while his children view him with newly wary eyes; he is the forcefully jolly character in the playground trying to elicit as many precious laughs from his kids before his allotted time is up.

O'Connor readily admits that he made for a hopeless husband, and that his wife had every right to turf him out. But he insists that he was never a bad father, merely an all-too-absent one. It was the breakdown of his marriage that effectively shocked him into taking belated responsibility for his sons, and throughout the lengthy sepa-ration process, all he really craved was sufficient access to them in order to right his wrongs.

But this was not to prove easy. Relations with Sophie were becom-ing, he says, "increasingly nuclear", and he reacted to the endless bureaucracy of family law by ranting and raving, often right there in court. He once even punched a barrister: "I was lucky I never got banged up for that one."

For a while, he was permitted to see his boys only within contact centres, venues normally used as a pick-up and drop-off point for children when relationships between an estranged husband and wife have degenerated irrevocably. "My lowest point," he says now. "Horrible places, completely and utterly degrading."

The situation did gradually improve, but only marginally. He was granted full Saturday access, one day in a week to somehow try to make up for those other six when he was elsewhere.

"You can't do it, it's impossible – and it's also an insane state of affairs," he says. "Think about it. My wife was free to set up home with any new bloke that took her fancy, and no one would impose any court-ordered check on *his* past. For all we know, he could be a murderer, a rapist, whatever, but he would automatically have more access to my children than I would myself. Now tell me, how can that be fair?"

He felt himself in a "hamster wheel" of misery, bled dry by all the emotional turmoil and feeling increasingly financially stretched, the legal proceedings as expensive as they were convoluted. After three years of court battles, he was ready to walk away.

"I'd just got so fucking traumatised by the whole thing that I thought the best thing to do under the circumstances was not to see my children again until they got older."

He explained this to a judge one day in his customary manner, his face purple, while his ex-wife, also present in court, watched on in silent horror. It proved a turning point for her, and over lunch they somehow managed to thrash out an agreement for access that had previously always eluded them.

"And so today," he beams, "I have as much contact as I want. I get to see them every weekend and on days during the week, and you know what? They are amazing boys. Somehow, these wonder-ful, bright, intelligent, vivacious children of mine have gone through this entire process, so far as I can work out, with barely a scratch. It's a miracle, and I'm grateful for it."

Four years on, and another unlikely development in his bitter battle with his ex-wife has emerged.

"We get on famously these days," he says. "Well, mostly we do. There are still occasional spikes of resentment that pop up every now and then, but mostly we get on just fine; we're friends. I can't stress just how important that is for everyone in this situation. You've got to remember the F word: forgiveness. You simply cannot afford to hate your ex more than you love your children, and so we all have to learn how to forgive. That's what I've done and, to her eternal credit, that's what Sophie has done as well."

At the age of 41, he is a new father all over again. He and his partner Nadine have a young son, two-year-old Alfie.

"I'll admit the pregnancy was never planned," he laughs. "In fact, it was anything but, just the result of a very rock 'n' roll weekend down in Brighton. She phoned me up a month later and told me and asked me what we should do. The blood drained from my face, much as you'd expect, but I told her she should just let it be. I said to her, I'm happy, you're happy, neither of us believe in abortion, so fuck it, let's go for it, and we did."

You'd think, I say, he'd be wary of entering fatherhood again given his past experiences, but O'Connor, cut, as he likes to say, from a certain cloth, was instead his customarily bullish self about it. But he was newly confident as well, and with good reason.

"I won't make the same mistakes again because I've drawn a line under that chapter in my life. I don't go out much any more, I hardly drink. I just want to be at home with my kids these days. That's what age and maturity do for you, I guess."

But while many of his old proclivities have been successfully reined in, one of them has remained in rude health: his ego. F4J may have made him a footnote in history, but he is keen to keep himself visible. The majority of his attentions these days are focused on the setting-up of a brand-new political party, which he, naturally, will lead, a libertarian one that will extol the need for greater civil liberties, greater democracy, greater privacy and strong family communities. O'Connor is convinced he will make for an unimpeachable political figure because, unlike so many other politicians, there are no skeletons hiding in his closet. Everything is already out in the open.

"And so I've nothing left to hide," he boasts, laughing. "I'm an open book. You know, I've learned a lot from everything I've gone through in my life, but it's my children I've learned from the most. And it's because of them that, ultimately, no matter what else I turn my hand to, I will never allow F4J to just disappear. Not when there is still so much important work to be done. Look at the statistics. We have a generation of children out there right now growing up without fathers. One in three carries a blade, and because so many girls grow up without fathers, their first relationship with men is invariably a sexual one. As a result, we have the highest rate of teenage pregnancy in Europe, along with an abortion epidemic…

"People will look back on this time and say of maniacal pioneers like me that we were ahead of our time, and it's true, we are. This is one fucked-up society we are living in, but we simply cannot afford to lose sight of fathers' rights or the importance of fathers in the lives of their children, not just for this generation but future ones as well. I've got three boys who may well go on to become fathers themselves. Do I want them to go through what I did? No, I fucking don't. I have a duty to help them and everyone else. We all do."

Eight

So how does a man bond with his child if biologically things haven't quite clicked instantly into place? This is in fact fairly common amongst men, and it is the cause of various levels of distress, from detachment to outright depression. Male postnatal depression can affect as many as one in fourteen of us. But this is a rarely reported statistic, much less one expounded upon within the medical profession.

"Father depression is indeed an underresearched area," Professor Lorraine Sherr, Head of Health and Psychology at London's Royal Free Hospital, tells me when I talk to her on the subject. "There have been a few studies but it remains rather neglected. Why? Well, we've asked ourselves the same question many times. It isn't that fathers don't want to engage in the subject, just that people haven't really bothered targeting them. There is a wealth of literature on mothers, but precious little on fathers."

Adrienne Burgess, from Fathers' Direct, offers one possible reason.

"It's because man, traditionally, is seen as the sturdy oak, someone who must not express how he really feels because, let's face it, his partner has enough to contend with as it is. So of course we don't focus on it. Why would we? To this day, motherhood still very much defines fatherhood, casts it in its shadow. It is, of course," she adds, "a lot of sexist crap. Men shouldn't be sidelined in this at all; they should be listened to, acknowledged."

Professor Sherr suggests that there are well-established links between maternal depression and behavioural problems in children, that the more depressed a mother is, the more likely the child is later on to display cognitive and developmental problems as a result. No one has bothered to gauge similar effects in the paternal equivalent. We are, then, an enigma, something to be brushed under the carpet in the hope it will go away or else, eventually, quietly, solve itself. In a men's magazine, I find the number of a helpline for those struggling with fatherhood. I call it, and get an answer machine message. I call it again several times over several weeks, but the message never changes: "Hello," a male voice says. "The centre is currently closed until I come back from holiday in August. Please leave a message and I'll get back to you." The fact that I am calling in January suggests that the helpline is, in fact, permanently unmanned, has perhaps run out of funding, or else offers very attractive holiday packages to its employees. I leave my name and number, but no one calls back. One day, I bring up the subject of male post-natal depression with a female friend. Her reaction is starkly unsympathetic.

"Excuse me, *male* post-natal depression?" she says. "What on earth do men have to be depressed about? It's the woman who goes through all the pain, all the changes, the removal from the workplace, and will likely never have a decent night's sleep again. So what, precisely, does the man have to get depressed about?"

It's an ignorant response, but an emasculating one. No wonder we rarely speak up about it.

During one of our now customary dark nights of the soul, looking down into the Moses basket at the foot of our bed with a mixture of fear and trepidation, Elena admits to me something I consider crucial to my own development in my new role: that she, too, has yet to experience the instant overflow of love that the parenting books so often suggest is natural, even mandatory. In its place, she says, she feels an immense need to nurture and protect, and from this, she believes, the love will surely flow. The same will be true of me, she predicts, and who am I to argue?

I take further encouragement from the fact that I feel no tangible antipathy towards Amaya, nor, mercifully, any more resentment, even after a succession of broken nights. And the nights are now endlessly broken for both of us, for I no longer sleep quite as soundly as I first did. Instead, we take turns to see to her nightly ministrations, which are punishingly regular.

Though becoming incrementally familiar, she is still the house guest that won't leave, the mysterious stranger with the antisocial night-time habits, and she will continue to remain largely unknowable to me so long as she is quite so reliant upon her mother for everything, so uncommunicative with me, so *alien*. Her appearance begins to worry me. She is forever malfunctioning. A few weeks after her birth, what little hair she did have has come out in clumps, leaving patches of baldness on her pale skull. She starts to suffer from spots, teenage-style yellowheads clustering angrily around her cheeks and forehead a full twelve years before her father's own affliction. She is always coughing, sneezing, hiccupping. She regularly vomits. Exposed to the harsh elements of life for the very first time, she seems to be reacting adversely to it, shutting down and then bursting back into bloom again, an incessant contradictory cycle, each day bringing with it a new flare-up, another abatement. Every morning, she looks and sounds different from the one before, having taken one step forward and two steps back, entirely human and also not, like something out of science fiction. One morning, she wakes with a virulent rash, swathes of angry red splashed across her body and face. She looks radioactive, sounds nuclear, and I fear picking her up in case something falls off.

And even when her metabolism has reached some kind of equilibrium, she remains at one remove, aloof and utterly unreciprocal. Everything is one-way traffic: we *are* for her and we *do* for her, while she simply soaks it all up and then demands more. I find myself desperate for eye contact, a smile, the tiniest morsel of acknowledge-ment. One morning, we take her to the clinic for a routine check-up, where she is stripped and weighed and measured, her chart filled out, her progress book amended, and as we are dressing her afterwards, I look at the mother alongside us, whose own daughter must be around the six to ten month mark. Her baby is gurgling and smiling, looking directly up into the woman's face and plainly communicating. When her mother tells her to sit up, she does. She raises her arms to make it easier for the removal of her vest, and then lies back down on the mattress ready for the next instruction. Elena watches me watching.

"Be patient," she says. "It'll come."

At home, Elena suggests I spend as much time with my daughter as work will allow, because how is a proper bond to develop otherwise? For the first few weeks, I see this as vocal encouragement, but I soon come to realise what it really is: a threat.

"I could do," she says, "with some help here."

And so I help. The three of us are together for breakfast, lunch, a mid-afternoon wander around town, dinner and bedtime. I don't manage this every day, of course, but mostly I do. Also now, on two or three evenings a week, I get to have her all to myself, and it is this that rapidly becomes the most rewarding time of all.

Though we are ostensibly a joint partnership in all this, there is nevertheless a pronounced pecking order: mother first, father second. I cannot help but defer to Elena's greater knowledge, which is instinctual rather than learned, so far as I can work out. There is, in addition, the fact that her very proactivity around the baby effectively renders me indolent. Why should I bother lifting a finger when she is busy lifting all of hers at once? She is so efficient, so all-encompassing. She doesn't need me.

But for these two or three evenings a week, while she is at the gym trying to regain some of her former shape, the baby becomes my sole responsibility. Finally, I am motivated into affirmative, independent action. This is where I can do as I please, and learn from my mistakes alone. If I drop her, or clunk her head on the door frame, or check my e-mails while she is wailing in my lap, no one need know. There is no outside direction or interference, no criticism. This is great, it's terrific. It gives me breathing space, an opportunity to test myself. And if I then start to thrive while we are alone together, things happening to my emotional levels I feared never would occur, then this can also for now remain private, a secret between the two of us, while I slowly process the mounting feelings for myself and consider what they might mean.

By this stage, several months in, she is beginning to show signs of cautious interaction. When she is not crying, she is smiling and laughing for what feels like much of the time. This isn't just biased parental reading, either: other people comment on it, that she appears to be a happy baby. Photographs we have of her from this time are all gummy and beaming, her perpetual bark of laughter sending drool spooling down her chin like thrown fishing reel. She has started to look directly at me, too, and the more clownish I am in her company, as instinctual to my behaviour around her as responsibility is to her mother's, the more likely she is to double up with giggles. I'll do anything to get her giggling. They say that there is nothing quite as joyful as the sound of a baby's laughter. Before, that never quite made sense to me. It's only laughter, I thought. The world is full of it. But it makes sense to me now.

We start our evenings alone with dinner. Our daughter is on solid food now, though the watery baby rice we feed her is more slop than anything else. She is still confused by the rubber spoon, its shape so unlike a nipple, and she fights the new requirement to let her tongue sit flat in her mouth rather than curling into a suckling position to such an extent that much of the meal ends up like abstract art all down the front of her top. Once dinner is dispensed with, the nearby surfaces wiped down, I take her upstairs to her room where we lie side-by-side surrounded by toys, and I try to make her laugh. But she has other ideas. She craves movement now, trying desperately to crawl, figuratively to run before she can walk, and forever wants to stretch for things beyond her reach. Everything is beyond her reach. Much of any given day is spent trying to roll over, and the competitor inside me wills her to do this, and to do it now, before the other babies manage it. I want to see the look of accomplishment on her face after all that expended effort, and I want to boast about it. (She eventually manages this, rolling over, about a month later while I am away for work. Elena informs me of the historical moment by text message.)

Her eyes, too, never sit still in their sockets, but instead continually rove, hungry to assimilate as much information as possible while her hands grasp hungrily onto this toy, that tube of cream, the lace of my trainers. After half an hour of this, I'm exhausted and I undress her for her nightly bath, a routine exquisite in its awkwardness, her plastic tub within our chipped porcelain one, the water having been tested once, then twice for appropriate temperature (an initiative laid down by Elena simply because one time I made it too hot, Amaya quickly letting it be known just *how* hot with an accusatory scream), and I place her delicately inside it, supporting her head with an arm while she deliberately flops left and right, learning to splash and throwing her plastic duck to the floor, gleeful with amazement when it is somehow returned to her moments later.

Establishing what will soon become a familiar pattern to our evenings for years to come, my daughter then fights encroaching sleep with such adamance that she can remain awake almost in spite of herself for hours. Much trial and error has taught us that the best way to get her at least in the mood is to first put her in a sling, a contraption that fits on to the parent's chest, the baby suspended snug within its harness, limbs dangling freely. I'm fairly sure that this was designed largely with men in mind, for the thing looks good on the male torso, and wearing it in public brings something out in women that all men are inexorably drawn towards. It makes us look sensitive and caring. I've had women in the street sigh at me when wearing it in a manner that seems almost postcoital, a reaction which of course prompts me to wear it as often as the weather permits. I'm not alone in this, either. I now spot men everywhere doing likewise, each of us clearly unable to resist showing off to a female audience, as if boasting about a latest toy the way we once did, well, with our latest toys.

At home, without the pleasure of adoring eyes, it is simply a useful way to get the baby to sleep. The intimacy it conspires between us is a by-product, but a lovely one. I switch off all the lights and turn on at low volume some appropriate music, Leftfield's *Leftism*, perhaps, the postmodern nursery rhymes of the Lemon Jelly EPs, or King Creosote's whispering *KC Rules OK*. And then, each of my index fingers clamped tightly within her fists, I begin the business of pacing. She needs the pacing if she is to go off; it is paramount to the entire exercise. The moment I dare sit down to ease the strain pulling at my shoulders is the moment she stirs back into life, suddenly grumpy, and kicking me as if I were a horse and she a mini Frankie Dettori. But the pacing is good: it calms us both and helps unwind the world around us. An hour goes by, maybe more, and at last her head is lolling heavily on my chest, her breathing steady and deep, a line of saliva soaking my sweatshirt.

At this point, things can become somewhat complicated. To detach her first from my fingers and then the sling before inserting her into the sleeping bag within the cot *without* waking her is as convoluted a process as this sentence is unwieldy, requiring as it does the dextrous unclipping of various clips while supporting her head and spine, and lowering her as horizontally as possible. But I've done it many times now and mostly manage it with little error.

By the time Elena comes home, in tight lycra and with a bright pink lobster glow to her face, I can barely keep the satisfaction from my voice as I relay the news that I have fed, played with, bathed and successfully put our daughter to bed *all by myself*. The boast is, of course, almost exclusively for my own ears. I'm trying to convince myself that I *can* do this, after all. And what a relief that is.

My very favourite part of the evening comes once she is fully asleep in her cot. I love to gaze down upon her in the low blue glow of the nightlight, when she is still and steady and finally quiet. I look at her and think her indescribably beautiful.

This, I believe, may mean I'm slowly coming around to her. I hope she is to me.

• • •

Most days, Elena attends one or other social morning gathering, which she has seen advertised in the local church hall or the doctor's surgery. Invariably, the advert will read *mums-and-tots playgroup* or, sometimes, *parent-and-child*, but the word *father* is usually nowhere to be seen. This is hardly surprising, given that while maternity leave stretches on for months, requiring multiple activities to fill each yawning day, paternity leave, for those that qualify, barely lasts a couple of weeks. These playgroups are places for women only, or women *mostly*. Elena invites me along occasionally, but I always decline, not just because of work but because, frankly, it's not my place. I'm not alone in the conviction, either: she very rarely encounters other fathers there, and those that do show up are remarked upon in whispers. In many ways, it is our role *not* to attend. We are upholding tradition.

"A woman is absolutely essential to a baby's well-being," Adrienne Burgess says in sardonic explanation. "Fathers are purely peripheral. Yes, it's all very nice if they are involved from time to time, but as long as mummy is there, then that's fine. Look at open days at nurseries or schools; look at your local crèches. It's almost always mothers; men having been thoroughly sidelined. That's our culture, and a long upheld one, but our culture very much has to change, otherwise we'll never move forward, and fathers will never get the look-in they deserve and very often crave."

This sidelining isn't, however, necessarily in place within the home as well. About a fifth of all fathers would qualify in the *high involvement* category today (perhaps because they work from home, or else are househusbands, of whom there are a growing number). The rest of us qualify as only *partially involved*. The way society works is partly to blame for this, Burgess suggests, but only partly. It's down to a mindset that needs an overhaul.

"If you, the average man, come home from a hard day at work and the kids are screaming and you think, *That's it, I've had enough of it today as it is, I need to shut myself away and allow my wife to put them to bed* – as society has long allowed us to think – then you are giving out a powerful statement to your family. That has to change. The way we work has to change. When you, the average man, come home, you have to think differently. You have to think that your next meeting is with your children, and that the meeting after that is with your partner, both accordingly important and essential to your day. You shouldn't come home and expect to put your feet up, unless, of course, you are happy to be marginalised from the family set-up. Then you can put your feet up all you like."

It is vital, she continues, that fathers remain as highly involved as they possibly can. This has a benefit over and above the mother's efforts because the mother is already highly involved herself. When we share the responsibilities, we lift the burden from our partners, thus maintaining the status quo and also, in some cases, a grip on sanity. But a father's involvement also *improves* the relationship between a child and the mother because, by giving her a break, she does not get as stressed and exhausted as she otherwise would. Thirty-eight per cent of children who stay at home with their mothers alone, Burgess says, end up having an insecure attachment with them for this very reason: "If mothers are allowed to become overstretched, then what do you expect? The father who is able to assist in all the daily duties, not just today but continually, as a matter of course, can be of enormous benefit to the child's upbringing. We shouldn't underestimate that."

This is one of many reasons Fathers Direct was set up, to highlight the role we men should be playing within our families. Nevertheless, much of its current online traffic comes from women. Another website, called Raising Kids, which has over 200,000 hits a month, is also used almost exclusively by women, as much as 90 per cent. Look around for any fathers' groups, meanwhile, and you'll find precious few.

In Richmond, south-west London, I come across a local, council-sponsored support group aimed specifically at young fathers and run by Ahmed Saliu, an enthusiastic 22-year-old, single and fatherless himself but keen to help change society's perception, he says, "that young fathers haven't a care in the world. They have". He has been running his workshops for three years now, targeting fathers as young as seventeen, many of them jobless, still living at home and keen not to be. Sometimes he meets with them individually to discuss any issues their new responsibilities have raised. And sometimes he offers group therapy sessions where, in theory at least, these young men can come and talk over their problems together, a very unBritish thing to do.

"The groups are mostly tiny," he admits with a sage smile. "And even those that do turn up find it difficult to talk. Why young dads can't talk openly about their feelings in the way that young mums do – and the young mums' groups are always full – I'll never know. I tend to get around three to five guys at most, and mostly all they want to do is sit around talking about football, music; safe things. But that's okay, because being in a social environment is in itself a positive thing, and eventually some do come around and start to talk, to share. It's never easy though."

In Hampshire, I meet Volker Buck, an area manager for Parentline Plus, a national charity that works for, and with, families. Buck tells me what is by now a familiar tale, that 87 per cent of calls come from women and that the Saturday dads' clubs are often typified by low attendances, especially if the local football team are playing at home that afternoon.

"Listening is our main tool," he says. "Just to be able to acknowledge the feelings of how difficult parenthood can be, especially for first-timers, can often be a huge help in itself. We do this for new mothers each and every day – and we get *a lot* of calls – but it is difficult to fully engage men. It's like there is a stigma in admitting that we have a problem, a weakness, or that we are a failure if we need support." He shakes his head. "We don't question it when we need to have our cars MOT'd, do we? Why should this be any different?"

A potential remedy, Buck says, would be if men were included a lot more in every step of the process, not just personally but professionally.

"Wouldn't it be better," he says, "if more men worked within the childcare industry? Why aren't there any male midwives, male health visitors? When was the last time you saw a man working in a crèche? Would it even be permitted? Were we to see men in these areas then I think it would perhaps bring about a gradual change in the traditional male roles. And though parenthood is currently high on the government's agenda, it is ultimately down to men themselves to learn how to express their feelings, their needs. At the moment, they don't."

Perhaps nationality really does play a part here, an example of a reserved nation doing what it does best: buttoning up. I'd presumed, then, that fathers' groups were probably things that flourished only in America, a land where any life choice is merely an excuse for people to sit around in a semicircle and discuss their feelings. Not so, according to one American I manage to track down.

Danny Singley is a psychologist who specialises in men's issues, and lives in San Diego. A 33-year-old father of two young boys, he was struck by the lack of parental classes for fathers when he first arrived in California from the east coast and so decided to do something about it. He founded his own and called it Basic Training for New Dads.

"What initially got me interested in the idea was entirely self-absorbed," he tells me in a bright, ebullient voice. "I'd had a somewhat frustrating experience at the hospital for the birth of both my sons, and so when we relocated to southern California, I thought to myself, Hey, where better to start up a father-oriented parenting class than in a state where everyone is supposed to be all super parent-centric?"

In Singley's experience, men are likely to have a wider but ultimately more shallow network of contacts, while women tend to have fewer but deeper and more emotionally based ones. This means that women are much more likely to get together and actually talk about the things that matter, specifically, in this case, he says, "about what is going on with you as a parent. I wanted men to achieve similar. In my classes, the idea was that new fathers could come together with our babies so that we could have the opportunity to interact as fathers while the moms were nowhere in sight. I wanted to encourage an atmosphere of, 'Well, if you can do it, I can too'. What I wanted most was to change the attitude that when a father looks after the baby in place of mom, it is not babysitting, but rather fathering".

At the time I speak to him, Singley has been running his classes for a year. He has been advertising locally, diligently and earnestly, but with little real success. His average class numbers no more than five, though sometimes, he admits, it can go down to just one.

"And so I've started marketing the course more towards moms. I say to them, 'Moms, want the morning off? Want your husband to learn a little bit more about what he has to offer? Then send him to me!'"

Basic Training for New Dads is a two-part class, his aim to teach and enlighten. But he is careful to keep it casual lest he scare anyone off. Sport is often discussed as a friendly icebreaker.

"I outline some potential topics at first, things like discipline, relationship changes, baby blues, post-partum issues, the changing of diapers and feeding, things like that," he says. "We as fathers have a unique parenting style which is complementary to what, stereotypically, mothers have to offer, but then we, of course, are stereotyped ourselves. Look at the media, the way fathers are portrayed. We enjoy a one-up position in society anyway, so it's okay to take potshots at us because, ha ha, dad is a buffoon, he doesn't understand this or that. But I try to explain how this can actually give us a negative mental image, one that we really should be fighting against."

The feedback he has received from those that *have* attended has been roundly positive, men having taken more from it than they thought they would. Only very few fail to turn up for the second class, which is more in-depth.

"In the second class we discuss social, cognitive and motor development, ways to understand what is going on with our babies, and ways to remove the mystery around them, how we can interact with them, become effective fathers and establish a bond. I also take them through more practical activities, like infant massage, which is about as California as you can get. The dads go bananas for it; they love it. It's something men can actively *do*; it's physical, and it's useful too, helping the baby's digestion and sleeping."

In today's global society, he says, fathers are caught between a generational squeeze. For the baby boom generation, a standard was set in stone: father went off to work to earn the money while mother stayed at home in charge of the family. He would play golf at the weekend and, at best, enjoy just two to three hours a week playing with the kids. Largely, he remained emotionally unavailable, the mother being the only one to express any real emotion other than anger.

"However, these days there is a much higher expectation of fathers to be more participative and intimately involved, but this causes a Perfect Storm effect. I'll explain. Okay, so you are a new dad; it is a transitional point in life, and brings with it some stress, in fact a lot of stress. And sometimes, as a result of all that stress, you will inevitably switch to autopilot and revert to some of the things your own father did. These may well have been appropriate and judged to be successful at the time, but they could well get us into hot water if implemented today."

All of which suggests there is much new fathers need to learn, and quick. He laments the lack of similar groups as his, not just in California, but right across America, the UK and beyond. He hopes that more people will realise this soon and act accordingly.

"It's a big thing, becoming a father, every bit as big as becoming a mother," he says. "A recent survey reported that 67 per cent of couples three years after having a baby are unhappy, and that's something we all have to tackle. Mothers go to groups, they read the books, they do the best they can. I'm sure men want to be just as effective. If they don't go to groups themselves, and let's face it, they probably don't, then I'd encourage as much personal introspection as possible and to have full and frank conversations with your partner about all your expectations, your hopes and fears. Don't bottle it up. Talk about it. That's all my little class offers. It's not a panacea or magic potion, just a way to help dads feel more confident, to get out of fatherhood as much as they put in, and to stay engaged."

Nine

I endeavour to take Danny Singley's advice to heart, almost literally. I stay engaged. By March, I actually go one step further. I get *married*.

When Amaya is three months old, we decide it's time to take her to visit her relatives, my grandparents in Italy, her extended family in Spain. This proves more complicated than we'd anticipated. The baby, we learn, will need a passport, but because her mother is Spanish, she, Amaya, doesn't automatically qualify for British citizenship. We discover that we are free to apply for it, but that forms need to be filled and that, due to a current backlog, the application may take several months to process. I explain to somebody officious in the British embassy that my grandparents are well into their dotage and may not have months left. Is there any way to fast track? Yes, I'm told. Get married. That way citizenship becomes instantaneous, the passport a mere formality.

I very much want my grandparents, effectively all the family I have left, to see their great-granddaughter before they die, and so I do the thing I never quite managed the morning of the five-month scan. I propose. I do it awkwardly, inelegant and stuttering over bacon and eggs on a Sunday night, an hour before *The Sopranos* is on. She says yes, surprising me with tears in her eyes and the loveliest of smiles. We push dinner to one side. We hug. I end up taping *The Sopranos*, to watch it later.

Given that we are entering into this more for bureaucratic reasons than romantic ones (though we will dress up on the day, exchange rings and swap warm sentiments), we elect to get married in a frowsy London registry office, albeit one famous for marrying rock stars (the kind who invariably later divorce). We ask just two of our closest friends, Ria and Gil, to be witnesses. The registrar's assistant, a woman of advanced years who smells of lavender, makes small talk before the ceremony and asks how long we've known one another. We tell her, and explain that we've recently had a baby.

"Oh, but that's wonderful," she says, clasping ringed fingers to her bosom. "And is baby back home with grandma right now?"

Grinning, I tell her that, no, actually we've left the baby outside on the pavement. I had hoped that she would laugh at this, because while it is factually true, I did mean it in a light-hearted way. Our daughter *is* outside, but not alone. She is under the supervision of two other friends, Richard and Julie, at least one of whom I would trust with my life. But the registrar's assistant looks horrified. I hurriedly explain myself in the hope that she realises I am not as cruel as my words suggest, merely an idiot.

The next day, we throw a big party. The majority of the guests gather in our oversized kitchen, some spilling into the garden whenever the rain stops. I get very drunk very quickly. Elena has also invited some of the mothers she knows from the local playgroups, and they have brought husbands and children with them. She insists I go into the living room, which they have commandeered, their buggies sitting alongside Amaya's, to say hello and introduce myself. Inexplicably, the prospect unsettles me. What will I say to them? Will we find any common ground apart from the obvious? I put it off for hours and remain in the kitchen, pouring and drinking champagne and overseeing the music.

Eventually, I do cross the gaping divide into the living room, and am quickly relieved. These are nice people, reasonable and sane, and one couple in particular, Clare and Jon, I feel an instant bond with. We chat amiably for several minutes until one of the babies awakens in its buggy and erupts into tears, the sound tearing the room apart and dampening the party atmosphere as effectively as flicking a switch. I turn to one of the mothers, raise my eyebrows and lower my voice until it is as deadpan as it will go, and say that I hope to Christ it's not mine. As soon as I've said it, I realise how it sounds. I try to explain that I didn't mean it, not really, but that, well, who wants a baby at a party in the first place, much less a crying one? My efforts are in vain. I have already caused offence and am being judged accordingly. The look this particular mother throws me could fell a bison. My mind scrambles for ways to backtrack, but I can think of nothing, and so I smile meekly, apologise, then stand and retreat quickly back into the kitchen and to my childless friends who, quite frankly, wouldn't have expected anything else of me.

I begin to view this behaviour of mine as a kind of Tourette's, an all-new ability to either say or do the wrong thing at the wrong time in front of the wrong people. A few weeks later, after one particularly nerve-shredding morning, Amaya crying with an edge to her wail so shrill that it sends us to the computer to read more on colic, Elena begs for some respite and asks that I take her out for a walk.

"Maybe the fresh air will do her good," she says desperately, "or maybe the motion of the pushchair. I don't know. Just try, just go, *please*."

I head straight for what I think is a local park, located through an alleyway I have only recently spotted at the end of our road. It in fact leads to a cemetery, but it is quiet and peaceful and so I head into it. We wander up and down its cracked and careless paths, her persistent cries disturbing no one but the dead and the crows that hunch like something out of Hitchcock on so many of the crumbling headstones. The clouds are low today and ominously grey, sporadically clearing their throats in an attempt to generate some proper thunder. They match my daughter's mood. Presently, my eye is caught by a collection of sparkly things in the distance. I head towards them, intrigued. As I draw near, I find that it's a small area dedicated to dead babies. Here, the graves are garlanded with balloons and ribbons, toys and mobiles that spin furiously in the wind. There are photographs of babes in arms, in their cots and on playmats, or in hospital beds with tubes running into nostrils, and many of the plots are decorated as if for a birthday party that the recipients didn't quite live to see. The headstones make for sober reading: *Harriet Swain, March 2, 2005, born and died*, one says. *Our darling Andrew: You left your baby footprints on our hearts and an ache in our soul*, says another. *Emma. You fell asleep the day you were born. Your mummy and daddy will always love you very much and will never forget you. See you again soon.*

I become aware of a woman standing nearby, looking intently at one of the graves. Her face is ashen, hollowed out. She looks up at me and smiles thinly, as if we shared something unifying, an unspeakable tragedy, the tie that binds. Inexplicably, I start to shake my head, adamant that she realise there is a misunderstanding here.

"Just looking," I quip, regretting the words the moment they leave my lips, turning on my heel and heading off, the pushchair rattling from the speed at which I am pushing. We leave the cemetery and head out towards the main road, Amaya now mercifully quiet. I reach a set of traffic lights and, checking that oncoming traffic is still at an appropriately safe distance, blithely cross the road. Behind me, an elderly woman starts shouting. All at once, I realise she is shouting at me, for crossing the road without the due care and attention required of one in possession of a pram.

"Stupid, stupid man!" she cries. I turn as cars rush past in a blur of tyres and exhaust, and see her shaking her head, wagging an accusing index finger in my direction. Pedestrians stop and stare. My cheeks redden.

At home, I recount the episode, expecting raised eyebrows and shrugged shoulders from an understanding wife, but instead I get anger and reproof. I am told that from now on, a lifetime of jaywalking is behind me, that our baby is fragile goods and that the woman was right to scold me. I must start setting an example, Elena says. I argue that she is three months old. It is unlikely she is paying attention to anything I do right now, much less when fast asleep.

"But you have to get into a routine of good behaviour," she counters, another homily expertly dispatched. "You may as well start now."

She also bans me from visiting the cemetery again.

• • •

"Haven't seen you for a while now," says Gil.

It is early April. My friend and I are talking on the phone. He wants to know whether I am free to meet up soon and whether my far-flung suburban station serves London on a weeknight, his sarcasm bleeding through the phone line like a haemorrhage.

Old friends, I'm beginning to find, rather fall away once you've had a baby. In our case, geography has certainly played a part, but that's not the only consideration. A house with a child in it holds very little appeal for those who don't have children themselves, and so once that first post-birth visit is over, it's a sacrifice they'll rarely repeat. To those without one, a family home becomes a no-go area of sorts, somewhere no longer convenient to hang out in, to eat and drink in until late and to sometimes stay over, but instead a newly sanctified place with a new set of rules and guidelines, and evening requirements for visitors to be quiet and also forgiving when we disappear upstairs for things like bath and bedtime and sudden crying jags. Dinner can often be delayed (our record is three hours), and there is little hope of any sustained conversation.

"So, fancy meeting up?" he asks.

I am exhausted almost all the time these days, but I make a point of saying yes to him. Elena and I had decided that this was essential if we wanted to maintain any semblance of our former selves. We've made a pact to each go out, separately, at least once a week, and also to find a reliable babysitter so that we can occasionally go out together.

So Gil and I go out for drinks. He asks me how I am, but I know he doesn't really want to know and so I make a point of not telling him. Childless friends don't want to hear about your children. And who can blame them? These are OPK, after all. Nevertheless, it is difficult not to stray on to the subject from time to time. There is so much to tell, after all.

"Christ, you've changed," he mocks. He's right, of course. I have. It's my job now to limit just how comprehensive that change is.

From here on in, unless I am specifically asked, I make a point of never discussing my daughter with friends. When people ask to see photographs of her, I claim I don't have one, if only to sidestep the awkward responses such pictures necessarily deliver: oh but she's lovely, so sweet, you must be so proud. It disrupts the tempo of a proper night out.

Tonight, with Gil, I make up for lost time in the manner of one without a care in the world. I live to regret it. The morning after comes at me like hammer and tongs. I feel like I've been peeled and rubbed raw, the baby's five a.m. bleatings machine-gun fire in my head.

Elena proves unsympathetic.

The hangover is but one reason that our pact to go out socially once a week never quite comes to pass. We decide to relegate it to once a month instead, but the sad truth is we come to forget about our social lives altogether. New parents generally do. In its place, home becomes everything. Ours certainly has. The new fridge has finally been delivered, filling that sad and lonely space in the kitchen with its fat, voluptuous contours reminiscent of a 1950s Chevrolet, the first fridge I have ever purchased in my life, and more expensive than a holiday in Mauritius. But it's worth it because it becomes the centre of all things almost immediately. Previously, the fridges in our succession of dingy rented flats had been tiny and mostly bare, containing little more than half-drunk bottles of wine and margarine cartons, the occasional remains of an already forgotten takeaway. But our new one is full of goodness on every shelf, Elena now ordering online and buying in bulk. The food she has chosen she has chosen wisely, for its health quotient, its calorific boosts, its vitamin count, its roughage value. I look in the fridge every morning, amazed anew each time by how plentiful it is. It tells me that I won't be going out to restaurants any more. It tells me that life is now something that will mostly happen within these four walls.

Because we are now buying in such quantities, I no longer have to pop out to the off-licence for a bottle of wine or two when the mood takes me. The fridge carries upwards of ten bottles at any one time, and because Elena is off alcohol for the duration of her breast-feeding, that means twice as much for me. This seems like a good deal until we see a news item on the television reporting that the nation's most common binge drinkers today are no longer teenagers necking alcopops on a Saturday night but rather middle-class types stuck at home with the baby and nothing but a bottle of red to mollify them. I immediately cut down on my nightly intake, if only to avoid becoming a statistic. Or an alcoholic.

If we really are to be forever surrounded by these walls and little else, we decide, jointly, to make the most of it. Specifically, we have to start having regular sex again. We had been told by the doctors and midwives to leave it for a good while after childbirth, but to be honest, they needn't have been so stringent with their advice. In the weeks after the baby's arrival, sex had effortlessly paled into memory, referred to now only fleetingly, and in the past tense. Elena was exhausted. She had eyes only for her daughter. I was so deep into my woe-is-me confusion that arousal was the furthest thing from my mind, and the lowering of testosterone levels ensured that I had no erotic dreams during those long weeks of abstinence. If I mastur-bated at all, then it was only for the sake of dwindling habit and a brief cloudburst of solace. But while the physical urge had abated, the mental one hadn't.

Approximately six weeks after the event, the baby asleep and with nothing of great import on the television, we decide to try. Both of us are hesitant, a novelty in itself that brings about a not unpleasant level of excitement, as if we were teenagers all over again. We eschew the by now damp lure of the matrimonial bed in favour of my room upstairs and the recently delivered sofa bed, which we do not unfold. We close the door and dim the lights. She sits, I kneel. We do some kissing, which we haven't done for months now, and we take our time, caressing and stroking until it can't be put off any longer. I enter her, but gently, with exaggerated care. There is bruising to consider, a new (and temporary) scar to negotiate, to say nothing about my knees on the carpet below.

Afterwards, in the absence of cigarettes, we sit side by side and agree that it's still there, we've still got it, and that whenever our daughter's sleeping patterns permit, and whenever our exhaustion lifts, we will try it again.

The trouble is, we never quite manage it as much as we, or as much as *I*, would like. The looking-after of Amaya takes precedence to the extent that we occasionally need reminding. Conveniently, one such reminder does come, but at a cost.

It is several months later, and a quiet weekday afternoon. I have no pressing work to occupy me. To pass the time, I go online. With the whole world at my fingertips, I nevertheless plump for the obvious. Online porn is interesting these days for perhaps the first few moments only, before it quickly palls in the way everything does when you are given unlimited access to it. But because I have nothing else to do right now, I click on a succession of links. I do this for maybe fifteen minutes, clicking more out of boredom than excitement, clicking for the sheer sake of it, when something happens: the screen freezes, then goes bright white and then bright green. My face matches its colour as my panic expands. I click the x in the corner of the screen, attempting to lose it, but by now images are overlaying on top of one another at terrific speed, each page giving way to another more lurid one, huge breasts followed by enormous erections and gaping labia. I shit and fuck and Jesus Christ and pray to God, but the images keep self-reproducing. I ctrl, alt and delete repeatedly, but nothing happens, and so I turn off the computer at the mains without shutting it down properly and stagger away. I splash water on my face in the bathroom and hope against hope that I haven't just killed my computer. After what I deem a safe time away from the machine – the technophobe's reasoning is nothing if not blissfully illogical – I turn it on again, awash with relief to find that everything appears back to normal. But when I double click on Microsoft Word, I don't get the anticipated empty screen with its invitingly flashing cursor but rather more tits, cocks and cum, and an advert for bored housewives in New Malden who are ready to fuck me now.

Later, during dinner, I suggest to Elena that it is perhaps time I upgraded my computer. She takes this news with raised eyebrows. I know nothing of computers, so the very concept that I would feel my "system" requires an "upgrade" is laughable, preposterous. I tell her that a friend says I need more RAM in these days of high-speed broadband, and I'm grateful that our daughter's inability to consume a plate of pasta without mishap means that Elena's attention is divided.

"Well," she says distractedly, "you have had it for a very long time now."

"Exactly."

It's a shame I didn't think this through more thoroughly, that transfering all the files from the old PC to the new one would require my wife's help, and that when she turned it on she would see the real reason why I'd felt the need to upgrade and would want to have this out with me, in detail, once Amaya was fast asleep in bed, but then this was hardly my fault. My daughter had pasta all over her face. My attention was also divided.

It is often suggested that there are two main times in life when you make true new friends. The first is during school and university, the second after you've had children. Elena has already found herself a new peer group amongst a selection of new mothers in the neighbourhood, and rarely comes home from her afternoon walk without having made another new acquaintance, women with pushchairs somehow unavoidably drawn to one another, keen to connect. One day, she starts talking to a woman in the park who turns out to live half a dozen doors down from us and has a son two months younger than our daughter. A dinner date is swiftly arranged, despite the fact that our only discernible link outside of a shared postcode is that we are new parents. I am reluctant to meet them. I've already insulted one new mother; I'd rather keep the rest at bay. I refuse to go.

I interviewed an actor once, a ruggedly handsome American popular with housewives, whose hit TV series had made him a household name comparatively late in life. He was 42. He told me that one of the downsides of having children – and he had three – was all the new people you were forced to pretend to become friends with on account of them, something he found harder than most, he argued, given his celebrity. If he failed to look peppy and enthusiastic in front of them at all times, the whispers would start.

"And I gotta say, I resent it," he told me. "You spend all your days working, and then in the evenings and weekends you have to go to the houses of these *fuckers* you would never normally be seen dead with just because your little Annie is friends with their little Sally. My wife and I argue over it all the time. She says I have an unreasonable attitude. Hell, maybe I do, but with good reason, trust me."

I liked this man; I felt his pain. His words never left me, and they don't now, even while I am still flat-out refusing to have dinner with our neighbours as we are making our way from our front door to theirs, a bottle of wine in hand, Amaya out front on her wheeled throne, ever curious to new surroundings and oblivious to my socially awkward pain.

"What am I supposed to talk about with them?" I say.

"Work, life, TV, babies, whatever." Elena frowns. "What's so wrong with meeting new people anyway?"

I have no easy answer to this. Eventually I say: "Because they are parents. I don't know any parents."

"Well, you do now."

Much later, as I am running home to fetch another bottle of wine from the fridge, I will wonder to myself why I'd been quite so resistant. Jane and Morten are terrific people, she an illustrator and teacher, he a newspaper cartoonist. They are the first set of parents I've met similarly willing to confess just how hard the transition into mother and father can be. Unlike the others I have spoken with (albeit fleetingly, so perhaps I'm judging in haste), they haven't suddenly become paragons of virtue and responsibility, but would instead rather hold onto the people they were before Junior came along. Jane is upfront and funny, has a filthy sense of humour, and Morten is cool, laid-back and Norwegian. I'd envy him more if he weren't so likeable. While we eat and talk over music, their son sleeps soundly upstairs and our daughter does likewise in her pram in the hall, both of them failing to rouse, despite the fact that we get louder and louder. By the time dessert is dished out, the third and final bottle of wine is spent, at which point I'm dispatched home for more. We trade stories about childbirth, post-natal depression and foreign in-laws late into the night, but we talk about everything else as well: sex, food, travel, the discomfort of thrush. We don't leave their house until one in the morning, and we are all very drunk, the best night out we've had in ages. We vow to do it again, and again.

But there is a postscript. While Jane and Morten do indeed become friends, we each individually come to realise that our first evening together represented a kind of watershed for us all, a semi mythological one-off for like-minded souls. In the months to come, we will enjoy dinner together several times, and lunch, and we will take our offspring to the local farm and parks, and sit in one another's houses and enjoy our gardens in the summer. But every time we consider whether to open a second or third bottle of wine again, we will look from ourselves to our young charges, and an ultimately necessary caution will descend. *Best not, eh?*

That first evening, then, was us letting go of something for the greater good of the people we have subsequently become, a terribly sensible thing to do in the circumstances.

Even just typing that last sentence now brings a lump to my throat.

Ten

In the first twelve months of my daughter's life, she makes more trips abroad than her mother did in her first twenty years This is because the only family she has aside from us happen to live several countries away. It may not be particularly convenient on those evenings when we suddenly fancy going out and would love the services of an impromptu and, crucially, unpaid babysitter, but there are several benefits to the enforced distance as well, distance being merely the most obvious. But the worst thing about our situation is the necessity of air travel in order to see them. There are always more and more Spanish people claiming to be relatives requesting an audience with their latest second cousin twice removed, something Elena is more than happy to arrange, and in my case, the prevailing reason we got married as quickly as we did, I simply want my grandparents to get to know their great-granddaughter before it's too late.

The first time she boards an aeroplane, bound for Milan, Amaya is just over four months old. We had been told by battle-scarred parents to prepare for a torturous trip, a crying fit prompted by either the unending queues at the airport, the unfamiliarity of the plane itself or, most likely of all, the sudden change in air pressure on take-off which would cause our daughter's ears to pop painfully, something she wouldn't hesitate to articulate in decibels.

In the event, we are lucky to make the flight at all.

Where solo I remain almost pathologically incapable of being late for anything, as a family unit I find that the entire concept of time-keeping has become a thing of whimsy. Great hoops through which we must jump have now sprung up between us and any destination, and if it takes us half an hour to ready our daughter for a trip to, say, the corner shop, then it takes an entire evening and the morning after to prepare for a weekend away. By the time we finally leave for the airport, we are weighed down with all manner of impedimenta and are forced to rush madly to the bus stop. This has become commonplace since her birth: we rush everywhere. I'm sure our daughter thinks that we can only ever get anywhere by running at great speed and then collapsing onto the train we have only just made by minutes, if not seconds, sweat-soaked and exhausted. We really must buy a car.

This morning, we miss one bus and are forced to wait upon another. By the time it arrives, inevitably late, it is already packed. Nobody offers up a seat. The middle-aged woman sitting at eye level with Amaya, heavy and squirming in her mother's arms, decides to regale us with her entire family history, the telling of which is as long and endless as the traffic jam we are stuck in. We reach Heathrow in a state of advanced panic, convinced our flight is about to leave without us. I dash to the nearest helpdesk, where a man gives me his best stern airport official look, shakes his head and taps his watch. I in turn point to my new secret weapon, a howling daughter to whom I had moments earlier given a quick thigh pinch. It works wonders: a drawbridge suddenly appears between us and he beckons us over to the upper-class check-in, where we are permitted to jump queues. By the time we get to the gate, they are in the process of boarding, two hundred bodies surging impatiently forward. But another quick pinch, another painful howl, and the mass parts like something biblical. We glide through, the first people on the plane, helpless with wonder and awe.

The two-hour flight is unexpectedly free of further incident. Someone wise had recommended that Elena feed Amaya as the plane takes off and later as it lands, as her swallowing would help keep her ears unblocked. It works like a dream. But our success lulls us into a false sense of security. Subsequent flights will not pan out like this. By the time she is walking, she will refuse to sit at all, viewing a parent's lap like a prison from which she must escape. Instead, she will run endlessly up and down the aisle, crashing into the legs of her fellow passengers and the drinks trolley. Thin-lipped cabin staff will tell me that they would very much prefer it if I could keep my daughter under control.

I will tell them that they are not the only ones.

Landing in Milan brings an overwhelming sense of relief, a small dream about to be fulfilled: we are here; they will meet. My grandfather has been convinced of the imminent approach of his death since the age of 60, but now that he is in his 90s, such grave predictions no longer seem quite so hollow. I, meanwhile, have become belatedly aware of the importance of family. Amaya will never have very much of one herself on my side, and it's likely she'll never remember her great-grandparents. But I want interaction now all the same. I want photographic evidence that in the absence of a paternal grandmother, grandfather, uncles, aunts, nieces, nephews and cousins, she at least had them, if only for a short while.

Age has come to suit them rather well, successfully dampening any fires that may have raged within my grandfather back when he cack-handedly attempted to raise my mother with his ridiculously outdated values. My mother could never fully forgive either of them for dispensing their love with so much criticism, but when I look at them today, all I see are two sweet, kindly souls, their faces full of unspoken regret and remorse, both so very keen to remedy as many of their mistakes as time left will allow. As a consequence, they smother me with love and support whenever I visit. And if there is still the sound of distant thunder in my grandfather's voice from time to time, then it is merely that: distant.

Time has stood still in their small rented flat on the outskirts of Milan for as long as I can remember. It has all the same furniture that

I grew up around each summer as a child, and the living-room clock continues to mark every half-hour as if the passing of time were something worth noting in their empty, empty days. They have been retired for what feels like for ever, three decades at least, he from a local factory, she from part-time nursing, their roles in retirement long set deep in stone. Like so many Italian men, he spent his first few years of leisure seeing his wife much as he had during his employment: at mealtimes and night only. The rest of the time he was out playing bowls, a slow-motion sport whose appeal, as I see it, is that it never need end. But one by one, his bowling partners died off, the ground passed on to new management, bringing with it new players and new rules, all of which he took unkindly to. Thereafter, he began more and more to stay at home, initially pottering about the house fixing things that didn't need fixing, before graduating full-time to what he does today: filling out crossword puzzles while falling asleep, open-jawed, in front of wretched Italian television.

My grandmother, meanwhile, remains the quintessential 1950s housewife, a role she continues to undertake today with as much conviction as she ever did, presiding over three square meals a day and polishing the place until it shines like something out of an advert for domestic cleaning products. He complains about everything, as is his habit, and she takes it all with a mostly silent, embattled smile upon her face and an internal zest that refuses to fade. Each evening after dinner, the table is cleared for espresso, boiled sweets and a game of cards that can go on for hours, while a dubbed *Columbo* rerun plays out on the television behind them, their minds still sharp, aware and full of cunning. It is here where they best reveal their continued love for one another, with sly asides and mocking admiration for whoever wins each successive hand.

These days, I manage to visit them only in small doses, a long weekend usually, simply because the pace of life here is so extraordinarily slow that exposure to it for more than three days can drive me insane. While growing up, I would spend most school holidays here, long, hot summers that threatened never to end. Now I see them perhaps three times a year, and whenever I take my leave of them at the top of the stairs of their small block of flats, I, like them, am convinced it will be for the last time.

This visit, then, has much riding on it. By the time we have landed, transferred first onto a coach, then a tube and finally a fifteen-minute walk to their neighbourhood, Amaya is as ratty and exhausted as her parents, and desperate for all the motion to cease. The first sight my grandparents get of her is with her mouth wide open, pink and stretched and screaming. And though she quickly settles, the vigorous life she brings with her into a hermetically sealed flat more used to peace and quiet causes such shock waves that my grandfather at least never really regains composure. While his wife of almost 60 years coos over the baby with the joyful exaggerated fuss I'd anticipated, he remains on the perimeter, eyes wide, his wariness palpable. Each time she cries again, no matter how briefly, he becomes freshly unsettled, perhaps secretly wishing that she should be seen, yes, but rarely heard. As far as he is concerned, babies at this age are exclusively the female's domain. If his limp permitted (he fell off a chair a year ago; the bone refuses to heal), he'd disappear to the bar for respite. Instead, he is imprisoned here, fearful and unable to join in. This is something I know he feels will only change when she gets older, if, of course, he lives to see such a thing.

For the time being, he does, and by her fourth visit, a year and a bit later, she is hyper with toddler activity. One morning, she decides to bring him apples and oranges that my grandmother keeps, inexplicably, in a cupboard on the balcony. He is in the living room puzzling over his latest crossword as she does this, methodically, one by one, and soon the dining table is full of ripe and bruising fruit. He puts his pencil down, lowers his reading glasses down his Roman nose and appraises the blonde granddaughter his own daughter never lived to see. A hand reaches out to cup her cheek and a smile swims from his eyes to his mouth and back again. I watch on from the doorway in silence. It is a moment I will treasure.

●●●

Like my grandfather, I begin to warm to my daughter the more recognisably human she becomes. Leaving behind all the gubbins that babyness is so unavoidably beleaguered with, her new toddler status heralds the onset of behaviour patterns I can identify with and readily relate to. I like her now; I like her a lot; more it seems each day. To watch her interact, process and learn from the world around her on a minute-by-minute basis is unendingly fascinating. It feels like a privilege. Much of her waking hours are spent crawling from one point to the next, her limbs pumping so fast across carpet and floorboard that she resembles something out of a speeded-up film. We fit kiddie guard gates on the stairs and remember to close doors behind us, and we learn to live in a house of perpetual chaos as she discovers the secret of drawers and cupboards: that they can be opened and have things concealed inside them, things like pens and paper, knives and forks and tampons, items she can either chew on or toss around at will, laughing maniacally as she does.

Shortly after her first birthday, which passes entirely without her knowledge, despite our best efforts, she begins the task of trying to stand up, lifting herself up first onto her knees while holding tightly onto the nearest available adult leg. It appears to be an entirely natural instinct, this drive of hers for mobility and independence. She soon casts aside the adult leg, and launches herself into the unknown, teetering on tiptoe rather than the flat of her feet, which predictably does little to promote balance. She falls over almost immediately. What isn't instinct to her yet is the need to break her fall with outstretched hands. Instead, she breaks it with her face, and when she goes over, she goes over hard. But even through howling tears and blossoming bruises, she is up again quickly, pushing free again and taking another tentative step into new territory. Each evening, we encourage her more and more, though encouragement is the last thing she needs. This is a game to her, and she giggles as she propels herself forward, foolishly confident each time that we will catch her when she falls, despite the fact that we so often don't. On one occasion, she dives too quickly and my arms are too slow. She crashes in a heap on my lap, my testicles bearing the brunt of the force in an explosion of pure pain. Another time, she falls onto the door frame and very nearly knocks herself out.

Meantime, to help stem the house's descent into a pigsty, we decide to get a cleaner. This isn't an easy decision for either of us. It feels rudely middle class, ostentatious and somehow decadent, the kind of thing our mothers, who seemed always to cope with everything, would frown at. But we are stretched all the time, and the place is showing advanced signs of neglect. Its mess is something we argue over, and it's the arguments that seal the deal whether we can afford it or not. I call a local company and make an appointment for someone to come the following week.

The morning of the cleaner's arrival, I find I am so nervous that I go through every room tidying frantically so that what she arrives to is essentially a clean house. She has brought reinforcement: another woman. Both are hard-looking 30-somethings, both buxom and barely constrained in white lycra. They set about the place with a lethal efficiency, moving from room to room as if in a race to finish, and leave behind them the commingling smells of bleach, polish and sweat. I hide in each successive room they vacate, unsure of what to do with myself. Over the course of 90 minutes, I hear the breaking of a cup and at least two plates. In the living room, they move the sofa from the wall in order to dust beneath it, but they don't lift it; they drag it, the sofa's legs tearing the floorboards beneath and leaving a deep and ugly wound. Because I am frightened of them, I say nothing about it. I pay up, and never see them again.

Our next cleaner is better. Her name is Eva, she is 27 years old and Bulgarian. She speaks good, crunchy English. She has nice teeth. Over successive weeks, she tells me about herself, about her business degree, the bureaucracy of British employment agencies, and about how she is currently estranged from her husband back in Sofia, one of the country's biggest rap stars. She got tired of the lifestyle there, she says, the press attention, the touring, the American-aping east-versus-west rap wars that her husband became mired in, and so she got out, leaving it all behind, including her three-year-old daughter.

She comes to clean every Friday morning. Perhaps because she misses her own child, she never fails to ask of the whereabouts of my daughter, whom she has seen only in photographs. My answer is always the same: she is at the crèche where she spends every weekday while my wife works. But on one occasion, Amaya stays home because of a visit from the mother-in-law, and so finally Eva gets to meet her. By this stage, myself and the cleaner are practically close friends. Each time she comes, we spend a good half-hour talking and laughing over coffee. I know all about her hopes and dreams, how she loves to dance and how much she misses her daughter, whom she hopes will join her here soon. In the meantime, she tells me, she would happily be nanny to ours. I need only ask.

Amaya has been very nearly walking for a week now and carries the bruises on her forehead to prove it. Eva adores her instantly, her maternal instinct grateful for this new focus. After hugging her, picking her up and swinging her through the air, she sits on the floor in the kitchen and suggests I do likewise, facing her, legs apart. She then tells Amaya to walk towards each of us in turn, and encourages her in a voice so full of enthusiasm it practically yodels. Amaya, arms above her head for balance like an orangutan, an enormous smile on her face, walks between us, back and forth, and doesn't fall over once, Eva and I moving incrementally further from one another, thus requiring her to take yet more bold steps. We clap and she giggles, and I am so very proud. She shouts "more!, more!", the first word she will feel fully in command of, and she laughs. We all do. In time, the noise draws the mother-in-law into the room. I look up at her and suddenly see the scene from her eyes: her son-in-law with a woman who quite pointedly isn't her daughter, the pair of us unashamedly prompting a key moment in her granddaughter's development. This is inappropriate behaviour. It is suggestive of something else. Eva gets up quickly, places her empty coffee cup in the sink and fetches the hoover. I retreat upstairs and get on with some work.

"So, I hear she walked properly for the first time today?"

It is evening and we are in the kitchen preparing dinner. The mother-in-law has her back to me, facing the cooker, and Elena is sitting at the table opposite me, her daughter on her lap. She appraises me with suspicion. I ask her what her mother said about Eva.

"That she has nice teeth."

I wake the following morning half convinced that the mother-in-law has placed some kind of hex on me. I have a high fever and a throat as dry as the desert. I am boiling hot and freezing cold. There is deep muscle ache everywhere, and I cannot move without being ravaged by pain. But suddenly I need to, and quick. The mass evacuation from either end of me keeps me in the bathroom for a full hour. I'd groan, but I don't have the strength.

• • •

Illness finds me many times over the coming months, and with raging virulence. First I have a cold, then another. Then it's a fever, flu, aches and shakes. I contract conjunctivitis. I endure bouts of diarrhoea and vomiting, I cough all the time, am forever weakened. I lose count of the pre-dawn mornings I spend curled up on the sofa in my room, unable to sleep and slick with sweat and shivering pain. It's a lonely business, and one I'm not cut out for. Elena feeds me soup, lots of it, but it alleviates nothing, and instead passes through me like lightning. I lose weight; people notice. One month, I board an aeroplane to Brazil for work. I am sick in the airport toilets beforehand, and for much of the fourteen hours on board, I shit myself senseless in a cubicle I come to know intimately. Upon arrival, instead of enjoying a caipirinha on the beach at Copacabana, I am kneeling in my hotel bathroom, some toilet tissue pressed to my open mouth. Another month, an ulcer on my palate suggests I may have contracted hand, foot and mouth disease, which I had previously thought only affected cattle.

Though I don't know it yet, this is a pattern that will hound me for the next eighteen months at least. The reason, quite simply, is my daughter. It's her fault. Since beginning at the crèche, which she attends five days a week from nine until five, she has been exposed to all manner of viruses, each of which is new to her and to which she is helplessly prone. Germs breed in, on and about her all and every day. She then brings them back home where they socialise and disseminate. Given our daily proximity, I am virtually a sitting duck. Even Elena, who had previously been impervious to all common ailments, is now regularly ill herself.

"Your average crèche is a hotbed of viral activity," a doctor tells me. "But then this is good news. Children need to be exposed to all these illnesses in order to build up their immune systems. It will benefit them in the long run."

But what about my immune system? Shouldn't I be more resistant myself?

"In theory," the doctor says, "yes. But you are at a disadvantage right now because you are tired and stressed and run ragged from parenthood, which means that you're far more likely to catch things. It should settle down within a couple of years, though. Unless of course," he adds, and I wish he hadn't, "there is actually something seriously wrong with you."

In all the printed arguments we read about whether one should or should not send their child to a crèche, the subject of illness never came up. Illness is just a bonus to file alongside all the other surrounding controversies. I remember reading in the Oliver James book, *They F*** You Up*, of the arguments for and against sending children into day care. He referenced theories that suggested if a parent of a child under three were physically absent on a regular basis, then that child could become anxious should his attachment needs not be met. A good carer, it was agreed, could alleviate this problem, but studies have shown that children who experienced day care when young were nevertheless more likely to display poor emotional well-being, aggression and antisocial behaviour. Upon reading this, I decided immediately that we would never consign our daughter to such a cruel fate. But then I read on. More arguments came at me, counter ones this time, studies that claimed stay-at-home parents faced a very real risk of depression if no longer engaged in the workplace or within the adult world. This could also affect the child negatively. To muddy the waters further, it was then claimed that day care wasn't actually bad at all. No, quite the opposite. It could help develop social skills earlier; it could encourage independence. Yes, but it could also lead, in some cases, to early sexual promiscuity and perhaps even juvenile crime...

It was at this point that I closed the book and walked away, profoundly confused.

Ultimately, we chose to send our daughter to a crèche because we had to. After eight months' maternity leave, Elena needed to return to work for financial reasons. More pertinently, she wanted to. There is a crèche on site at her place of work, which makes it more convenient than we could have hoped for, and as for the arguments for and against, we decided, rather conveniently, to put our faith in the suggestion that exposure to other children would help develop her social skills, surely a good thing. At home, meanwhile, we would endeavour to shower her with an excess of love and attention in the hope that she wouldn't end up pregnant, joyriding or cooking up heroin by the age of fourteen. And anyway, if you follow the logic that all parents make all kinds of mistakes with their offspring irrespective of their efforts, then this was merely to be one of many to come. As Oliver James himself concludes, quoting Larkin: they fuck you up, your mum and dad.

To our great relief, our daughter seems to love the crèche, and it certainly exposes her to a wider world. On that first morning, we had expected tears at the point of handing her over to a stranger. Perhaps we had even hoped for them as confirmation that she needed and wanted us. Instead, she barely noticed our departure. This was a magical place filled with toys, noise and activity. In one corner, there was something she had never seen before: a sandpit. She was sold, and off she went. Already we were losing her to outside temptation.

But though she liked it, the crèche very quickly took away her innocence, replacing it with, amongst other things, the spectre of violence. On her fourth day, this was written into her logbook:

"Amaya had a wonderful day today playing in the sandpit and reading stories. Unfortunately in the afternoon there was an incident. Amaya was lying happily on the floor playing next to another child when for no reason another child bit Amaya on the right cheek. A staff member immediately applied a cold compress to the bite. Teeth marks and bruising was left."

The crèche has a policy of never revealing the perpetrator of any crime, and so retribution was not a possibility. Elena brought our daughter home that night, having forewarned me of the incident on the telephone. The bite mark was big. It covered much of her cheek, and started just millimetres beneath the right eye. The bruise that grew and swelled was a dark purple that, over the ensuing weeks, faded gradually to black, then blue and finally a nicotine yellow. The last things to fully disappear were the tiny red marks left by the tiny teeth of a demon child.

"Unfortunately, biting is very common in toddlers this age," lamented Linda, her kindly care worker. Linda's words would ring true. Our daughter would be bitten again. Soon, as is the way in this world, she would start biting back.

In addition to the loss of innocence comes the loss of her otherwise perfect health. A week after her first day comes her first cold, thick green snot coagulating at her nostrils, a hacking cough that keeps us all awake at night. The cold never seems to fully abate, but instead hangs around like a bad habit, often gestating into something worse. But she proves a fighter, her rampant energy levels refusing to be so easily dampened. I only wish I could say the same of me. Everything she passes on lays me low and my only real course of action, aside from popping completely useless vitamin supplements, is to grumble. I spend months slumped over my desk feeling sorry for myself. But then I'm often slumped over my desk feeling sorry for myself. At least now I have a definable reason for doing so.

John Simpson, the older father

When he became a father for the first time, John Simpson was just 25 years old. This was a lifetime ago, the 1960s. His career as a journalist at the BBC was just beginning and, as he admits to me now, "I rather had other things on my mind." These days, an entire generation on, he is distinguished, venerable, and a grandfather to boot, and he is sufficiently old to consider retirement, a pension and a house by the sea. Instead, at 63, he is a new father all over again. His son, Rafe, is two.

"To be honest, I think I'd have been happy with just my two daughters [now in their late 30s], focusing instead on having a nice, gentle time of it for the rest of my life," he says, "but my wife [Adele Kruger, a journalist and television producer nineteen years his junior, whom he married in 1996] was very keen on having a baby. I do think when you marry someone you have to listen to what they want, don't you? I could hardly have lain down the law and said that it was out of the question, not least as I imagine it would have created much future resentment."

Simpson has agreed to meet with me to discuss fatherhood on a crisp autumn morning at his local café in Chelsea. He was initially difficult to pin down, his PA telling me that today was the only day this year he'd be free – between wars, presumably. But the moment he arrives, he is friendly, relaxed and highly likeable. He butters and marmalades his toast and adds first one spoonful of sugar into his coffee before, having tasted it and winced, adding another and then another still.

"And so anyway, yes, now we have Rafe, and I have to say that I am completely and utterly besotted with him."

John Simpson is, of course, one of the UK's most well-known and respected journalists. He carries *a lot* of scars. He has been shelled in Afghanistan, and close to the line of fire in Tiananmen Square. In 2001, he famously "liberated" Kabul, and two years later was injured by friendly fire in Iraq when an American aircraft bombed the convoy he was travelling with. A member of his crew was killed in the incident; he was left deaf in one ear. A tough man hardened to the ways of the world, then, but as he is so prone to do whenever talking publicly about his new son, he can also become unabashedly emotional. He is doing just that before me now, directing his words towards the window and out at the traffic, as if in the hope that focusing on the passing cars will perhaps still his trembling lower lip. Of all the people I speak to on this subject, Simpson is by far the most sweetly sentimental about it.

"I wrote about him for one of the papers recently, and I have to say, there were tears running down my cheeks and onto the keyboard as I typed," he recalls with a shy smile.

Within the first year of his son's birth, Simpson had written a series of articles for the broadsheets on his new status as elderly father, features defined by their candour and honesty. They proved popular, so much so that he then did a three-dimensional version for TV, on the BBC's *From Our Own Correspondent*.

"And rather humiliatingly," he says, "I just couldn't get through it. I kept having to ask the cameraman to stop filming so that I could collect myself. In the end, I had to go through it sentence by sentence because I kept welling up. I don't know why, but I find it all terribly emotional."

Fatherhood, he readily grants, is hardly a rare occurrence: "It's not exactly an unusual human experience, but it still touches me profoundly. I think the reason is probably buried rather deep inside me, perhaps linked to various things in my past, perhaps due to all the time I spent in Iraq, but it's as if I've only now become aware of the very vulnerability of life. Having said that," he continues, "I have come to learn that it is often anything but. In the course of my travels, I have seen children born in all sorts of situations: in wars, in air raid shelters, and often with no one to help and always against the odds, but they somehow survive. It makes you realise that they are, in fact, as tough as old tyres."

Nevertheless, he recalls how fearful he was when his first daughter was born back in 1968: "She was this weak little thing, and I remember watching her as a little girl and feeling so very worried about how someone as seemingly fragile as she could possibly survive. She not only survived, she thrived: she now rows for Oxford, is a marathon runner and has three kids of her own."

Rafe may well have been the culmination of a dream come true for Simpson's wife, but before he finally came along there was much trying and failing, and the ghosts of multiple miscarriages.

"We tried for ten years and had all sorts of tests," Simpson recounts, "all of them intrusive and painful, and yet all of them, and each of the miscarriages as well [there were four], only made us even more determined, somehow, to succeed. And then, in the stupid way of these things, having tried all the technical and medical help available, it just happened, and it happened in a lovely, a really *nice* way. Everything that had been a problem before suddenly faded away. The foetus was never less than robustly healthy, always strong, and certainly stronger than any of the others. Very quickly, it became obvious that this at last was going to be okay, the one that lived."

It also brought him something of a surprise. His first two children were both girls, as were each of the four miscarriages. But when they attended a five-month scan for Kruger's latest pregnancy, they saw something that marked this one out as different.

"There it was, an unmistakable dick in the picture," he says. "That took a bit of coming to terms with, a while for me to get my head around. I was used to girls, you see, but a boy? A boy was going to be completely new to me."

And what of his age in all this? Simpson would have qualified for an old*ish* parent back when they first started trying for a child a decade previously. But by now, he was comparatively ancient.

"Well, these days, 61 – as I was when we had him – is not really so old, is it?" he argues. "I work as much now as I ever used to, in fact, often more than many of my colleagues, and in nastier places, too. But I will give you this: one does get increasingly aware of the passing of years as a result of fatherhood. I have, anyway."

He suggests that as we get older, we each become increasingly aware of our running out of time, that we see the end of the road hurtling towards us, and all the signs that say Do Not Pass, which we go ahead and pass anyway.

He sighs. "I think it rather sharpens the whole sense that your kid will ultimately represent a little bit of you when you've shuffled off," he says. "My son looks terribly like I did at his age, which makes me realise this fact all the more, and I do suppose that his youth cannot help but make me feel my age. I often wonder how old he will be when I finally snuff it. I'll be *80* by the time he reaches university. All these things come together in my head and make me feel depressingly sentimental and lachrymose. Trouble is, I don't want to be like that at all. I want to be jolly and play cricket with him, but I now realise that I'm going to have to carry this baggage around with me for the rest of my life. You know," he says, allowing a piece of toast to dangle between his fingertips, "when I'm on my deathbed I'm going to feel really and properly upset that I won't get to see more of the little chap."

Back in the late 1960s, John Simpson wasn't so consumed with the art of navel-gazing. He was young and robust and gregarious, full of ambition, and newly married to an American artist, Diane Petteys. He had trained to become a sub-editor within the BBC, and was just two years shy of his first promotion to the position of reporter. His first daughter, Julia, was born at home in Greenwich, a bohemian enclave of south-east London, and so while their choice of home birth was somewhat frowned upon by their local GP, it was permitted nonetheless. Denizens of Greenwich, sandal-wearing creative types mostly, were prone to such radical choices. And when his wife's waters finally broke after an interminable nine months, Simpson made another radical decision: to be present at the delivery.

"Though it was bloody hard to convince them of that," he says of the visiting midwife, who had insisted he should instead remain in another room pacing. "She was convinced," he huffs, "I'd faint."

But Simpson was never the fainting kind. He ultimately persuaded her of this and was allowed to stay.

"She insisted I make myself useful and boil some water, so I did, and thereafter I stood in the corner of the room out of everyone's way."

After the delivery, the midwife and her small team of nurses tidied up, offered tacit congratulation, then promptly departed, leaving behind them two very bewildered new parents.

"Suddenly it became clear that this squalling creature, who was, by the way, hideous, absolutely hideous, purple spots all over her face – though I should point out that she's a real beauty today – was our exclusive responsibility and that it was about to make the most tremendous demands of us. I quickly became convinced I'd ruin its life somehow, make mistakes, get everything wrong..."

Very much a man of his era, Simpson could make head nor tail of nappies.

"They were the size of bath towels back then," he complains, "and needed to be wrapped in a special sort of way. I tried it, I really did, but I was always pricking the baby or myself, and generally got it all wrong. And even on the few occasions I did fashion something that looked more or less correct, there were still gaping errors because – well, because I hadn't plugged all the holes properly. Wee would run down the poor thing's legs."

And so he gave up, a decision happily sanctioned by his wife.

Although to all intents and purposes a feminist, Diane Petteys, a Californian, was still of the belief that certain traditional roles were just that for a reason: "And all this [nappies, feeding, *babies* themselves] she considered woman's work. The bloke could help if he really wanted to, but basically, she had her job and I had mine."

This is true: Simpson very much had his. By now, his career was beginning to take hold. After 1970's promotion, he was soon to go on to become first political editor, then diplomatic editor, then roving foreign correspondent, news anchor for a short while and, ultimately, world affairs editor. There would be endless dispatches to war zones where he endured the perennial whistle of flying bullets and the crump of mortar attacks. There would be plaudits and triumphs, a CBE, and books, lots of published books. At the height of his success, Nelson Mandela declared himself an admirer.

"My career was never one in which, alas, you could opt to stay at home," he says. "In fact, I was talking to my oldest daughter about this just the other night, about how sorry I was that I was so absent-minded towards both her and Eleanor, her sister, for so much of the time while they were growing up. They'd come to see me in my study when they were young, but I'd be so involved in my work that I'd tell them to go and bother Mum instead. Not that I didn't love them both very dearly, you understand, but just that I had so many other things on my mind."

Work was so pressurised, he continues, that he lost his patience often at home and frequently shouted at them, he forever on deadline, his daughters, with little clue, concept or interest in deadlines, simply keen to be with Daddy.

"That doesn't mean we didn't often have great fun as well, because we did. I used to read to them most nights, and I was about a fair amount because I never travelled anywhere near as much as I do now. So I was a presence in their lives, then, just not as focused as they wish I'd been."

Shortly after his oldest daughter had become a teenager, Simpson took the decision to walk out on his family.

"When I left their mother," he tells me, eyes on the road again, "I felt really pretty awful about it. My children were twelve and fourteen, a really bad time to go, and – well, you know, I'm not proud of myself at all. But fortunately, my wife didn't badmouth me to them. In fact, she openly encouraged them to continue seeing me, and so I remained a part of their lives. I was still pretty guilt-ridden over walking out, though. It must have been brutal for them. But somehow we got through it and we have a very close relationship today, far closer," he adds, his voice a whisper, "than I think I deserve, quite frankly, and that's something I put down to their niceness, their forgiveness, their sense of family loyalty."

And how did they greet the news that their father was to become a dad all over again? He thinks a while before answering this question, and the gentle smile reaches his mouth before any words do.

"They like it, I think. Yes, I really think they do. They're rather amused by it."

It's all different this time, of course, and not just in terms of the nappies, which he approaches with gusto, and even enthusiasm. Simpson has learned from experience and is now intent on being the ideal parent, spending as much time with his new son as he possibly can. He is also coming to terms with the fact that retirement will never quite be a viable option.

"Having a baby at this stage of life means I'll have to keep on working long after I'd have liked," he shrugs. "Bringing this kid up, educating him, is all going to cost money, so I can hardly afford to retire. I'm also aware that when I'm deep into my 70s, I'll have to face things like teenage rebellion, slammed doors in my face, his ghastly friends, his awful music…"

But these are minor quibbles, not even really quibbles at all. Simpson can't wait for fatherhood in all its guises, good, bad, challenging and exhausting. Mostly, he just wants to be here for all of it, every last drop, healthy, alert, *alive*.

"Who knows, he may turn out to become an arsehole," he muses, "but it doesn't seem to be that way at the moment. If anything, he seems rather suitable for elderly carers, which I'm very grateful for. He can be boisterous at times, but he is also sort of nice and quiet right now. When he wakes up, for example, he just lies there until we wake up and go to fetch him. He doesn't just sit there in his cot going *waaa!*, which, when you're 63, is precisely what you don't want, trust me. But really, I am as fully prepared for whatever comes as I can be. There is no point grumbling about any of it. If I was going to grumble, then I really shouldn't have got myself into all of this again in the first place. But I have, and I have done so willingly."

Rafe, he is relieved to report, is sleeping through the night now, but for the first six months of his life he would wake up routinely between midnight and dawn, three, four times a night, and each time a pitiful *waaa!* was his only form of communication. Though Simpson likes to suggest that the older parent needs much less sleep than their 30-something counterparts, these nightly interruptions left him wrecked the morning after.

"But then, mercifully, I went to Baghdad," he beams, "and I had a fantastic time. They are quite a lazy lot over there, you see. Mostly, they don't start bombing until seven o'clock in the morning, so I'd get a good night's sleep every night and wake up fully rested. I came back home after a fortnight feeling completely refreshed. Unfortunately, my poor wife had had no such luck…"

Ask him whether he ever feels moved to take a safer job now that he is needed more at home, and he shakes his head no.

"I can't suddenly climb out of the trench and take a desk job after all this time," he says. "And I don't want to, either. I want my son to know who I am, what I am, and I want him to appreciate and accept that this is what I do. My wife agrees with me. Coming from journalism herself, she doesn't necessarily see my time away from home as a burden on her, but rather as a great opportunity for me, and that's just wonderful, to be able to count on that kind of support. That said, I wouldn't mind if there was a little less travelling from now on, if only because I want to be with my son first and foremost, wherever and whenever possible."

Nowadays, he says, he won't let anyone come between him and his family.

"Occasionally, senior people at the BBC will ring up and say that they are having a meeting tomorrow afternoon and that they need me to attend. In the past, I would have dropped everything to go, but these days I often just come up with an excuse. I still have quite a bad back, you see, a persistent injury from having been bombed in 2003. Sometimes I can use that on the BBC to operate on their conscience – I never asked for compensation – but mostly I don't even lie about it; I simply say I'm not available. I'd rather be at home, at home with Rafe."

And here he goes again. At the very mention of his son's name, the lower lip begins to corrugate and tremble, and the great man is forced to turn away.

Of late, Simpson has been thinking a lot about his own father and about how it is inevitable that we all turn into a version of our own. His parents having broken up when he was seven, he elected to stay with his father rather than his mother, chiefly, he says now, because his father was so distraught at the thought of being left alone (his mother already had two children from a previous marriage). Roy Simpson was a Christian scientist and genealogist who changed jobs regularly and had a forever fluctuating income.

"We moved house on average once every six months," he recalls, "and at times we had a live-in staff, a cook and a driver, things like that. But the good times never lasted long and the staff would have to go. We moved from small flats to big houses and then back to smaller places all the time."

Wherever they lived, each temporary home was filled with music, pets and beautiful women, the young Simpson free to roam wherever he chose, bedtime a discipline for other children only, never him. His father would frequently drive him crazy, acting more the wayward teenager than a sensible adult. And yet today, the older he gets, the more he realises the growing similarities between them.

"We all need to come to terms with our own fathers," he says, citing that his wife also had a fractured paternal relationship and was angry with hers for a long time before Simpson encouraged them to get back together. "They are terribly close now and that, I feel, is so very important. Even if we haven't seen our fathers for years, even if we meet up with them and still consider them a stupid bastard or a selfish bastard or whatever, learning about where you come from, *who* you come from, is all part of knowing who you are, and having your kids know who you are."

A few days after our conversation, he will set off again, back on an aeroplane bound first for Pakistan, then Zimbabwe, on the trail of wars, genocide and injustice. While bravado has identified him for much of his professional life, John Simpson has never had a death wish. He concedes that his job can be a perilous one, but then he draws attention to a small story that ran in the newspapers a few days ago, about a Filipino nanny walking down the Kings Road in London, mown down by a Porsche, the driver having suffered a heart attack and ploughed into her.

"So there's danger everywhere, isn't there?" he asks rhetorically. "I'm not particularly scared of dying, but I know that I very much don't want to right now. I want to see this kid of mine grow up. I'd feel really bad about it if I sort of switched off like a light bulb when he was still just a child. I want to see him grow up; I want to see what sort of person he turns into. That's my only wish."

The window and the mid-morning traffic consume his final thought.

"I very much hope my wish comes true."

Eleven

It is a blazing April day when Elena leaves me fully alone with our daughter for the first time. She is going to a hen party in Dublin and will be gone an entire 36 hours, promoting me to sole parent. She may have certain misgivings about this but, wisely, she keeps these to herself. I'll be fine, she tells me. Of course I will. Amaya is sixteen months old now, walking and almost talking, a daily wonder to me. Parenthood has finally become fun.

If, before they reach one year old, babies aren't exactly *boring* – they are the architects of far too much incident to prompt such a passive response – then it is nevertheless true to say that they aren't particularly interesting either: too demanding, too inert, too much take and not enough give. But by sixteen months, she is more entertaining than TV, more involving than sport, and prompts a well of emotion within me that compares favourably to music and books.

Naturally, I have been left alone with her on many occasions before now, but never for an unbroken weekend, from first thing in the morning and, if necessary, all through the night as well. This will be my biggest challenge yet.

I read in a book recently that parenting styles are not determined by how much time fathers spend with their children, but the amount of time they spend with them *alone*.

I've long enjoyed Elena's gym nights for this very reason, so I find I'm rather excited by the prospect of an entire weekend with her all to myself. There is slight terror in this mix too, I'll admit it, but right now it's a 60/40 split. I'm optimistic.

• • •

A soft, warm, toothpaste kiss to the cheek wakes me at seven on Saturday morning. She is ready to leave, she says, and I tell her to enjoy herself. Confident by now in my middling ability to look after our daughter without mishap, she nevertheless can't quite help herself, and tells me to remember to feed her at regular intervals, to put a jacket on her if we go out, and not to neglect a nappy when it needs changing. She has left food in the fridge, she says, there is lots of fruit in the fruit bowl and, our daughter's current addiction, boxes of raisins in the cupboard. I'm to make sure she has plenty to drink. She needs to sleep after lunch or else she gets grumpy. "I've left enough of her clothes out for you, washed and ironed," she says. "And don't forget to take extra nappies with you when you go out. And make sure you do go out. She needs air."

I make the appropriate affirmative noises, then drift back off into a pillowy sleep as the front door clicks shut quietly downstairs.

A quarter of an hour later comes the familiar staccato cry from Amaya's room. I bound out of bed with an enthusiasm that scarcely represents my usual morning self, cross the landing in three steps and burst into her room. She is standing up, wailing from what she considers unforgivable inattention, but promptly breaks out into a sunshine smile at the sight of me. This bodes well. Her new teeth glint in the morning light, and I draw attention to them by placing my little finger between them. I rarely find teeth cute, but hers I do. She in turn draws attention to them by biting down hard. My scream can be heard next door. A plaster stems the blood flow, and I take her upstairs with me where I shall have my shower.

Whenever Elena is on early-morning duty, which is more often than not, she tends to forego the luxuries of her daily routine in order to give the baby full care and attention. Her argument, admittedly a sound one, is that she can brush her teeth and cleanse later. But I am a creature of habit. I have certain requirements that need to be met upon waking, and a shower for me isn't so much a luxury as a necessity. Without one, I am incapable of functioning. That ritualistic blast of hot water is the only thing that enables me to face the day.

Amaya, meantime, roams around my room, pulling open successive drawers until she finds what she is looking for: my desk diary and some pens. These she brings into the bathroom and, while I work shampoo into my hair, my eyes narrowed into slits, I watch as she stands at the toilet, lid down, and scribbles all over Wednesday and Thursday of the coming week. Once she has done this, she leaves the bathroom, despite my pleading, and walks over to the alphabetised CD racks back in my room, where I hear her begin to remove as many as she can, one by one. Sometimes, she likes to take out the inner sleeve and subject them to a Biro attack. Other times, she can be more aggressive still, either throwing the discs as if they were frisbees or else trying to bite chunks out of them. When I come out of the shower now, a towel wrapped around my waist, the disc I gently remove from between her teeth is a promo of Radiohead's first-ever release, the *Drill* EP. I saw a copy of this in a record shop recently, in far less pristine condition than mine. It was priced at £180.

After a breakfast of Weetabix, which she fast loses interest in, we sit in the oversized playpen that dominates half the kitchen, and she climbs all over me while I keep at least one eye trained on Channel 4's *Transworld Sport*. It's early yet, barely nine o'clock, but I'm feeling the distinctly pleasurable tang of novelty. Elena is a wonderful mother, and undoubtedly encouraging of the development of my own parental skills, but whenever we preside over our daughter together, I inevitably defer to her in everything. I can't help it. She is clearly the boss, with me as second-in-command, a hierarchy even Amaya has picked up on. If she enters a room to find the both of us, it is her mother she will run to first. But Elena is somewhere over the Irish Sea right now, her corrupting significance diminishing with each successive air mile that springs up between us. Amaya appears not to notice her absence, and I become the sole recipient of all her forceful attention. I love it.

An hour later, Julie texts to ask how I am doing, the unwritten suggestion that I'm flailing already. After I'd told her the story related to me by the man who came to fit our new Venetian blinds last week, she was convinced that my time alone with my daughter would end in similar chaos. He'd arrived, this Venetian blinds man, early on Tuesday morning. I invited him in and made him coffee, immediately aware of the coiled tension that came off him like vapour, a tension that knotted his shoulders and transformed his features into a pinched frown he seemed incapable of relaxing. Unprompted, he began telling me how much he hated his previous job in telephone engineering, and how this current one was scarcely any better: "But I do it all for my kids," he said. "You got any?" I pointed to the playpen. "I've got two myself," he continued. "Twins, girls, two years old now." We chatted about children for a while. I told him about being alone with mine this coming weekend. "First time my wife left me alone with mine," he said, "they got ill. Diarrhoea. Diarrhoea like you wouldn't believe."

It never ceases to amaze me quite how the subject of children can open up lines of communication between a couple of strangers. For a country whose people are noted for being socially awkward, we nevertheless love to discuss our kids in explicit detail, no matter how intimate or messy. The only other topic, in my experience, that can instantaneously unite strangers in such a fashion is illness. When my mother was dying of cancer nine years ago, I'd told very few people, but those I did almost universally responded with uncomfortably candid stories of their own. An old editor of mine, who would only ever discuss music with me, responded to the news that I wouldn't be able to do my column that month because I had to spend time with my mother in the hospice, by telling me about how cancer had worked its way through several members of his family, and how he increasingly feared for his own health as a result. His soliloquy on the acceptance of mortality was unaccountably moving for a Monday morning, and I didn't quite know where to look. At its conclusion, neither did he. Shortly after my mother's death, I had cause to visit a carpet shop where she had ordered a new carpet for the living room she knew she'd never return to, hoping to cancel the order. The owner displayed immediate understanding, then lost all composure, tears pouring down his cheeks. He told me of his own mother's death from the disease two years previously and that he had yet to get over it. As I made to leave, he offered me a consoling hand to shake, then pulled me towards him in a hug. "Be brave," he said.

In my sixteen months of fatherhood, I had experienced many comparable situations, the faces of total strangers lighting up at the slightest mention of my child. Sitting next to someone on an aeroplane bound for Los Angeles once, my aisle-seated neighbour clocked my new wedding ring, asked a few strategic questions, and began telling me about his son's diet and his fondness for the local paddling pool, "which he pisses in unfailingly". At a dinner party where we knew only the hosts, a late-arriving couple sat next to us and explained that their baby was vomiting all the time. "*Projectile* vomiting at that," she specified. "He's got this thing in his throat that makes it come out at, like,100 miles an hour." I interviewed a pop star in Havana a while back, a man infamous for his hatred of journalists (the feeling was mutual). Our conversation was progressing poorly, he implacable behind a pair of wraparound sunglasses and more interested in his cigar than he was my questions. Towards the end of our meeting, by now clutching at straws in the hope of making some kind of connection, I mentioned that my girlfriend was six months pregnant. Instantaneously, his frown lifted. He removed his sunglasses and his clear blue eyes pooled. He shook me by the hand, called for drinks and offered me a Cuban cigar, revealing that he and his partner were also trying for a baby. For the next half hour, that's all we spoke about. The subject had transformed him into someone capable of expressing emotion for one other than himself, a side of his character no one had previously witnessed, at least in public.

And now here I was having to hear about the out-of-control bowel movements of a pair of twins.

"No idea how they got it," the Venetian blinds man continued, "but I've never seen anything like it. The poor darlings. They just stood there on the kitchen lino, naked from the waist down, legs open wide. Out it came, like hot brown soup."

My own daughter has yet to succumb to the runs, but she is actively courting danger as if it were her birthright. We are in the garden now, because it is unusually warm for April, and she is standing proud on the garden table. Her mother would never let her stand on the table, but her mother isn't here. Laughing, she runs to the edge and launches herself into the air and my awaiting arms. She does this again and again, laughing loud and clear with each jump, a sound so intensely delightful that I find I'd do anything to perpetuate it. When I texted Julie back to tell her that I was doing fine, no calamity yet and certainly no diarrhoea, I also invited her over for lunch, knowing that she'd turn me down, given the late notice and my current circumstance. But she said yes to the invitation, and so I now invite Richard as well, convinced I could get a mini college reunion going here. He says yes, too.

It is only as I'm walking to the train station an hour later to pick them both up that I realise this means I will no longer be all alone with my daughter this weekend. I wonder whether what I'm doing here is calling in the cavalry, perhaps doubting my own potential for coping without assistance. Even worse, have my friends so readily agreed to come and see me at the drop of a hat because they too fear for my daughter, home alone in the company of a man who hasn't a clue?

● ● ●

It feels strange not to be walking out with a pushchair – the pushchair once so alien to me, now practically an extension of my fingertips

— but because Amaya is upright these days, and because I rather want to show off just how well she can walk, I leave it at home in favour of the new reins I've bought, which are strapped to her torso and effectively act like a dog leash. She totters enthusiastically in front of me, often tripping in the pavement's cracks. Whenever this happens, I simply yank the leash up and she dangles before me like a puppet. It's quite comical. Much like the baby sling, this method of transport garners me much attention from passing shoppers, mostly women, who each smile at me with forceful emotion, cooing at the doting father with his cute daughter. It's an addictive feeling, the attention doing wonders for my ego. Briefly, I toy with the idea of striking up a conversation with one of these women, one of the prettier ones, and suggesting to them that I'm actually a lone parent bringing up my child by myself, the sadness conveyed in my voice indicative that a tragedy has perhaps occurred to put me in such a position. It strikes me that this could be the most powerful chat-up line in the entire canon, instant confirmation to an available female of my strength of character, and the commitment I am so evidently capable of. It is not a train of thought I entertain for long, though. My flirting could lead to an affair, which in turn could lead to another pregnancy, another baby, some new reins and, one day not too distant, another Saturday afternoon alone with the infant, another conversation with another pretty woman, and a vicious circle that knows no tangible end.

Julie arrives. As we catch up, my daughter tugs at her leash, and I allow her to sink to her knees for a canine-like examination of the pavement. When she stands again, she looks up at us both, grinning broadly, to show us what she has salvaged from the ground. Between her lips is a blackened cigarette stub. A passer-by offers her a light.

Richard arrives shortly after, and we wander home via the supermarket, where we pick up provisions. Back in my garden, my guests prepare an al fresco lunch, while in the fridge I find some mineral water and a half-carton of orange juice. Behind a cauliflower on the bottom shelf, I discover a forgotten bottle of champagne. I open it.

Some time after lunch, following a 90 minute nap that I'm inexpressibly grateful she took, Amaya awakens and seeks attention from three people for whom cold champagne on a hot day has proved debilitating. We need coffee and a change of scenery, so I suggest the local child-friendly café. When we arrive, my friends look at me in open derision. Of all the places we could go to on a day like today, they seem to be saying, we end up in this, a part-café, part-crèche concoction, full of screaming children and nursing mothers. They'd rather go elsewhere.

I tell them that it's either this or nothing. Along with restaurants and bars, cafés have become no-go areas for us, particularly as our child is the kind who seeks calamitous adventure beneath every table. Which is why this particular coffee house is a godsend, a lifeline for beleaguered parents, because here you can sink into comfortable armchairs while your offspring runs riot in comparative safety. The parents here all look the same: grateful and relieved, the mothers chatting amongst themselves, the fathers hiding behind newspapers. Richard and Julie seem uncomfortable to be here, but I don't, not any more. These are my people now.

I never used to feel this way, not least when I came here with Amaya alone on weekdays. During the week, this place is dominated entirely by mothers, many of them breast-feeding without compunction, and consequently unhappy to find a man within their midst, especially a man whose innocent staring can so easily be misconstrued.

My daughter, of course, has never had any such reservations about the place. She loves it. The moment she is freed from her reins now, she bolts off towards the other children. We watch on with amusement as she kisses a toddler she has never, as far as I'm aware, previously met. I buy the coffee, and we sit around chatting until Julie alerts my attention to something. Amaya is sat at a wooden kitchen set – cooker, sink, an assortment of cutlery – and a boy older and broader than her approaches, attempting to shoulder her away from the pots and pans. My daughter stands her ground with admirable tenacity, but the boy grabs her by the hair and pulls her backwards until she is on the floor and crying loudly. Richard and Julie turn to look at me, intrigued as to my next move. I look back, wondering much the same thing. I still have no clear idea quite what the correct response to such an incident is. Instinctively, I want to smack the little fucker against the far wall for daring to lay a hand on my girl, but his father may be bigger than me, so I don't. Elena would know what to do, but Elena is in Dublin, and though I am tempted to phone her to ask, I don't have the time. Affirmative action is required. Slowly I stand, my hands clammy with nerves. I take a single step forward.

Fortunately, I am not compelled, this time, to do anything further, because a young mother rushes up to what is clearly her son, and forces an apology out of him. By now, Amaya has quite forgotten the incident and is striding off towards a vacant plastic chair. When she gets there, she finds another girl has beaten her to it. But this is no longer a deterrent. She grabs the girl by the hair and sends her tumbling to the ground much as she had been just minutes before. Dog eats dog. She sits, her expression one of sublime achievement. My friends look at me once more, grinning. I stand again, breathe deeply, and walk forwards.

The more time I spend in this place, the more I come to understand how we all end up the way we do.

●●●

Richard and Julie had originally intended to stay only for lunch, but somehow it is now eleven o'clock at night and they are still here. Amaya is fast asleep upstairs, the kitchen table is strewn with the remains of a Japanese takeaway, and we are horizontal after a second bottle of wine. The running theme of our conversation is how I am effectively drunk on duty, and failing to exhibit anything even resembling fatherly responsibility.

"Elena would kill you if she knew," Richard suggests as they leave.

As if to taunt me, Amaya breaks two full weeks of uninterrupted nights' sleep by waking at 3.30, wailing plaintively. The room spins when I clamber to my feet, then turns liquid and sideways as I try to make my way towards her. I fall to my knees at the cot, and she soon quietens as I commence rubbing her back, an apparent preference of hers when combined with repetitive shushings. I'm praying right now that she falls asleep quickly, that her howls are not indication that she is in fact ill. I don't want to consider this possibility; it's too terrifying, because if I have to take her to hospital now, the medical staff will smell the alcohol on me. Elena will divorce me; I'll be lucky to be granted weekend access by a judge keen to set an example. I make my repeated *shh* noises, whose top notes become increasingly shrill with pleading. The longest twenty minutes of my life elapse until her breathing becomes steady, and she goes under again. I return to my room and collapse onto the mattress. Relief puddles around me.

If there is a more potent motivator for the sudden pursuit of goodness than an overwhelming sensation of guilt, then I'd like to meet it. In the morning, I am up and showered before my daughter has even stirred. I banish my hangover with jets of cold water. I can't afford to feel bad today. I have responsibilities, and I aim to meet every last one of them. By the time I tiptoe into her room, I find that she is already awake and sitting up, leafing through a book and smiling at me as if last night never happened. I lift her up and take her over to the window, where I open the curtains to a bright Sunday morning. Looking down into the garden, her eyes grow wide and she begins to point to one corner with mounting excitement. There, we see a mother fox and her six cubs, tiny and gorgeous, the colour of autumn and full of the bounce of new life. We are captivated by the sight until, after ten minutes, she wants to get down and do something else. I place her on the floor, where she starts to play with her plastic cups, which she likes to stack and stack again. I stay by the window to watch the mother fox tending its young. From behind me, I hear a sound that I don't quite register, a kind of strangled gasp for breath, a muffled choke. Looking at the foxes, I remember that I always wanted a puppy as a child, but growing up in a block of flats prevented that. I'm wondering now about the possibility of adopting one of these cubs. Amaya would love it. The choking noise comes again, and this time it reaches me fully. I turn around.

I see my daughter still on the floor, her face now a bright and urgent purple, mouth gaping. Her eyes are huge with panic, and she is gesturing at her chest. I drop to the floor and begin to pat her back, gently at first, then harder. Nothing. I have no idea what I am supposed to do, and for several painful moments I draw a complete blank. She continues pointing. I tilt her head back and look inside her mouth to see that something large and yellow has become wedged at the opening of her throat. I insert an index finger and manage to get quick purchase on the object, which slides out with merciful ease. It is half of the plastic casing of a Kinder Egg surprise, slippery with saliva. Amaya is now breathing freely. She pants like a dog. She clambers up onto my lap and hugs me tightly, pressing her hot body against mine. She has never done this before, and I hug her back with equal force, an avalanche of guilt mixing with overwhelming relief. Elena always says that we should never take our eyes off her, not even for a moment, but I'd always responded that this was impossible and impractical, and that she was overcautious and overreacting. Humility is a painful thing to navigate early on a Sunday morning.

I think I read somewhere once that your child's first firm memory doesn't come until they are at least three years old. This is good to know. I've got two years to stop making reckless mistakes like this, and to ensure that she never turns round to me one day as an eighteen-year-old to remind me, in a room full of people, that I'd once inadvertently almost let her choke to death.

• • •

For the remainder of the day, I am a model parent. I feed her, play with her, keep the television off and the volume of my iPod at an acceptable level. I even sniff her arse regularly to check the state of her nappy (something I see many mothers do, Elena included, but *never* fathers), and I change her every couple of hours so that she is always dry and comfortable. We go for a walk along the river where I introduce her to the ducks and swans, and I buy her a yoghurt drink that she pours all down her T-shirt and onto her jeans. We spend 30 minutes at the playground which, like the café, feels far more female than it does male, despite the proximity of adventure and danger. There are several mothers at the swings and slides, each of them relaxed and confident with one another and fully interactive with their children. Those fathers that are present look much more awkward, uncomfortable in a way I imagine many of us are in nightclubs, unsure of just how uninhibited we can allow ourselves to be in this public place. Many of us are consequently tense-limbed, hands firmly in pockets. But not me, not today. Today I make an extra effort, pushing her high on the swings, accompanying her on the roundabout until we very nearly see my Japanese takeaway from last night again, and helping her up and down the slide until the sun sets and the temperature drops. At home after dinner, I give her her evening bath and allow her to soak the sponge and push it into my face repeatedly, something she finds helplessly amusing. The day, uninterrupted by the influence of selfish childless friends or alcohol, has been perfect.

At eight o'clock, she is lying in her cot in her growbag, with only the light from the rotating musical mobile keeping the room from total darkness. In the shadows, her eyes find mine and lock on. A beautiful smile melts slowly across her face, filled with benevolence and unambiguous sentiment. This, I become convinced, is reciprocal love finally asserting itself. Tears flood my eyes.

I sit on the floor by the bars of the cot and allow her to fall asleep with my finger in her grasp, setting an unwise precedent for the nights to come, but right now I don't care. I just want to be right here alongside her, to draw out the moment for as long as I can.

Fatherhood does strange things to you. It ages you prematurely and denies you sleep, sex and a social life, but it softens you as well and makes you sentimental in ways that rarely look good in print, but that in the flesh feel so very valuable, injecting warmth into the parts where previously there resided only cold.

Once she is fully asleep and I have managed to remove my finger from her fist, I head downstairs to watch television. *Kolya* is on, an Oscar-winning Czech film about a confirmed, late-middle-aged bachelor whose life is turned upside down when he has to look after a young boy. I first saw this film several years ago, and though I found it mildly diverting, I considered it ultimately a lot of mawkish guff. Now I find it almost unbearably profound, and its poignancy knocks the wind out of me. Elena comes home towards the end, at the moment the man has to return the boy to his mother, who has come back to whisk him off to a brand-new life in Germany. He is utterly bereft at the child's departure, and as my wife bends down to kiss me, she sees the tears streaming down my cheeks. Instantly, she panics.

"What is it? Is it Amaya? What happened? What have you done?"

I shake my head, smiling. I decide not to tell her about the drinking and the choking. It'll wait.

The film's credits roll, and then I speak.

"I think maybe my daughter loves me," I say.

She looks at me, confused. "And you've only just realised?"

Twelve

I may have been a little rash, actually, because my daughter may not, after all, love me, at least not in any proactive way. Granted, she uses me frequently as facilitator, which usually involves me lifting and carrying her wherever she demands it, but then she promptly discards me once I have fulfilled my limited purpose. She is far too busy circumnavigating her unfolding new world to bother much with me, frankly, and she remains at heart, for now at least, her mother's girl. When I am not in the house, Elena tells me, she regularly asks for Daddy, her voice a pleading, heart-tugging cry. But when I am in, it's Mummy all the way. Where once we used to take turns in putting her to bed at night, she has begun to insist that this is done solely now by her mother. If I try to overrule, she lets out a murderous shriek and collapses in a heap on the floor at my feet, repeatedly intoning *Mummy, Mummy, Mummy*. It is difficult not to be mortally offended.

But then our daughter is twenty months old now, and becoming abjectly wilful, experimenting with temper and attitude, pushing boundaries and pressing buttons. Gradually, I come to see this for myself, and it is to my great, point-scoring relief that she soon displays similar unfeeling towards her mother as well. When she picks her up from the crèche these days, Elena tells me, Amaya at first ignores her, then wags a finger in her face, saying "*No!* Don't want to. *Go!*" And then attempts to push her out the door.

And yet at other times, she is an absolute skyscraping delight, so full of giddy good humour and a desire to be dangled upside down that it is difficult to believe I could be having a better time with anyone else anywhere else in the world. If only it lasted. She will change again, abruptly and apropos of nothing, her mood swings increasingly schizophrenic, each day her face a new mask that we try hard to discern, understand, second-guess.

One evening, I cycle to pick her up from the crèche. It is a dark autumnal night, the clocks having gone back at the weekend, not yet properly cold but pleasantly cool. The ride through the park is an exquisite velvety black, the proximity of rutting deer making the journey more exotic than suburban London has any right to be. As I arrive, I spy my daughter and her friend Lizzie in one of the play-rooms, walking on top of a set of low tables pushed together, soft mattresses surrounding them. Lizzie is leading. I stand at the door watching them both for several silent moments before she notices me, this cute little girl with the severe fringe. She stops dead in her tracks and peers inquisitively through wary brown eyes. Behind her, Amaya stops and also now sees me. She lets loose a scream of what I hope is pleasure and gives her friend a forceful shove in the back to get her out of the way, then runs towards me at full pelt. Lizzie flies forward and slices through the air, falling flat on her face. Her care worker reaches for another incident report, her umpteenth of the day.

"She's been quite hyper today…" she tells me afterwards, stroking Amaya's head as Amaya holds onto my leg in an attempt to yank me towards the exit, the bicycle and home. The care worker is tired; her silent ellipsis speaks volumes. Though she doesn't ask for it, I apologise profusely for any trouble caused.

Amaya lets go of me and now runs into the bathroom. The crèche bathroom is a bemusing place, built as it is for infants, its toilets and sinks standing no higher than my shin. My daughter is obsessed with water at the moment, the drinking of it and the pouring of it from one receptacle to the other and all down her clothes and onto the floor. I watch her fetch a paper towel from the dispenser, then run to the taps and soak it. Now she begins to clean the wall methodically, then throws the sodden towel into the kiddie-sized bin. She does this two, three times, before moving back into the playroom, me following with her coat and a pleading expression. Here, she spies a toy in the white-knuckle clutches of a blond boy. It's not her toy, but such subtleties are lost to her right now. She wants it. Two things happen simultaneously: the boy lifts the toy out of her reach, and I begin to force her outstretched arm into the coat sleeve, before bending the other at the elbow. In this fleeting instant, she is transformed beyond all recognition. Her face turns scarlet. It explodes at the nostrils, the noise immense. People turn to watch. She wants the toy, but the boy won't budge. He smiles. I lift her up, her body squirming like an eel, and stagger into the next room. Her rage increases, her cries becoming more shrill until they break through the sound barrier altogether, now silent to everyone except dogs. I lose my grip and she slides to the floor, banging her head on the wall as she goes, which prompts the crying to drop an octave and become audible once more. A suited man walks past, his placid daughter's hand in his. He looks down at me with sympathy.

"That's a relief," he smiles. "I thought only mine did that."

Summoning up hidden reserves of strength and patience from God knows where, I manage to zip up her coat and drag her out to the bike. I buckle her into the child seat and cycle away from the scene as quickly as possible. We ride through the dark park, dangerously close to the nodding antlers and the bambi young that daringly cross our path. Such things normally make her sigh with joy, but not tonight. Tonight, she is still choking in apoplectic fury behind me, her thrusting body causing the bike to swerve and sway. The path widens as we approach the exit, and I almost hit a woman trailing a golden retriever on a long leash, both only partially lit by the street light that hugs the pavement beyond the perimeter wall.

"*Dog! Dog!*"

Suddenly, the crying has stopped and her melodic voice has broken back through, like sunshine cleaving through storm clouds. I turn to see her pointing and exclaiming at the animal. The rage has gone, promptly vanished into thin air. Her face may be red and blotchy, but she looks happier than I have ever seen her before. Of course she does. She has just seen a dog in a park. Could life get any better than this?

The first time we lose our daughter is a key moment in our distinctly separate development as parents, six minutes of mounting horror that her mother and father deal with in two very different ways. I am already yawning as we enter the department store, where Elena needs to buy something suitable for a wedding. She takes three possibilities with her into the small changing room, and Amaya, desperate for freedom from the pushchair, goes with her. But the changing room is small and fails to contain her for long. Soon she is back out front with me, trailing sticky hands over successive rails of clothes, while I watch on fondly. After a moment, Elena emerges in pale blue, low-cut silk, with ornate detail on the sleeve and hem. She is barefoot but, she says, "Imagine me in heels, like this", and rises herself up on tiptoes.

"Where's Amaya?" she asks suddenly.

I point into what is now thin air, as she has already moved on. I remain entirely calm.

"She's just running around," I say.

"Yes, but *where?*"

She doesn't wait for a response, but bunches up the party dress in a tight fist and begins to run. She goes that way, I the other, and the further we get from one another the louder I can hear her voice calling out our daughter's name. I don't call out at all, not simply because I know she never responds to "Amaya" if she doesn't feel like it, but also because I don't want to draw attention to myself. Plus, if I allow myself to panic, then that would suggest that she is indeed gone, vanished. Trouble is, she really is nowhere to be seen.

"Have you found her?"

"No."

Elena begins to ask people, sales assistants and customers, whether they have seen a little girl, blonde, in jeans, a pink top, tiny trainers with flashing lights on the heel. Suddenly, I see myself at a press conference before television cameras, asking for my daughter to be returned to me safe and sound, *please*.

"I thought you were supposed to be watching her?" she says to me sharply.

There is terror in her face now, and I've never seen that before: a kind of blind, helpless panic. It is horrible.

"I was."

Because this happens shortly after the time of Madeleine McCann's disappearance, people everywhere are on an exaggerated high alert when it comes to the safety of their children. I think it distinctly unlikely that our local department store harbours in its midst someone with a propensity for child snatching, but then no doubt the McCanns thought likewise in Portugal. And yet still I don't run, swallowing any fear and determining to remain as level-headed as simple logic tells me I should. She can't have got far; we'll find her soon enough. I watch, at Elena's insistence, sales assistants radioing one another Amaya's description. Store detectives are told to keep an eye out. Elena is off again, scouring aisles, still in the dress she has not yet paid for. The blue suits her. Whenever she catches my eye in our search, her look is reproachful. This is *my* fault.

On this occasion, our daughter re-enters our lives on the hip of a heaven-sent shop assistant, an innocent smile on her face. I'm aware of every last fibre in my body unclenching. Elena fights back the tears, relief and anger combined.

"She was all the way over by the exit, about to leave the shop," the sales assistant is telling us. "Lucky I found her when I did."

One would think I'd learn from a fright such as this, but I don't. I baldly refuse to keep her on a tight leash. Children roam; it's part of childhood, isn't it? Elena thinks otherwise, and it is on this subject that we clash over more than any other in early parenthood.

I wasn't invited to the wedding for which Elena required the blue silk dress, but I am invited to the reception afterwards, our daughter too. It is held in the grounds of a beautiful countryside hotel on a high summer's day, and we arrange ourselves across the tables in preparation for a long, pleasant meal. As we eat and drink, a band plays wedding favourites while the assembled children, of which Amaya is by far the youngest, attempt to dance.

Before we'd arrived, we had agreed to take turns in looking after our daughter while we mingled. Elena would have her through the starter and main course, and she would be all mine during dessert and grown-up dancing. But Amaya is excited to be surrounded by so many new people and is difficult to contain, seemingly intent on introducing herself, as only twenty-month-olds can, to everyone individually. She spends much of the afternoon and evening wandering the tables, simultaneously charming and annoying the guests. I have trouble keeping up with her.

By the time our table has opened its fifth bottle of wine, I haven't so much forgotten about her as sidelined her in favour of conversation with those around me. We are miles from a busy street, in what seems to be a totally safe environment. She is surrounded by other children.

And so the shriek, when it comes, is out of all proportion, a hysterical reaction from one of the guests whose name I never quite catch. But this guest is a parent herself, and this is what counts to everyone else. She is standing tall and shouting for the parents of the little girl in white who has strayed, alone, towards the small staircase at the perimeter of the hotel's manicured gardens, steps that lead down to an unmanned swimming pool.

Elena gives me a look of unadulterated censure, and so I stop talking to the man beside me and, aware I am being watched, stride casually over towards my daughter. Together, we walk down the steps and over towards the pool, which is cool and pale blue in the early evening light. We stoop at its edge and dip our hands into it, and she laughs when I flick droplets of water at her. We then walk back hand in hand up the stairs and across the lawn, back to the table, where she sits in my lap and helps me finish the chocolate mousse that, in truth, I needed no help in finishing.

Amongst this group of people, many of whom I'll never see again, we are subsequently referred to as the Bad Parents (Elena was *most* unhappy about the use of the plural), the kind you read about in papers, who one day allow their children to run amok near hotel swimming pools, and the next to play chicken on public railway lines. Towards the end of the wedding night, the shrieking mother decides to chastise me for my lack of responsibility. I can smell the wine coming off her.

"Seriously, you should never take your eyes off them. And neither should your wife. There's no second chances if things go wrong, you know."

I wonder what this woman would have thought of me a year on, during our first family holiday together, when Amaya takes it upon herself to suddenly flee the beach, where we have been building sandcastles, and climb the 150 snaking steps that lead to the nearest Spar, where she helps herself to a Chup-A-Chups lollipop? I don't make an initial chase for her, not just because 150 snaking steps is a lot for a 39-year-old to manage in the punishing heat of a Spanish afternoon, but because I had initially thought she was simply return-ing to the Postman Pat ride in the nearby beach café. But Amaya is quick, very quick, and fools me.

She comes back down minutes later, beaming, and demanding I unwrap the shoplifted lollipop for her. Elena sees my face break out into a proud smile at this feat of derring-do, and refuses to talk to me for the rest of the afternoon.

• • •

This remarkable wilfulness, I soon learn, is typical of her age. They call it, the experts, the terrible twos. I've been warned that they are not particularly numerically correct, that they can, in fact, stretch all the way from one to three and beyond. With our daughter, there was a brief window of sublime pleasure between the ages of twelve and sixteen months, a time when she was still wholeheartedly dependent on us, beguiling and adorable. But now she is heading for her second birthday, and already busy asserting her independence. We live in a perennial state of power struggle these days, each of us trying to assert an enduring dominance. She no longer wants to be fed by us, for example. She'd rather do it herself, even if much of her food ends up on the floor. She gets irate if we attempt to apply toothpaste to her toothbrush in the evening because that is something she now does alone. If we dress her in a pair of socks that she doesn't for whatever reason like, she will yank them off and toss them over the side of the changing table. She chooses which shoes to wear on any given day, irrespective of whether her mother thinks they match the colour of her clothes. I once dressed her in a nappy with Tigger on it when, as any fool knows, she'd wanted the one with Winnie the Pooh. She became instantaneously livid. And she is beginning to issue instructions to the both of us, which she does not anticipate will remain ignored for long.

I am lying in bed, or perhaps I am sitting at the kitchen table. I may even be relaxing on the sofa. Wherever I am, I'm enjoying a brief respite that I invariably feel I deserve. But my daughter has decided that she wants something that, like so much of what she wants, continues to lie just out of her reach. She approaches me, grabs a finger in her bunched up little fist and threatens to pop my knuckle unless I get up and follow her. She requires assistance, and why else am I here? She will require assistance on any number of occasions during any single day, as curious as she is tireless. She wants cheese triangles from the fridge, water from the tap, a bread knife from the drawer, and then she is off again. Occasionally, she will dispense a little tenderness along the way, a grateful look here, a brief hug there, but already she knows to deliver these sparingly, aware perhaps of their currency, their power, and mindful never to overdo them. The best way to keep me keen is by giving me back affection in morsels only, knowing full well that I will do anything for that brief, fleeting, narcotic high.

In this fashion, she has become the very epicentre of our world. Not in a cloying, sentimental way, but simply because she demands it thus. Mussolini would have admired her dictator-like qualities. From me, she gets what she wants and when she wants it. The cost of ignoring her or, worse, resisting her, is just too high. Though her mother fights to maintain a kind of hard line, sensibly adamant that she learn manners and etiquette and decorum, I am considerably the weaker parent. True, I do it largely for a quiet life, but I'd be lying if I didn't say that I do it also simply to see her smile, to bask in the reflected glory of a temporary happiness that I alone have bestowed.

A weekend's worth of all this boundary testing can take an inevitable toll, and by early evening, I am feeling old, broken and depleted. Thank God, then, for those children's TV channels and a merciful half an hour in front of a soft putty world of honking puppets and dayglo colours. I am sat alongside her on the sofa for this, and she is pressed up tight against me, my arm around her, my hand in both of hers. My gaze falls not on the television but rather her profile, in all its button-nosed perfection. She is quiet and concentrated, her expression rapt and bewitched. It's a temporary state only, but a wonderful thing to see.

Elena watches me from the doorway.

"You adore her, don't you?" she says. "You absolutely adore her."

For reasons beyond me, I'm not ready to admit this out loud, not just yet.

But she's right. I do.

John Duerden, the absent father

I have no real defining memories of my father, and those I can muster he probably wouldn't thank me for. There are few remaining photographs of him, but those I do possess picture him as young and blond and self-consciously good-looking, whippet thin and posing behind a pair of sunglasses. In these photos, he seems as open and gregarious as my mother is tight and closed, the free spirit to her domesticity and good sense.

I remember him only in snippets: coming home from work one night in a bad mood, his temper made worse to find his sons fighting. He roared. I remember him lost behind a newspaper on Sunday afternoons, a pint of beer by his feet, and him asking me to massage his head in return for all the change in his pocket, which I could then add to my Manchester United piggybank. I remember him telling us to be quiet, that he was watching the news, *Upstairs Downstairs*, had had a long day at work and just wanted a moment's peace, was that so much to ask? And I remember the late-night arguments he would have with my mother in the kitchen while my brother and I lay unsleeping in our shared bedroom, all too aware of the raised voices, the slammed doors, the wretched weeping. After particularly bad arguments, he would disappear for days on end, with no word of contact until his sudden return, always unannounced and out of the blue, beaming, laughing again, a force of nature, with a brand-new camera to dazzle us with or, one time, a stylish white Rover with cracked leather brown seats. This would send my mother half crazed, money we didn't have spent on luxury items we couldn't afford.

The contradictions between them were vast, and often unnavigable. With him gone, we'd be barely scraping by, my mother eking out a vegetable casserole for several days because the fridge was otherwise empty, as was her purse. With him back, we'd be pushing the speed limit down quiet streets in the kind of car we normally saw only on *The Sweeney*. He dressed well, above his station, in camel hair coats and leather jackets, Sloane Square stylish in a pocket of London where few could ever afford to be. On our council estate, he stuck out like a sore thumb. I remember – and this was an odd sensation for an eight-year-old – being mildly embarrassed by him and his swagger.

I remember good things, too. Him introducing me to Laurel and Hardy, The Beatles, Spike Milligan and *Fawlty Towers*. He could draw beautifully, and would often help two-dimensionalise on the page Jao and Jingsdoo, the imaginary monsters I'd decided were living in the front-door frame of our flat. But mostly, I remember his absence. He kept long hours at work, and was required to travel frequently.

And then one day, a day that must have seemed inevitable to us at the time, he stopped coming home altogether. We were a one-parent family now, positively fashionable. They spoke of our kind on the TV news.

Something else I remember were the visitation rights, or rather how they never happened. One day he was around, the next he wasn't. There were no uncomfortable trips to the zoo, no awkward lunches at the old Wimpy's down the road. But this didn't matter. He had never been around very much in the first place. Now he was around even less. On my first birthday after my parents' separation, he was due to pay us a visit. My mother had baked a cake, and we wouldn't light the candles until he arrived. He was late, but we waited. We waited until long after my bedtime, until it became clear that he wasn't going to show at all. There were no phone calls offering explanation or apology the following day, just a swelling silence. And that was the point for me, at ten years old, when I drew a line under the relationship between my father and me. I could do just as well without him, and would. My mother was going to be relying on me from now on. I had to be strong, if only for her sake.

A year later, maybe more, he called out of the blue, saying he had three tickets for the Charity Shield. I forget now who was playing, but football was everything to me then and I wasn't about to turn down the opportunity of going to Wembley. I brought a friend with me (safety in numbers), but it didn't help. My father and I were strangers now, the tension so thick that it remained unbreachable for the full 90 minutes and all the extra time the world could throw at us. When he dropped me off at home afterwards, my mother hovering anxiously by the kitchen window, it felt like we'd come to a definitive parting of the waves. I would hear nothing more from him until my teenage years were almost over.

At eighteen, like all eighteen-year-olds, I was desperate for the onset of proper adulthood, and all the independence that that implied. I had spent much of my adolescence necessarily old before my time, an earnest co-parent to my younger brother and an emotional crutch for my mother, whose clinical depression would not be diagnosed for another decade at least. I craved freedom, breathing space, some time at last for myself. I was done with families.

The morning I came of age, a letter arrived. A birthday card with, inside it, a photograph of a man, woman and young child, a girl. I didn't keep it for long, and I never memorised its contents, but I do recall the gist of it today: "Hello son, happy birthday, an adult now, water under the bridge, I've a new family (see photo), what say we meet up and start over?"

This was the father that had abandoned me several years previously, the man who had smashed my mother's heart and left inside her a bitterness from which she would never recover. By this stage of my life, I was all too aware that my mother was hardly a saint; in fact, she was a difficult woman, at once inspirationally strong for her sons but also mired in self-doubt and self-hate, and so very full of sadness. My father, the way I saw it, was surely partly responsible for this, but only partly. And though I was always too stolid a person to ever actively feel hatred towards him, there was little warmth flowing his way either. I could never have have entertained the idea of meeting him again, even if I'd wanted to. It would have destroyed my mother. And so I wrote a letter back, polite but curt, saying thanks but no thanks.

I never consciously missed him, never knowingly thought about him. I hadn't ever really got to know him in the first place, so there was precious little to pine after, to mourn. But now, as a late 30-something, after having become a father myself and started on this project, I'd spoken to other men who'd told me how having children themselves had made them reassess their own paternal relationships. This resulted, in some cases, in them appreciating their fathers in a way they never had before. Ashley Walters told me getting to know his dad was one of the most valuable things he had ever done; John Simpson was amazed I had not contacted my own father sooner. Adrienne Burgess told me not to waste any more time, to track him down, ask him whatever the hell I wanted to, to demand answers, explanations, and also, just in case, to have a therapist's number on hand should it prove confusing, complicated and unravellingly painful.

I was adamant, however, that I wouldn't, my reason simply that I'd never done so before. If I didn't need him then, I certainly don't now. Friends considered me odd, cold, in denial; Elena wondered aloud whether I wasn't being a little rash. And so, initially for the sake of the exercise, I decided to sit down and write him a letter. It had been 30 years since I'd seen him last. I didn't quite know where to start, so that's precisely how I eventually did: *I don't know quite where to start. But I'll try nevertheless.* Writing, *Hello, John, it's Nick, your son,* sounded melodramatic to me, but then I suppose that if this isn't a perfect excuse for melodrama, what is? I finished the letter, read it over, put it to one side and got on with my work. My daughter's birthday was looming, her second, then it was Christmas, then New Year. I forgot all about the letter – on purpose, mostly – until January 2nd came along, traditionally a quiet time of the year, with little to fill it but remembering things previously discarded. I read the letter again, found an envelope, a stamp, and sent it to the last known address I had for him.

A day later, my phone rang.

I was on my bicycle when he called, cruising through a red light and swerving past pedestrians. In my free hand, I carried a large baguette, still warm from the baker's oven. I'd already bitten off the nub, and it was busy melting on my tongue as the phone vibrated. I stopped pedalling, swallowed hard and reached for it. The screen said private number.

"Nick? It's…" And in that hesitant pause, I *knew*. "… it's John. Your father."

Our conversation was brief, formal and polite. His voice didn't trigger any aural memory; he could have been anyone, his accent educated, his sentences economical, not a single word wasted. He said he could meet for lunch, and I suggested the following day. *See you tomorrow* had rarely sounded so seismic.

He has chosen to meet outside the Victoria Palace Theatre in Victoria at 12.30. He is there before I am, and as I approach from a distance, still two traffic light crossings away, my gaze passes quickly over the neatly dressed old man standing to the left of the main exit doors as I try to pick him out amidst the lunchtime crowd. But by the time I make it to the second crossing, I realise, of course, that it is him, that this old man is my father. I would not have recognised him. He is my height and still comparatively trim. He is wearing the colours of autumn: brown and beige, in corduroy and cotton. He carries with him a man's handbag of the kind perennially popular in Milan but that never quite caught on here. I have a sudden memory that hits me out of nowhere: of him carrying a similar version of this back in the late 1970s. It crippled me with shame then, not simply because I was, and remain, terribly self-conscious, but also because our part of town didn't look favourably upon metrosexual men ahead of their time. I feel no such shame now.

I walk up to him. We make eye contact. The seconds slow to minutes as we take one another in. Beneath a flat cap I imagine speaks volumes of his Yorkshire youth, I see what is essentially my brother's face almost perfectly reproduced, albeit considerably older. He wears glasses and a well-tended beard, pure white. He smells faintly but pleasantly of aftershave. I say his name.

"John?"

He looks shocked and surprised and happy at once, and is very likely as nervous as me. He removes a glove and shakes my hand.

"I wouldn't have recognised you," I say to him for want of anything better to say, and he responds, "No, I suppose you wouldn't. It's been... it's been a while."

We settle upon an Italian restaurant a minute's walk away. I'm grateful for its proximity, but it is still a minute of palpable awkwardness: what to say, how to say it, the vague niceties required of two strangers suddenly forced to make small talk. When we are shown to our table, he removes his hat to reveal a full head of hair. I take encouragement from this. Perhaps I'll avoid baldness, too?

"Shall we get the order out of the way first?" he says as the waiter presents us with menus. We order pasta, a glass of wine for me, some fizzy water for him, and then we are left to our own devices and a conversation that has to fill in the gaps of three full decades and an awful lot of respective incident.

Given that my brother was someone I could only ever communicate with through argument, I find it disconcerting, and slightly troubling, to look into much the same face. But physical similarity aside, they couldn't be more different. My father is cordial, courteous and polite, and somehow restrained, as if fearful perhaps of putting a foot wrong. His eyes are still the light blue I remember from my youth, gentle and soft and, right now at least, slightly cowed.

When I think of it later, the lunch seemed to speed by in no time, but it actually endures a full two hours. I ask him tame questions at first, and he fills me in with fleeting episodes of my forgotten early life. He tells me that when I was just four weeks old, my mother, who had occasionally worked as an interpreter, landed a job with Cliff Richard, then at the peak of his fame. He was planning an assault on the Italian charts and wanted to sing one of his songs in the native language. He required not just a literal translation of the lyrics but also coaching on how to get the cadence just right, while still being able to curl his lip like an imitation Elvis. My mother received £50 for the evening's tuition and came away convinced he was the perfect gentleman. That night was also the first time my father had been left alone with me in the small studio flat they would soon move out of. He was terrified, he says, of the colossal responsibility, and had nothing to help him cope except for some expressed milk in a bottle and a mental list of instructions on what to do in case I cried, crapped or worse. Instead, I did all three at once, sending him into a panic.

"But then I reached for Dr Spock," he says, and for the briefest of seconds I fear he is talking about *Star Trek*, "a parenting book *this* thick, but full of useful information. Anyway, it told me exactly what I needed to know to settle you. I've been grateful to him ever since."

We move on to more recent times, and he tells me that he spent much of the 1990s fighting illness, before contracting a superbug in hospital, the combination of both very nearly finishing him off. By the time he had fully recovered, his career in the travel industry had gone on without him and he was forced to look for something else. He now works in a funeral home. Having spent much of his professional life sending people off into the sun, he is now preparing them for an altogether different kind of journey. He tells me about his parents, my grandparents, and reminds me that they died back when I was in my early teens, he from bowel cancer, she from Alzheimer's. John – and he was always John to me, never Dad – is 64 now, three years shy of my own estimate for him, and twelve months away from retirement. He has been married for almost 30 years, lives in south London, and has a 22-year-old daughter, my half-sister. She is currently at university studying some or other ology, and is clearly his greatest achievement.

I learn a lot from him, but judging by our plates, it seems I may be doing more talking than he, because while he has finished his pasta, I'm barely a third of the way through mine. I worry, privately, that perhaps I am waffling on. I have a habit of doing so. He is clearly a good listener. He never once interrupts.

Eventually, I come round to asking him about my mother, their marriage and eventual separation. As he talks, picking over his words now with extreme care, the crows' feet around his eyes deepen. He says that he doesn't want to tell me anything that may contradict what I already know, and that he is fully appreciative that my mother is no longer here to contradict. But I encourage him anyway, and what he tells me does indeed contradict much of what I had come to regard as fact. No, my father never did cheat on her, though she forever had her suspicions. He says he felt loathed by her, and that she was increasingly jealous of the life he had outside of the family home. "I was very committed to my career, perhaps mistakenly, I realise now."

Their arguments made her angry, permanently so, and by the time they separated, she endeavoured to make the process of gaining access through the courts so protracted and painful that in the end he thought it best for all sides to give up and walk away.

"The worst thing I ever did," he says, adding that, "my failure as a father is something I will never recover from."

He tells me he has no memory of the no-show at my birthday and claims my mother never told him about it. He remembers the Charity Shield match and how much I had grown apart from him by then, acting as if I no longer wanted to know him. It hurt him deeply.

I ask him about the lack of letters and phone calls, and he says that my mother had explained neither would be welcome. She was punishing him, and in this she proved tenacious. Perhaps, I think to myself, he should have overridden all this, no matter how painful, and simply seen her anger for what it was? All those Fathers 4 Justice men never let any such obstacles deter *them*, but for whatever reason, they did my father. Perhaps, I also feel, he ultimately found it a little too easy to walk away and start again, although seeing him today, the way he looks at me with such regret, it doesn't seem as if anything that happened back then could be pronounced *easy*.

I'm not quite sure what to do with this new information, whether it should make me feel any different towards my mother. Instinctively, I want to honour her memory and think of all the mitigating circumstances. She had a lot to feel unhappy about, after all, ending up a mostly impoverished single parent in a block of flats in a downtrodden part of London. And so I don't think it does. She did what she did; she had her reasons. She and my father were not a natural match; I'm glad they separated. Rather than remaining in a loveless marriage for the rest of his life, my father decided to do something about it, and I can hardly blame him for that. I'd like to think I'd have done much the same thing in similar circumstances. If anything, I feel so very sorry for the both of them, though inevitably more for my mother, because my mother never did go on to find happiness a second time. My father did and, truly, good for him. His second marriage has been an enduring one and he has proven himself a good father, after all. Who could deny him the opportunity of that? Not me.

When I'm in the toilet, he pays the bill.

"The very least I can do," he says. "Allow me that."

The crows' feet deepen again now, and as they do so, I'm reminded that this meeting is, in so many ways, perhaps far more significant to him than it is to me. I don't mean this in an unfeeling, heart-as-stone way, but simply because a parent will always have more unconditional love for their child than a child ever will for their parent. I know my daughter will probably be much the same. I'm already trying to brace myself for the future agony of that.

The table is cleared. I look around to see that the restaurant has emptied.

"Right," he says, timid, hopeful. "Where do we go from here?"

All I know at this very moment is that I'm headed back to the station and home, but it's a good question. Where *do* we go from here? How do I find space in my life for a man of 64, to all intents and purposes a stranger to me? If I didn't feel I needed a father back then, can I possibly feel otherwise now? I ponder whether we have enough in common – outside of a barely tangible bloodline – to keep us in contact. He says he'd very much like to meet my wife and daughter, and for me to meet his family, just as he did all those years ago on the morning of my eighteenth birthday. I smile encouragingly, but when you've been without a family for so long, it rather makes you wonder how you'd fare if you found yourself having to endure one all over again. It's absolutely nothing like riding a bicycle. You do forget; I have.

I am glad I met with him today. It was a cautious meeting, inevitably, but a good one. He isn't the demon I'd decided he was all those years ago, but rather someone far more fragile and human than that. He's a nice man. In truth, I'm a little surprised. I'm also relieved.

But I've really no idea where we go from here and, as politely as I can muster, I tell him.

"Well, I'll leave the ball in your court," he says.

We walk back out together into the grey afternoon. He tells me to call him if I'd like to, but if not, then that's alright as well. Outside the theatre, we shake hands. He is heading that way, I the other. I say goodbye and turn to face the road.

The lights are red for pedestrians, but I see a break in the traffic and decide to make a run for it. Unfortunately, the bus I had thought was going straight on is actually turning left, and it swings hard and fast towards me. I'm forced to pick up pace, head down, legs up, and bolt for the safety of the kerb ahead. It's only afterwards that I think about what this must have looked like from his point of view, had he been watching me go. It would have looked as if I were running away from him, just as fast as my legs could carry me.

I hope he didn't think this. It would have been misleading.

Thirteen

Long before I ever had children myself, I thought I had them all worked out. They took from you and they took from you and then they deserted you, much like we had done with our own parents to a greater or lesser degree. What perplexed me was why anyone still bothered to have them in the face of this knowledge and that when they did, even amidst all the suffering and hardship, they would still stubbornly insist that it had all been worth it. Yes, children could be a nightmare and, yes, they brought with them so much stress and strain, but it was worth it. The good, they said, always far outweighed the bad.

And now I am one of them. Having children *is* hard. It's harder than I ever thought it would be, even more so than the parenting books would lead you to believe, and they hardly suggest it's a walk in the park. When Elena and I first got together, I committed myself to learning Spanish within a year as a public sign of my love for her. I soon gave up, however, not because my love had foundered, but simply because I thought it too much effort. I've always wanted to run the marathon but ultimately scotched any plans of actually doing so because the training seemed too much bother. Who wants to struggle into a pair of trainers at six in the morning for a pre-breakfast training run in the rain?

But both of these things are nothing to having a child, whose daily challenges are so myriad, and so bluntly and cruelly expressed that one is continually reminded just how steep a task it is, and how unending too, with its unfolding frustrations and fresh taunts. I am continually amazed now that so many people manage it at all, and it has given me a new-found respect for anyone that does. What selfless people they are. How gallant their readiness for sacrifice.

"I'm always surprised at the image the media feed us about having children," Professor Lorraine Sherr told me when we spoke recently. "They are always publishing photographs of women back in their bikinis and looking amazing five minutes after having given birth. It's terribly misleading when the reality is actually so very different. Having children is a destructive process, and no matter how much you prepare for it beforehand, you are still ultimately unprepared, if only because there are so many things to endure, many of which are akin to torture: food deprivation, for example, or sleep deprivation, both of which are the norm after having had a child. It really is a pronouncedly fragile time, and so why do the media do it? Why do they put happy pictures in magazines when the reality is quite so different?"

Sherr suggests that those new mothers and fathers that *do* thrive so soon after the birth of their child only manage this thanks to a coterie of nannies and carers and personal trainers and PAs. The rest of us have to make do with the occasional grandparent, in our case, very occasional. In the weeks and months that followed the birth of our daughter, clawing our way back to a kind of recognisable normality was so riven with obstacles it seemed impossible. Elena's bikini remained at the back of the cupboard, and not just because it was winter. One day, she bought herself an exercise DVD complete with its own exercise mat. She followed the workout's squat thrusts for about twenty minutes before running upstairs to breast-feed. I ejected the DVD for her and placed it on the shelf, where it began to collect dust. Exercise, downtime, *fun* – for the first few months they were all banished in favour of something else: duty.

The broken nights were the worst. In an ideal world, nobody

should have to become forcibly conversant with what life looks like at four o'clock in the morning. It's a cold and unfriendly time, and lonely with it, standing in the kitchen in the dark, waiting for the microwave to warm up the emergency milk, which the baby may well refuse, likewise the offer of Calpol or Infant Nurofen or anything else that could help assuage her while her sapped parents go out of their minds with worry that her cries could be a sign of illness or, at the very least, are likely disturbing the poor man who lives next door.

I'd thought that the nights would eventually get easier to cope with, but no. It never does get any less brutal to have your unconscious stamped on by the sudden wail of a distraught infant. For the first few months, Elena was mostly the one to tend to her, if only because it was her breast that the baby craved, but when the reasons for her crying became more unknowable, I was required to pitch in too. Mostly I did, but some nights I would feel it a physical impossibility to drag myself from my warm bed. And so I wouldn't, instead keeping my breathing steady and heavy in the hope of convincing Elena that my sleep was deep and needed to remain so, thus forcing her to get up in my place. But this was no way to maintain a happy marriage, and so we eventually established a rota, one night on, one night off, then arguing about it the morning after. I'm relieved, frankly, that Professor Sherr refers to these sleepless nights as a sort of torture, for if I had, I'd be accused of exaggerating. But it surely couldn't be described as anything less.

Life becomes so very full when you've had a child. There are no gaps in our days now, no time for boredom even, and where once the weekends offered an extended period of leisure, pleasure and occasional excess, they are now dominated by the swings, duck feeding, games, toys and falling asleep in front of idiotic evening TV shows at the very time, two years previously, we'd have been getting ready to go out. For a long time, I tried desperately to hold onto the vestiges of our old life, but a baby doesn't like to go ignored for long. A wife likes it even less.

But experience has made us cunning. Our cultural life may well have telescoped of late, but we still manage intermittently to pore over the Sunday newspapers, if only to read about the films we'll never see, the exhibitions we'll never attend and the far-flung countries we won't, now, travel to until retirement. Where once the Sunday newspapers took up much of a Sunday morning, we now time our reading of them to coincide with our daughter's post-lunchtime nap. As soon as her eyelids lower, I make a mad dash to the corner shop, then a mad dash back. Elena makes coffee, spreads the various sections of the paper between us, and we go to work, speed-reading if necessary. Every now and then, our eyes will meet and a mutual sympathy will pass between us, as if to say: *Look what's become of us.* Here we are at a kitchen table full of tiny hand prints rimmed with cream cheese, dried milk and snot, while discarded toys, empty raisin cartons and encrusted tissues lie dead and dying around us as if they had fallen from the sky. From upstairs comes the incessant rumble of the overused washing machine, while the clothes dryer in the corner of the kitchen strains under the weight of vests and pyjamas and babygros. The chaos spreads over into the living room, too, where the Charles Eames armchair forlornly sits, unsat upon for months and used solely now as a place to pile yet more clothes, these ones washed but pending ironing. The ironing board stands right alongside it, a constant presence, never folded away, and garishly suggestive of yet more domestic drudgery to be done, always more. It makes an already small living room smaller still. No wonder we spend so little time in here. When we were househunting in this neighbourhood, the estate agents would never call the kitchen a kitchen, but rather a *family room*. Now I see why.

Sometimes, the pressure of a hectic weekend will reach boiling point and we will buckle, Elena accusing me of not pulling my weight, of not helping out as much as I could, exasperated that I still fear nappies the way small children fear the dark. I fight back, convinced I have fared better than either of us could have dared expect. I am up each morning at seven to help ready our daughter for crèche,

I pick them both up in the evenings, I cook, wash up, I'm around for bathtime and bed, and I mostly no longer feign sleep in the middle of the night when she cries. But my wife has a point. This is hard for her too, she says, not just for me, and though she is far better at dealing with it all *without* the need to vent every step of the way, steam nevertheless accumulates and must find a way out. Perhaps this is why she is screaming right now, frightening our daughter and putting the fear of God in me, before storming upstairs and slamming doors. I've never seen her quite as furious as this before, and I can't quite remember what I did to prompt it.

"Mummy sad," Amaya says.

Eventually, the tears, raised voices and recriminations give way to a painful silence which, when I've done with all my sulking, in turn gives way to reciprocal apology, both of us making promises we mean to keep.

"We never go out on dates any more," she tells me.

We vow to make more use of our babysitter, to eat out more, to see the occasional film, to catch up with friends. Nothing too special, just life as it once was.

But then there are the other times, when the pressures of the weekend can cause an entirely different outcome, welcome ones. When there is a temporary lull in the fullness of the day, Amaya snoozing angelically in her pram, we will cast the papers aside because, at the end of the day, it's only the papers – they'll wait – and instead we nip upstairs for sex, the kind of electric stolen moment that we hardly have any more, and it's all the better for it.

When she wakes up, Amaya is smiling, her batteries recharged, her universe reopened to infinite possibilities. She sits herself up in her pram and looks at me through half-open eyes, her blonde hair every which way, her cheeks pink and criss-crossed with the pattern of the safety strap.

"Hello, omelette," she says to me with inexplicable wisdom.

And just like that, I'm sold on her all over again, a thunderbolt of extreme joy passing right through me and settling in my expanding heart. Any exhaustion or sense of mourning over the loss of our freedom is suddenly banished, replaced with something so much richer and more precious. She is awake now, my daughter, and I realise that I have missed her while she slept, and that I want her to be here to call me omelette for ever.

Those parents were right all along, then. It *is* hard, and children *are* so often a nightmare.

But the good always far, far outweighs the bad.

• • •

It is January, the southern English countryside, and a wedding Richard Curtis would be proud of. It's taking place in an elegant hotel in its own expansive grounds, with a winding, crunchy gravel drive and a golf course out back. Mulled wine is served for each guest upon arrival, even those guests that show up late for all the by now usual reasons. Our daughter, the invitation suggested, was more than welcome, but we, her parents, had other ideas. The Spanish mother-in-law was due a visit anyway, and the suggestion that she could have her granddaughter to herself for the weekend was all the temptation she needed. She booked the next flight. Elena and I hired a car, packed an overnight bag (for we'd been invited to stay over), and were gone.

We've never been away together without our daughter before, and it feels odd, but in a good way. The novelty of temporary freedom rings in our ears. We drive in excess of the speed limit, windows down, music blaring.

Our friends Steve and Gemma are getting married. While the bride-to-be and her mother spent several months arranging all the finer details – the venue, the menu, the seating arrangements and the service – Steve focused exclusively on the day's soundtrack (and the wine). As we walk into the ceremonial hall at shortly before one o'clock this afternoon, a string quartet is playing a Beatles medley of inexplicable loveliness. The doors open and a beaming, beautiful

Gemma walks down the aisle on her father's arm. Steve, wiping tears from his eyes, smiles back at her, despite everything.

I'd met up with Steve a week earlier. He'd said that there was something he needed to discuss, and I could hear the anxiety rife in his voice. My first thought was that he was suffering from cold feet. Perhaps he was having an affair, or had been diagnosed with something nasty. Over a cheap Italian meal and two bottles of wine, his worry unravelled until it eased and plateaued and eventually abated. He'd recently made a discovery in the kitchen cabinet, he told me, of something called Pregnacare Plus, a big box of serious-looking vitamins for women hoping to conceive, the very same brand Elena had used. He'd known that Gemma had wanted to try for children at some point but hadn't realised that she was quite so serious about it. Trying for children meant for him, as it had for me, nothing more than an excuse for regular sex. He could deal with the sex. But the presence of these vitamins in his house, coupled with her recent decision to abstain from alcohol and increase her intake of fruit and vegetables, brought him up short and slapped him about the cheeks.

As he spoke of his reluctance and fears, I was swamped with waves of déjà vu. I couldn't help smiling. Steve was where I had been a couple of years previously. And much as I had sought advice and comfort from my friend Peter, ahead of me in fatherhood by a good six months, so Steve now needed similar from me. He had no doubts about his future wife; this was the woman he wanted to spend his life with. But the spectre of babies suggested the loss of freedom and youth, and the arrival of overwhelming responsibility. He worried about money and work, and seriously doubted his paternal abilities. But then, he said, he'd seen how well I'd fared, and this was what was now giving him hope.

I may have been slightly drunk by this stage, but this fairly knocked the wind out of me. *He'd seen how well I'd fared.* I still wasn't sure whether I knew what I was doing or was simply making it all up as I went along, but the fact that a close and trusted friend thought I *was* meant the world to me. If I could convince him, then perhaps

I could convince myself as well. We spent several hours that night talking about what now seemed inevitable, and I could hear this voice coming out of me making a series of unambiguously positive statements, saying wonderful things about my daughter, the pride she brought out in me, the barrelling love I felt for her. At times I came close to tears, but hid them well. I meant every word of what I said, I knew that, but to speak them out loud acted as public confirmation. I was a proper *father* now. The epithet no longer unsettled me.

And now here he is on this sparklingly cold day in January at the altar, knowing that the woman who is about to become his wife actively wants to turn his world upside down, as only the arrival of a baby can, and he is smiling, but really smiling, and ready as he will ever be.

After the service, we are seated at a table with eight others, people I've never met but who, thanks largely to all the champagne, very quickly seem like old friends. I'm sitting next to a man whose wife is eight months pregnant. She isn't drinking. Nor is she smiling. The way they interact together suggest that the pregnancy has been hard on them both. The man has bags under his eyes and a faintly defeated air about him. When his wife gets up to go to the loo, waddling duck-like through the tables at a snail's pace, the man leans towards me and starts talking in a covert whisper. Steve had told him about me, apparently, and suggested perhaps that I would be useful to chat to. Fuelled by drink and the freedom created by his wife's absence, he says that he wants the benefit of my experience, no holds barred. He asks me a series of questions, about pregnancy, about sex, about the birth and beyond. I try to be as honest with him as I can, and as I talk I watch him go pale and drawn. An hour later, his back to his wife, we are still at it, chuckling regularly. Eventually, music starts. The worst part of any wedding has arrived. There is to be dancing now.

"Thank you," he says, as we make to stand. He is gripping onto my hand and pumping it. "Thank you."

I'm not sure what I've done, or whether what I have said has

made any sense or brought about any comfort, but I like the gratitude and with it the sensation of my having travelled from there to
here. Though I've done nothing particularly special by entering into
fatherhood, have, in fact, done what in many ways is the most predictable and inevitable thing for anyone to do, I have emerged from
it a changed man, changed in all kinds of ways, and some of them for
the better. It has given me what I imagine Americans call *perspective*.
That is, I think, a good thing.

I am far from complacent about it, though. A recent survey suggested that the average age at which men get divorced in the UK is
43, and that divorce rates tend to peak at around the fourth year of
marriage. I'll be coming up to both landmarks, however reluctantly,
before long. So it's all very well talking a good fight to a stranger at
a wedding, but I've got to back it up with cold, hard graft. I don't
want my marriage to end in divorce, not simply because the whole
business seems like so much protracted unpleasantness, but because I
know that Elena is the one for me, the one I love. I need to remember
this, and perhaps to remind her of it more often, too.

A few months later, I receive an early-morning e-mail from Steve.
Gemma has just taken a home pregnancy test and a blue + has
appeared in the window. I phone him immediately and listen to his
faraway voice, still dazed and not quite connected. I check in on him
throughout the day, perhaps overly keen to be there for him and to
make sure he is alright. But of course he is. He'll be a terrific parent.
By late summer, he is playing Bob Dylan to his wife's stomach in
the hope that the singer's nasal poetry will have an osmotic effect
on his unborn child, and that it will come out creative and musical
like its dad. I tell him I did similar with Amaya, playing her New
Order, Stone Roses and New Fast Automatic Daffodils, so that she
could recognise greatness early on. (Criminally underrated band,
New Fast Automatic Daffodils.) It seems to be working. The other
day, Echo and the Bunnymen's best song, "The Cutter", came on the
radio. I turned the sound up loud and she danced along to it. At its

gloriously dramatic conclusion, she jumped up and down and asked for "More! More! More!"

My proudest moment yet.

•••

Suddenly, all around me, people are having children. Friends, family, complete strangers. This has ever been the case, of course – there are six billion of us and rising, after all – but I never really noticed it before, my head too full of me to really care. My head, admittedly, is still mainly full of me. I've not suddenly transformed into a caring, sharing metrosexual poster advert for New Dads and I don't much intend to, but I've accepted my new role and have even come to embrace it. I have a daughter, and she is everything to me, the world and more. I'm glad she's here. I used to be filled with a terrible foreboding of the idea of fatherhood and the responsibilities that came with it. But right now I'm holding it together. Perhaps in time my general ineptitude will further recede and I'll even come to flourish. Who knows? All I do know for sure is this: the pessimist in me is starting to get optimistic. And I wasn't, once.

The only thing that could disrupt this blissful equilibrium now is if we had another one.

Epilogue

It is late March and, according to the weather forecast, at least six degrees colder than it should be at this time of year. Snow flurries as heavy as rainfall are pouring into our garden, settling on the flowers whose names I can never remember and weighing down the petals until they break and fall. Spring is elsewhere.

We are at home. The mother-in-law is *in situ*, scrubbing our kitchen until its surfaces gleam and sparkle. Elena is moored on the living-room sofa, reading a book between catnaps. I am upstairs, fielding intermittent job offers, all of which, to my barely concealed distress, I'm forced to turn down – just in case, in the event of.

The reason? For the second – and final – time, Elena is pregnant. She is nine months gone, full-term and ready. In fact, she's been ready a week now, her due date Good Friday. It is now the following Thursday, Easter passing in an agonisingly slow long weekend during which, because of the weather and Elena's lack of mobility, we sat around watching our fingernails grow.

Two weeks previously, a midwife had suggested that the baby, already engaged in her estimation, would likely come sooner than later. A fortnight on, following a procedure called a *membrane sweep*, which effectively removes the final safety net from the baby's head at the mouth of the birth canal, it was confidently predicted that it would arrive within 48 hours. A hospital appointment a week hence was made just in case, but the midwife told us we wouldn't need it. We would be parents again by then.

We took her at her word, and so anxiety ran rife throughout Good Friday. We became increasingly expectant on Saturday, every twinge in her abdomen (or mine) a potential contraction. Bags were packed; we were ready to go. But the tenterhooks gradually began to retract as Sunday unfurled like a cat's yawn, and by Monday, then Tuesday, then Wednesday, we were beginning to feel thoroughly down and defeated. It was abundantly clear now that our second child wouldn't be coming into this world of its own accord. Assistance would be required.

• • •

The plan all along, vague though it undeniably was, was always to have two children. If we were going to go to the bother of starting a family at all, went our reasoning, then we may as well do it properly. Jonathan Ross – no oracle of modern life, it's true, but a vocal public voice nonetheless – once said that you weren't a proper father if you had just the one child (he has four). One was easy; anyone could manage that. Another was the real test of a man's mettle, the point at which you could fully consider yourself a true dad.

It is probably unnecessary at this late stage to relate that when it actually came to putting our plans into action, I was reluctant. But I was, profoundly. The prospect of having to go through it all again filled me with a barrelling trepidation. Nevertheless, we started earlier than we would have strictly liked, believing that if it had taken a year to conceive the first time, then it was likely to take even longer now. But this time was different. During our second month of trying, late on a weekday afternoon, Elena announced her suspicions. The pregnancy test was a mere formality, but she took it anyway. We were upstairs in my study, the room still hot and musty after a day of unbroken sunshine. She came out of the toilet and sat next to me on the floor, our daughter standing between us.

"Ready?" she asked.

Before we even had time to focus on the result, Amaya snatched the stick from her mother's hand, pulling off its lid, convinced it was a pen. Shaking it in the air sent a golden arc of pee up between us. When we eventually wrestled the thing back again, the + was there in its little screen, indelible in blue.

Elena turned to me. "You're not going to cry again, are you?"

I didn't, not this time.

This time, we sat on the news for very nearly three months before telling most people, and when we finally did inform friends, by now deep into autumn and Elena beginning to show, their responses were more mixed: "That's wonderful," gushed Ria. "So soon?" asked Julie. "What, *again*?" said Gil. "Your life is over."

When you are pregnant for the first time, it's a gift, a miracle, cause for celebration. By the second time, it's already old hat, friends who have gone through the motions once not about to do so quite so fulsomely again.

In truth, we felt much the same way about it. It was no longer a novelty for us either, and for weeks at a time we made no real reference to it because, frankly, what was left to say? We had said it all, exhaustively, the first time round. After five months, we began to introduce the topic to Amaya, and though she did become rather taken with her latest bedtime book, *What's in Mummy's Tummy?*, she could hardly be expected to put two and two together just yet. We didn't bother with any antenatal classes this time, and it was only somewhere around the eight-month mark, Elena now huge, that it began fully to dawn on both of us that life was about to become properly complicated.

The earliest Easter in some 90 years brought with it an Arctic wind, snowstorms and the arrival of the mother-in-law, brisk and efficient as ever, and raring to become a grandmother again on the eve of her 60th birthday. We'd made no provisions for either occasion, if only because we had fully anticipated spending Easter in hospital, but now that it was upon us and the fridge bare, we were forced to feast on scraps found at the back of one of the kitchen cabinets. Amaya, by now two years and three months old, quickly developed cabin fever as the day dragged inexorably on. For minutes at a time, she amused us by indulging in a new favourite crèche game that comprised spinning round and round in a tight circle, then trying to walk in a straight line before the floor became the ceiling and smacked her full in the face. We watched bits of *The Wizard of Oz* on television, and the mother-in-law attempted to entertain her by singing, first Spanish nursery rhymes, then, inexplicably, a heavily accented version of Bob Marley's "No Woman No Cry".

In the early evening, the snow having lifted, Elena and I went for a long walk. It remained cold, but we walked for over an hour, up towards the hospital and even as far as its entrance in the pitiful hope that proximity to the maternity ward would prompt some kind of physical effect. Over the past few weeks, we'd tried all the old wives' tales to bring about labour – spicy food, raspberry tea, pineapple chunks, sex – but none managed to bring about even the ghost of a contraction.

One night, we decided to claim back a little semblance of real life and went out for the evening. At a local Thai restaurant, Elena sweated her way through the hottest green curry, and we then went to the cinema. If any film's title alone could ever hope to bring on a mercy dash to A&E, then it was surely *There Will Be Blood*. But even three hours of Daniel Day Lewis going mad failed to kickstart anything. During the journey home, we drove over every pothole the tarmac offered up.

And so now it is Thursday and we are at the hospital appointment that last week's midwife confidently predicted we wouldn't have to keep. Another membrane sweep is performed, and the nurse asks us whether we have tried the long walks, the spicy food, the pineapple chunks and the sex. She then asks us whether we have tried tweaking Elena's nipples.

"Some people think it's a crazy suggestion," she concedes, "but it is another way of producing oxytocin, which is the hormone necessary for contractions to begin."

We try this shortly after lunch. It has more effect on me than it does on her.

A further seven days pass. Friends call, text and e-mail for news, and life becomes unbearably stagnant while we impatiently wait in hope. Even Amaya has grown bored of any anticipation she may have been feeling, and has turned against the baby doll we bought her a month earlier in preparation for the coming event. This morning, I watched as she dragged it out of her room by its head and casually threw it down the stairs.

•••

Thursday, March 3, is a day punctuated by slow clock-watching. Today is the day of the induction. We have a 7.45 appointment, and are told to call an hour earlier to confirm. We rise at dawn, shower and have breakfast. Elena calls. The receptionist tells her that the ward is full, and to call back in three hours. At eleven, she is told to call back at one. At 2.30, we are finally summonsed in. At four, Elena's waters are manually broken with a fiendish plastic hook, and by nine, she is four centimetres dilated. At midnight, that number has shrunk dispiritingly to three. She is hooked up to a drip now to bring about the contractions that her body will not muster naturally. Pain comes quickly, like floodgates opening. She requests an epidural, gets it, then sleeps off and on throughout the night. At 6.24 on the morning of Friday, April 4th, our second daughter is born. She has a head full of black hair and the look of a widow from the old country about her. We experience a moment's blessed relief. And then comes panic.

Our midwife, who has been wonderfully composed all night, blanches. She pushes a button on the wall for assistance. Elena, she explains to us, is losing blood. The blood flow increases, she blanches more and now hits the alarm bell hard with the flat of her palm. It screams piercingly throughout the maternity ward. Half a dozen nurses pound through the doors within seconds. I hear the word *haemorrhage*, but then become aware of an abrupt tempo change. As quickly as the emergency had arrived, it departs.

"That's a relief," says one nurse, and I almost pass out.

Our daughter is finally here. She has no name yet.

A day and a half later, I drive to the hospital to pick them up and bring them home. I have carefully prepared for this moment, spending hours in front of my CD collection before picking the perfect song with which to usher our child into the outside world. We strap her into the car, and I cue up the song, Goldfrapp's "Clowns", which I've chosen specifically because it sounds so fresh out of the womb itself. She sleeps throughout, oblivious to its glistening whispers.

We arrive home and transfer her gently to the Moses basket that sits ready on the living-room floor. Amaya wanders in from the kitchen.

"What's that?" she says.

"This is your sister," I tell her.

Her eyebrows arch up and she makes the sound she uses for confusion, a sort of mumbled *hngg*. "My sister?" She comes forward. "I want to see."

She falls to her knees and *hnggs* again.

"Baby?" she asks.

For balance, she rests both her hands on the rim of the basket, promptly upending it, and the baby rolls out onto the floor. Her eyes pop open to reveal shiny, black, alarmed marbles. She frowns, then starts to cry.

The phone goes, and my mobile vibrates with an incoming text message. The mother-in-law wants to pick up the howling infant. Amaya wants to kiss her on the forehead. A brief struggle ensues. There comes a knock at the door, an eager neighbour keen for news.

My iPod sings faithfully to me from its speakers in the kitchen. The phone rings on. And over this commotion, Elena's eyes meet mine, a brief moment of connection before we are both pulled in separate directions, necessary positions we will have to keep for some time to come now, but that, hopefully, shall remain parallel and, perhaps once in a while, might even merge as one.

Acknowledgments

I'd like to thank everyone who took the time to talk to me, particularly: John Simpson, Ashley Walters, Alex James, Matt O'Connor, John Duerden, Adrienne Burgess, Dr Danny Singley, Dr Pat Spungin, Dr Lorraine Sherr, Volker Buck and Ahmed Saliu. Thank you to Aurea Carpenter and all at Short Books, to my agent Patrick Walsh and also to Robert Dinsdale. Thank you to my original Reluctant Father commissioning editors: Liz Hoggard, Michael Harvey, Luke Leitch and Sue Peart. To Peter Hall for his softly spoken wisdom, and to Steve Price for his camaraderie, moral support and for always wanting to order a second bottle; to Morten Morland, Jane Webster and Jonas; to Julie Clark and Mark Cahill (the almost aunt and almost uncle); and most of all to Elena Sanchez, for her love, support and understanding, and also for her permission.

Nick Duerden is a wide-ranging newspaper and magazine feature writer. He lives in London with his partner, and their two daughters.

In case of difficulty in purchasing any Short Books
title through normal channels, please contact
BOOKPOST Tel: 01624 836000
Fax: 01624 837033
email: bookshop@enterprise.net
www.bookpost.co.uk
Please quote ref. 'Short Books